ELISABETH LAMBERT ORTIZ

A Taste of Excellence

RECIPES FROM THE BEST
OF BRITISH CHEFS

ELISABETH LAMBERT ORTIZ

A Taste of Excellence

RECIPES FROM THE BEST OF BRITISH CHEFS

FOREWORD BY ANTON MOSIMANN

COLLINS

Dedication

For Elizabeth David, C.B.E., whose books have given much pleasure to a multitude of readers, and inspired a multitude of cooks

First published 1987 by
William Collins Sons & Co Ltd
London · Glasgow · Sydney
Auckland · Johannesburg

British Library Cataloguing in Publication Data
Ortiz, Elisabeth Lambert
A taste of excellence.
1. Cookery, International
I. Title
641.5   TX725.A1

ISBN 0 00 411254 7

Line illustrations by Jane Strother

Text set in Galliard
by V & M Graphics Ltd, Aylesbury, Bucks
Printed and bound in Great Britain
by Robert Hartnoll (1985) Ltd, Bodmin

Contents

Foreword

I first met Elisabeth when she interviewed me for an article she was writing for *Gourmet* magazine in New York. She told me then of her interest in the new young chefs with whom she knew I was deeply involved, as many of these young cooks of promise were working in my kitchens at The Dorchester Hotel. We talked of my interest and belief in British cooking and in the attitude of the public to food. She met sous-chefs in my kitchen, many of whom have gone on to become head chefs in their own right.

I think Elisabeth has done a splendid job in collecting recipes created by the many gifted young chefs she talked to and whose cooking she enjoyed. She has interpreted the philosophy behind their cooking, and above all she conveys her enthusiasm for cooks who are seeking to provide good healthy dishes, and whose real satisfaction comes from the enjoyment they give. She also shows their enthusiasm for what is very hard work.

The recipes are written in a clear and easy to follow style suitable for home cooks. They sound delicious. I am pleased that Elisabeth, whose work I admire, regards me as a valuable influence on the British kitchen, and as her friend and mentor.

Elisabeth makes it clear that chefs have not abandoned the disciplines of classical technique. They have adapted the greatness of the past to contemporary needs, using modern foodstuffs and modern kitchen technology. And she has not hesitated to keep favourites of traditional cuisine, or to value the work of older chefs who were the pioneers of today's new cuisine.

It is not always easy to translate a recipe from a chef's kitchen to a domestic one, but this she has done admirably without falsifying the chef's intention. She also suggests ways for the health and diet conscious to cut down on such temptations as heavy cream by using other dairy products, for example, junket cheese. I think she has understood the profound revolution that has taken place in the British kitchen. Young, creative chefs are meeting the challenge of today's needs with wonderfully innovative dishes that are nevertheless linked with the traditions of the past in the continuous process of renewal and change that is the heart and essence of good cooking.

Anton Mosimann
Maître Chef des Cuisines
The Dorchester Hotel
London

Introduction

Not so very long ago travellers came to Britain to see historic houses, castles, museums, cathedrals and theatre. Now they come for food as well, especially to the restaurants of the country house hotels, small, elegant places converted from country mansions and manor houses, too big for modern families. The hotels are luxurious and in exquisite taste, the dining rooms are not large and they are usually very beautifully furnished and filled with flowers, often from the hotel's own gardens. They are presided over by gifted young chefs whose cooking has caused a revolution in our attitudes to food.

I first found out what was happening when I met Anton Mosimann, the brilliant young Maître Chef des Cuisines at The Dorchester Hotel in London, author of two important cookbooks and a fervent believer in our cuisine. He encouraged young cooks in his kitchen to turn into important young chefs. He is so devoted to his profession that he founded Club 8, a group of eight young London chefs who meet once a month to eat, to exchange ideas, discuss recipes and help each other to raise standards. His club inspired the young, gifted chef Nicholas (Nick) Gill, when he was at Hambleton Hall in Rutland, to found Country Chefs Seven with the same aim of raising culinary standards.

Nick, in fact, has now left Hambleton Hall and hopes to set up his own restaurant soon. The others of the Seven, Murdo MacSween, Ian McAndrew, John Hornsby, John Webber, Shaun Hill and Michael Quinn, have all moved to other country house hotels, or to restaurants, and are still cooking sublime dishes. Michael Quinn was then at Gravetye Manor, but left the Sussex countryside to become the first British chef ever at The Ritz in London and has now returned to the country at Ettington Park, near Stratford-Upon-Avon. These Seven, and a host of talented young men and women, cooked for me and were generous enough to give me their recipes for this book. There are also recipes from great cooks like George Perry-Smith, Francis Coulson, Kenneth Bell and Joyce Molyneux, older men and women who pioneered the change, and helped train and inspire many of today's young chefs. When George Perry-Smith opened his first restaurant, The Hole in the Wall in Bath, it was an oasis in a desert of indifferent food. Now there are very few desert areas in Britain, from Cornwall, where George now has a Restaurant with Rooms in Helford, all the way north to Scotland. I made a gastronomic pilgrimage round the country, meeting chefs, and eating well. It took some time as chefs are no longer thin on the ground. This book is the result of those happy journeys. My only regret is that I wasn't able to visit more of these talented chefs throughout Britain, and that some of the recipes gathered from those I did meet have sadly, for reasons of space, had to be left out. I have tested all the recipes in my own kitchen, and without changing essentials have written them so they will work coherently in a domestic kitchen rather than in a kitchen with a brigade of cooks. The home cook may lack many of the advantages of a restaurant kitchen, especially trained helpers, but we do have the advantage of a captive audience. In some of the recipes the chefs have suggested suitable accompaniments to their dishes and I have included these.

I have also taken the opportunity to suggest ways to avoid too much cream and so on, for today's health-conscious diners. In any event chefs do want to produce food that is not just good to eat but is good for one as well, so they are downright stingy with any sauce that is very rich thus palate and health are both satisfied.

John Webber, whom I met when he was head chef at Gidleigh Park and who is now at Cliveden at Taplow, near London, summed up the new attitude nicely for me when he said that we used to eat out when we had to, now we eat out for entertainment and feel privileged to meet the chefs in their tall starched white hats, stars of the kitchen, when they make their rounds of the restaurant to make sure they have pleased us.

I am immensely grateful to Michael Harris, proprietor of The Bell Inn at Aston Clinton in Buckinghamshire and an important authority on wine, for his generosity in suggesting wines to go with the recipes in the book. He feels strongly about the marriage of food and wine, one complementing the other. These suggestions, he stresses, are just that, suggestions, and should not be treated as more than guidelines, encouraging the diner to search for the wine that most pleases his or her palate. The world of wine is as wide as the world of food, and there are great rewards to be had helping the marriage of wine and food to reach happy fulfilment. Fortunately there is no shortage of choice, and helpful advice abounds.

Writing this book has been great fun and I hope readers will cook and enjoy the recipes as I have done.

Elisabeth Lambert Ortiz

Basic Recipes

Stocks

Many home cooks prefer to make their own stock and these recipes have been worked out to suit their needs. They are not as formal as those of a restaurant chef who has at his or her disposal not only the ingredients and special equipment but storage space that most of us lack in small kitchens. I have used Lyn Hall's excellent recipes for fish stock, and clarified fish stock, which should be used when a strong fish stock is called for. They add wonderfully to the flavour of fish soups, and other fish dishes.

Sometimes excellent canned beef and chicken stock are available in supermarkets or groceries. These are very helpful when kitchen time is short. There are also acceptable stock cubes for beef, chicken, lamb and fish, useful in a crisis, or to enrich a thin-tasting mixture. Unfortunately, they tend to be very salty so liquids to which they are going to be added should not be salted, and care should be taken with mixtures that are to be reduced.

TO CLARIFY STOCK

3 egg whites for every 1.7 L/3 pt stock
3 crushed egg shells

125 g/4 oz lean chopped beef (optional)
Stock (beef, veal, chicken, game)

In a large saucepan, beat the egg whites until they are foamy. Stir in the crushed egg shells and the beef if using. Mix thoroughly. Pour in the stock and bring to a simmer over low heat, whisking constantly. Simmer, partially covered, over very low heat for 20 minutes. Let the stock rest, uncovered, for 10 minutes. Strain it through a sieve lined with a double thickness of dampened cheesecloth into a bowl or jug taking care to disturb the crust as little as possible. The crust may be lifted off carefully with a skimmer before straining the stock.

CHICKEN STOCK

MAKES 2L/3½ pt

1.8 kg/4 lb chicken carcasses (raw or cooked), necks, gizzards, hearts, backs and wings
3 L/5½ pt water
2 carrots, scraped and chopped
2 stalks celery, chopped
2 medium onions, unpeeled, halved and each stuck with 2 cloves

1 leek, trimmed, split, thoroughly washed and chopped
Bouquet garni: sprig thyme, 6 parsley stalks, 1 bay leaf
6 peppercorns
Salt to taste

Combine all the ingredients in a large saucepan or kettle, bring to a boil over low heat and skim for 5 minutes, to remove any scum that rises to the surface. Cover and simmer over low heat for 2 hours. Strain the liquid into a bowl or jug. Discard the solids. Chill the cooled stock in the refrigerator and remove all the fat. The stock can be frozen.

BEEF STOCK

MAKES 2L/3½ pt

1.8 kg/4 lb oxtail, shank or chuck, chopped into 5 cm/2 in pieces
900 g/2 lb beef bones
3 L/5½ pt water
2 medium carrots, scraped and chopped
2 medium onions, chopped
2 cloves garlic, chopped
2 stalks celery, chopped
2 medium tomatoes, chopped
3 parsley sprigs
1 bay leaf
6 peppercorns
Sprig thyme
Salt

Combine all the ingredients in a large saucepan or kettle. Bring to a boil over low heat and skim for about 5 minutes. Cover and simmer over low heat for 4 hours, skimming from time to time. Strain the liquid into a bowl or jug. Discard the solids. Chill the cooled stock in the refrigerator and remove the solidified fat. The stock can be frozen.

To make Veal Stock, substitute 1.8 kg/4 lb veal trimmings (neck or shank), and 1 large veal knuckle bone, cut into 5-6 cm/2-3 in pieces. Cook as for Beef Stock.

LAMB STOCK

Lamb stock is not as much used as other stocks, and when it is needed it is usually for a sauce.

MAKES about 475 ml/16 fl oz

1 tablespoon butter
1 tablespoon vegetable oil
1 medium onion, finely chopped
1 small carrot, scraped and chopped
1 stalk celery, chopped
1 clove garlic, finely chopped
Sprig thyme
Lamb bones (from rack of lamb, or loin)
2 L/3½ pt water
Salt
Freshly ground pepper
2 teaspoons arrowroot (optional)

Heat the butter and oil in a saucepan and sauté the onion, carrot, celery and garlic over moderate heat, stirring from time to time, until the vegetables are lightly browned, about 10 minutes. Add the thyme and bones, stir and cook for a few minutes longer. Add the water, bring to a simmer, and cook, uncovered, over low heat for 30 minutes. Season with salt and pepper, strain through a fine sieve and return the stock to the saucepan.

If liked, the stock may be lightly thickened. Mix the arrowroot with cold water, stir into the stock and simmer until the stock is lightly thickened.

Chill the cooled stock in the refrigerator and remove all solidified fat. The stock can be frozen.

GAME STOCK

The carcasses of roast game make wonderfully rich stock which can be frozen and used to enrich sauces or gravies for the next batch of game.

MAKES about 475 ml/16 fl oz

Chopped carcasses of any game such as pheasant, grouse, partridge, etc., using 2 or 3 birds according to size and type*
2 tablespoons butter
1 medium onion, chopped
1 medium carrot, scraped and chopped
1 stalk of celery, preferably with leaves, chopped

1 bay leaf
½ teaspoon dried thyme or sprig of fresh thyme
Salt
Freshly ground pepper
1 L/1¾ pt water

*Any necks or giblets may be added with the bones as well as any leftover bits of meat.

Sauté the game bones in the butter in a large saucepan or heavy casserole. Add the onion, carrot and celery and sauté for a few minutes longer. Add the bay leaf and thyme, season with salt and pepper, pour in the water and simmer, covered, for 2 hours. Taste for seasoning and strain through a fine sieve. The stock can be frozen.

DEMI-GLACE

This has become part of the international repertoire though it originated in France. Cooks everywhere find it useful. It is not difficult to make, or time consuming.

MAKES about 475 ml/16 fl oz

1 tablespoon butter
1 medium onion, finely chopped
1 medium carrot, scraped and chopped
50 g/2 oz finely chopped mushrooms
2 sprigs parsley
1 clove garlic, chopped
1 stalk celery, chopped

Sprig thyme
1 small bay leaf
300 g/10 oz chopped tomatoes, fresh or canned
1.1 L/2 pt beef stock (see page 11)
50 ml/2 fl oz dry Madeira (optional)
Salt
Freshly ground pepper

In a saucepan, heat the butter and sauté the onion and carrot until they are soft and lightly browned. Add the mushrooms, parsley, garlic, celery, thyme, bay leaf, tomatoes and beef stock and simmer, uncovered, over very low heat, skimming from time to time if necessary, for 1½ hours. Strain through a fine sieve. Stir in the Madeira if liked. Taste for seasoning and add salt and pepper if needed. The demi-glace can be frozen.

FISH STOCK

This very good recipe for fish stock is from Lyn Hall, Chairman of Cuisine Creative in London.

MAKES 1L/1¾ pt

900 g/2 lb fish heads and bones of any non-oily white fish, cleaned and chopped
50 ml/2 fl oz olive oil
175 g/6 oz chopped tomatoes, fresh or canned
50 g/2 oz carrots, thinly sliced

125 g/4 oz onions, thinly sliced
Bouquet garni: sprig thyme, 6 parsley stalks, 1 bay leaf
1.4 L/2½ pt water
Salt
Freshly ground pepper
125 ml/4 fl oz dry white wine

In a large saucepan, sauté the fish heads and bones in the oil for 2 or 3 minutes. Add the tomatoes, carrots, onions, bouquet garni and water. Season to taste with salt and pepper and simmer, covered, for 30 minutes.

Strain the stock into a jug. Rinse out and dry the saucepan and return the stock to the pan with the wine. Bring to a simmer, skimming the froth from the top. Simmer for 4 minutes then strain through a sieve lined with a double layer of dampened cheesecloth. Cool and skim all the fat from the top. Measure and reduce over brisk heat to 1 L/1¾ pt to concentrate the flavour. The stock can be frozen.

TO CLARIFY FISH STOCK

Use whenever strong fish stock is called for in a recipe. This is also from Lyn Hall.

MAKES about 725 ml/24 fl oz

50 g/2 oz any non-oily white fish, skinned and boned
2 egg whites
1 L/1¾ pt fish stock

Salt
White pepper
Cayenne pepper

In a blender or food processor, reduce the fish to a purée. Scrape into a bowl. Beat the egg whites until they are foamy then gradually beat them into the fish purée. Pour the stock into a saucepan, add the egg white and fish mixture and whisk briskly. Bring to a boil over low heat, whisking. As soon as the stock comes to a boil, remove from the heat. Taste for seasoning and add salt, white pepper and a pinch of cayenne. The stock should be strongly seasoned at this point as the clarifying process thins the flavour. Return the saucepan to the heat and simmer gently for 20 minutes. Remove from the heat and carefully lift off the crust formed by the egg whites and fish with a perforated spoon or skimmer, then strain through a sieve lined with a double layer of dampened cheesecloth set over a deep bowl. The stock can be frozen.

SHELLFISH STOCK

This is a useful, easy to make stock for enriching the flavour of prawn, lobster or crab sauces.

MAKES 1L/1¾ pt

Shells and heads from 500 g/1 lb
   prawns, or 1 lobster, or equivalent
   crab shells, chopped
2 tablespoons olive oil
1 small onion, finely chopped
1 small carrot, scraped and chopped
1 stalk celery, with leaves, chopped
1 clove garlic, chopped

6 parsley stalks
1 bay leaf
Sprig thyme
3–4 sprigs chervil (optional)
Salt
Freshly ground pepper
1.1 L/2 pt water
125 ml/4 fl oz dry white wine

In a large saucepan, sauté the shells in the oil, stirring with a wooden spoon until they turn pink, 2–3 minutes. Add all the remaining ingredients, using very little salt as the stock will reduce. Cover and simmer for 30 minutes over moderate heat. Strain and measure. Return the liquid to the saucepan and reduce over fairly brisk heat to 1 L/1¾ pt, if necessary. Cool, refrigerate and remove any fat. The stock can be frozen.

ASPIC

Most stock will set into a light jelly when cold but this may not be firm enough for an aspic. Use a little unflavoured powdered gelatine to reinforce the stock. One envelope, about 1 tablespoon, will set 475 ml/16 fl oz of liquid into a firm aspic. One envelope will set 725 ml/24 fl oz of liquid into jellied soup.

To use gelatine, sprinkle one envelope of the powder on to 50 ml/2 fl oz cold water and let it stand until softened. Stir into the liquid to be jellied and simmer over moderate heat until the gelatine has completely dissolved, stirring once or twice, a minute or two. Pour the liquid into a bowl and refrigerate to set.

There are commercial aspic jelly powders available in speciality shops. These are flavoured and have salt. If using these do not salt the stock.

Pastry

PUFF PASTRY

This is an elegant pastry and though not difficult to make is time consuming. However, it has a great many uses, often turning an ordinary dish into a special one. It is available, frozen, in supermarkets and groceries, and is quite satisfactory. There is a simpler pastry, Rough Puff Pastry, that is very useful, and easier to make than classic puff pastry (see page 16).

MAKES 500 g/1 lb

250 g/8 oz bread flour, or use plain flour
½ teaspoon salt
2 tablespoons unsalted butter, cut into pieces

1 teaspoon lemon juice
125 ml/4 fl oz ice water, about
250 g/8 oz unsalted butter

Sift the flour and salt together into a large bowl. Work the pieces of butter into the flour with the fingertips until it resembles coarse breadcrumbs. Make a well in the centre and add the lemon juice and water. Still using the hands, work the mixture into a fairly stiff, smooth dough, adding a little more water if necessary. Form the dough into a ball, sprinkle lightly with flour, put into a plastic bag and refrigerate for about 1 hour.

While the dough is chilling, work the remaining butter into a square. Put it between 2 sheets of greaseproof paper and roll it out with a rolling pin to make a 10 cm/4 in square. Peel off the greaseproof paper, sprinkle the butter lightly with flour, wrap up in fresh paper and refrigerate until the butter is firm. On a lightly-floured board, roll out the dough to an 18 cm/7 in square and put the butter diagonally in the centre. Fold the dough over the butter as if making an envelope. Make sure the butter is completely sealed in. Turn the package over. Dust the board and the dough lightly with flour and roll out the dough gently and evenly into a rectangle 15 × 25 cm/6 × 10 in. Fold the top over all but the bottom third of the rectangle. Fold the bottom third over the top to make a square of three overlapping layers. This is the first fold. The process will be repeated making five folds in all.

Turn the dough so that one of the open ends faces you. Always turn the dough in the same direction. Roll the dough, gently and evenly, once more into a 15 × 25 cm/6 × 10 in rectangle. Do not roll right to the edges. Stop about 1 cm/½ in before the edge so as not to force the butter out of the paste. Fold up the dough once more into three overlapping layers. This is the second fold. Wrap the dough in greaseproof paper and refrigerate for 30 minutes. It is a good idea to mark the dough by pressing it lightly with a finger so that it can be turned from the correct position. Always have an open end facing you when rolling out the dough.

Continue to turn, roll out, and fold the dough, refrigerating if it seems to be getting the least warm and sticky, until it has been rolled out and folded five times in all. Chill the dough, wrapped in greaseproof paper, for at least 30 minutes after the last fold. It is now ready to be used.

The dough will keep, refrigerated, for about a week. Wrapped in foil, it will keep in the freezer for up to 6 months.

ROUGH PUFF PASTRY

MAKES 500 g/1 lb

250 g/8 oz bread flour, or use plain flour
½ teaspoon salt
125 g/4 oz unsalted butter, cut into pieces

50 g/2 oz lard, cut into pieces
6 tablespoons ice water, about

Sift the flour and salt into a large bowl. Work the butter and lard into the flour with the fingertips until it resembles coarse breadcrumbs. Pour all but 2 tablespoons of the ice water into the dough, mix with the hands and form into a ball. Add more water, if necessary. Wrap the ball of dough in greaseproof paper, or put in a plastic bag, and refrigerate for 30 minutes.

Following the same procedure as for puff pastry, roll out the dough into a rectangle and fold it up into a three-layered package. Turn, roll out and fold four times in all. Wrap the dough in greaseproof paper, or put it in a plastic bag, and refrigerate it for at least 30 minutes. It is now ready to be used.

VOL AU VENT

Carême is credited with inventing these very useful pastry cases using the puff pastry that is generally credited to the French landscape painter, Claude Lorrain, who lived from 1600–82. Vol au vent are sometimes available ready-made, needing only to be thawed and baked, or they can be made from frozen puff pastry also available from supermarkets or groceries. When I have time I much prefer to make my own puff pastry and use it for vol au vent among other things.

1 recipe Puff Pastry (page 15)
1 large egg yolk

1 teaspoon water, or double cream

Roll out the pastry to 1 cm/½ in thickness. Using a scalloped 7 cm/3 in pastry cutter, cut the pastry into rounds. Choose a slightly smaller plain cutter and carefully press it into the centre of each round down to about two-thirds of the dough. Chill for 30 minutes.

Mix the egg yolk and water or cream in a small bowl. Arrange the pastry cases on an ungreased baking sheet and brush the tops with the egg yolk mixture. Bake in a preheated, moderate oven (180°C/350°F/gas 4) for 40–45 minutes, or until the pastry is well risen and golden brown. Using a small sharp knife remove the centre rounds. With a small spoon scoop out any soft pastry from the shells. Fill, and replace the centre circle as a lid.

SHORTCRUST PASTRY

ENOUGH for a 25–28 cm/10–11 in pie plate
250 g/8 oz plain flour
½ teaspoon salt
6 tablespoons unsalted chilled butter,
   cut into pieces
2 tablespoons chilled lard, cut into
   pieces, or vegetable shortening
1 egg yolk
3 tablespoons ice water, about

Sift the flour and salt together into a large bowl. Toss in the pieces of butter and lard to coat them with flour then rub them into the flour with the fingertips until the mixture resembles coarse breadcrumbs. Mix the egg yolk with the water. Add it to the flour mixture all at once and quickly mix together. Form the dough into a ball, wrap it in greaseproof paper, or put it into a plastic bag, and refrigerate it for at least 1 hour before using.

For sweet pastry, add 1 tablespoon of sugar to the dough and reduce the amount of salt to ¼ teaspoon.

CHOUX PASTRY

MAKES enough for about 40 small puffs, 3.5 cm/1½ in diameter
250 ml/8 fl oz water
½ teaspoon salt
125 g/4 oz unsalted butter
125 g/4 oz plain flour
4 large eggs

Combine the water, salt and butter in a medium-sized saucepan. Bring to a boil over moderate heat, stirring once or twice. When the water boils, add the flour, all at once, stirring vigorously with a wooden spoon until the batter draws away from the sides of the pan and forms a compact ball. This takes less than 1 minute. Remove the dough from the heat and let it stand for 2–3 minutes. Beat in the eggs one by one until the batter is smooth and shiny. The pastry is now ready to be used.

For sweet puffs, add 1 tablespoon of sugar to the water, salt and butter mixture.

TO MAKE PUFF SHELLS

Make 1 recipe choux pastry. For puff shells about 3.5 cm/1½ in in diameter, use a pastry bag with 1 cm/½ in round tube and pipe circles of dough about 2.5 cm/1 in around and 1 cm/½ in high onto a backing sheet, 5 cm/2 in apart, or drop by teaspoons onto the sheet. Brush with egg wash made with 1 egg yolk beaten with 1 teaspoon water, slightly flattening the puffs. Bake in a preheated, hot oven (220°C/425°F/gas 7) for 15–20 minutes. Remove the puffs from the oven and pierce the sides with the point of a small sharp knife. Return the puffs to the turned off oven and leave, with the oven door ajar, for 10 minutes. Take out and cool on racks. To fill, use a pastry bag with a 0.6 cm/¼ in opening for tiny puffs, and a 2 cm/¾ in round tube opening for larger puffs.

BRIOCHE BREAD

I have been using this recipe for years, at least since the mid-seventies when I asked my dear mentor and friend Jim (James Andrews) Beard for a simpler brioche recipe as I just wanted to make brioche toast. He gave me this recipe which is reproduced here with only the most minor changes. It appears in *How to Eat Better for Less Money* by James Beard and Sam Aaron, a wonderfully useful book. I miss Jim, as indeed I think the whole world of cooks does, and it makes me happy to be able to remember him when I knead this delicious, easy, quick and wonderful bread.

The recipe can be halved.

MAKES 2 loaves

5 teaspoons (2 × 7g/¼ oz packages) active dry yeast
50 ml/2 fl oz lukewarm water
300 ml/½ pt warm milk
2 large eggs, lightly beaten
175 g/6 oz butter, softened at room temperature

50 g/2 oz sugar
2 teaspoons baking powder
2 teaspoons salt
625–750 g/1¼–1½ lb bread flour, or plain flour

In a large bowl, soften the yeast in the warm water. Add the milk, eggs, butter, sugar, baking powder, salt and 625 g/1¼ lb of the flour. Mix thoroughly using a wooden spoon and the hands. Turn out onto a lightly-floured surface and knead until smooth, about 10 minutes, adding the remaining 50 g/2 oz flour as needed.

Oil or butter two 23 × 12 cm/9 × 5 in baking tins and fit the dough into them. Cover and set in a warm, draught-free place to rise until doubled in bulk, about 1 hour. Bake in a preheated, moderate oven (180°C/350°F/gas 4) for 45 minutes, or until golden brown.

OATCAKES

Oatcakes are a Scots tradition. They make a pleasantly crunchy accompaniment to pâtés, terrines, or cheese, or are delicious just by themselves with butter. The catering staff at Hopetoun House near Edinburgh gave me this recipe when I told them how much I enjoyed their oatcakes.

MAKES 18 oatcakes
250 g/8 oz fine oatmeal (rolled oats)
50 g/2 oz plain flour
1½ teaspoons double acting baking powder
Pinch each salt and sugar
50 g/2 oz lard, butter or vegetable shortening
Milk

Put the oatmeal into a large bowl. Sift in the flour, baking powder, salt and sugar. Rub in the lard, or other shortening, with the fingertips to form a coarse meal. Add enough milk to make a fairly stiff dough. Form the dough into 18 patties, about 5 cm/2 in in diameter and flatten them slightly. Arrange the patties on a greased baking sheet and bake in a preheated, moderate oven (190°C/375°F/gas 5) for 15–20 minutes. Allow to cool before storing.

CRÊPES

(Pancakes)

This is a basic pancake batter for any savoury crêpe recipe. For dessert pancakes add sugar, or any other ingredients as indicated in the recipe.

MAKES about 12 × 15 cm/6 in pancakes
175 g/6 oz plain flour
½ teaspoon salt
4 large eggs, lightly beaten
4 egg yolks
250 ml/8 fl oz milk
1 tablespoon melted butter, or vegetable oil

Sift the flour and salt into a large bowl. Add the eggs and egg yolks, stir to mix. Add the milk and melted butter or vegetable oil and beat with a balloon whisk until the mixture is very smooth. Or, combine all the ingredients in a blender or food processor and process until the mixture is smooth and silky. It should be like double cream. Refrigerate the batter for 2 hours before using.

To cook the pancakes, have a non-stick frying pan with a 15 cm/6 in bottom diameter. Brush the pan with vegetable oil, or crumple a piece of greaseproof paper, rub it over some butter and grease the pan with it. Set the pan over moderately high heat and when it is almost hot enough to smoke, pour in 50 ml/2 fl oz of batter. A ladle or a measuring cup are best to use. Quickly tilt the pan so that the batter covers the whole surface. Cook for about 1 minute.

Lift the edge of the pancake to see if it is done. It should be very lightly browned. Turn with a spatula or the fingers, or flip over by tossing up in the pan. Cook the other side for about 30 seconds. Stack the pancakes until ready to use, greasing the frying pan for each pancake. The pancakes can be kept warm by wrapping them lightly in aluminium foil and putting them into a warm oven, or by setting them on a plate, covered, over simmering water in a saucepan. They can be made ahead of time and reheated when ready to use.

Sauces

BÉCHAMEL SAUCE

(White Sauce)

This is a sauce far less used by today's young chefs than it was in the past, but it is a classic sauce, and still has its place in the kitchen.

MAKES 475 ml/16 fl oz
3 tablespoons butter   **Salt**
20 g/¾ oz plain flour   **White pepper**
475 ml/16 fl oz milk

In a heavy saucepan over low heat, melt the butter and stir in the flour with a wooden spoon. Cook, stirring, without letting the mixture colour, for 2 minutes. Remove from the heat and gradually stir in the milk until the mixture is smooth. If there are any lumps, beat with a wire whisk. Season with salt and pepper and return the saucepan to the heat. Bring to a simmer and cook, stirring constantly, for 5 minutes.

VELOUTÉ SAUCE

Make as above using white stock made from poultry, veal or fish in place of milk.

HOLLANDAISE SAUCE

MAKES about 250 ml/8 fl oz

3 egg yolks
1 tablespoon cold water
250 g/8 oz butter, cut into pieces

Salt
Pinch cayenne pepper
1 tablespoon lemon juice

Combine the egg yolks and water in the top of a double boiler over hot water and whisk until they are light. Set the double boiler over very, very low heat and whisk in the pieces of butter, one by one, adding a new piece when the previous one has been incorporated into the sauce. Be very careful not to overheat the sauce as it will not thicken into a smooth creamy mixture if it is too hot. The water in the double boiler should not boil but be at just under a simmer. Remove from the heat if necessary. When all the butter has been beaten into the egg yolks, and the sauce is thick and creamy, season to taste with salt, cayenne and lemon juice.

Serve as soon as possible. The sauce is always served warm, not hot, and can be kept warm for a time over tepid water. If the water is too hot, the sauce will thin or curdle.

Hollandaise can also be made, with care, in a small, very heavy saucepan set directly over low heat.

BÉARNAISE SAUCE

This is a first cousin of hollandaise sauce. It is more strongly flavoured and uses vinegar instead of lemon juice.

MAKES about 250 ml/8 fl oz

50 ml/2 fl oz tarragon vinegar
50 ml/2 fl oz dry white wine
1 tablespoon mixed fresh tarragon
   and chervil, or 1½ teaspoons mixed
   dried
2 tablespoons finely chopped shallots

3 egg yolks, lightly beaten
Salt
Freshly ground pepper
250 g/8 oz butter, cut into pieces
2 tablespoons fresh tarragon, chervil
   or parsley, finely chopped

In a small saucepan, combine the vinegar, wine, herbs and shallots and simmer over low heat until the liquid is reduced to 2 tablespoons. Strain into the top of a double boiler set over low heat. Beat in the egg yolks, add 1 tablespoon cold water and continue to beat over low heat until they are thick. Season to taste with salt and pepper and beat in the butter, piece by piece until the sauce is thick and creamy. If it seems to be getting too hot, lift it off the heat for a minute or two. Stir in the chopped herbs and pour into a sauceboat.

BEURRE BLANC

(White Butter Sauce)

This is another of the sauces that has become an indispensable part of every cook's repertoire. It can transform an everyday dish into a special one.

MAKES about 250 ml/8 fl oz
25 g/1 oz shallots, finely chopped
50 ml/2 fl oz dry white wine
50 ml/2 fl oz white wine vinegar*
250 g/8 oz chilled butter, cut into
 pieces

Salt
White pepper

*Some cooks use strained lemon juice
 instead of white wine vinegar.

Combine the shallots, wine and vinegar in a small heavy saucepan and simmer, uncovered, over low heat until the liquid has reduced to about 1 tablespoon. Still over low heat, whisk in the butter, one piece at a time, adding a new piece as soon as the previous one has melted into the sauce. Continue until all the butter is used up, beating constantly. Do not let the sauce get too hot as the butter will turn oily. Simply remove the saucepan from the heat briefly if it seems too hot. When all the butter is used up and the sauce is thick and creamy, remove it from the heat and season with salt and pepper. Serve as soon as possible.

TOMATO SAUCE

If ripe, red tomatoes are not available, use the best canned tomatoes possible.

MAKES about 725 ml/24 fl oz
1 medium onion, finely chopped
2 tablespoons olive oil, or vegetable
 oil, or butter
1 clove garlic, finely chopped
900 g/2 lb tomatoes, peeled, seeded
 and chopped
2 tablespoons tomato purée
Salt

Freshly ground pepper
1/8 teaspoon sugar
1 bay leaf
1 tablespoon chopped basil or chervil,
 or sprig thyme, marjoram or
 oregano
125 ml/4 fl oz water

In a heavy saucepan or casserole, sauté the onion in the oil or butter until it is soft. Add the garlic and sauté for 1 minute longer. Add the tomatoes, tomato purée, salt, pepper, sugar, bay leaf and herbs. Stir in the water, cover and simmer for 15 minutes, stirring with a wooden spoon from time to time. The sauce should be thick and well blended. If it is too thick, add a little water, if too thin, cook uncovered for a few minutes longer. Before serving, remove and discard the bay leaf.

MAYONNAISE

MAKES about 475 ml/16 fl oz
2 large egg yolks
1 teaspoon Dijon mustard
Salt
Freshly ground white pepper

350 ml/12 fl oz oil (olive or vegetable or a mixture of both)
4 teaspoons vinegar (any type), or lemon juice

In a shallow bowl, whisk together the egg yolks, mustard, salt and pepper until they are well blended. Whisk in the oil drop by drop until the mixture is thick and creamy. When about half the oil has been absorbed by the egg yolks, whisk in the vinegar or lemon juice. Add the remaining oil, pouring it into the mayonnaise in a thin, steady stream and beating constantly with a whisk. When all the oil has been absorbed, taste for seasoning and add more salt and pepper, vinegar or lemon juice to taste. If the mayonnaise is too thick it may be thinned by adding a tablespoon of water or single cream.

OIL AND VINEGAR DRESSING

This is the basic salad dressing that is usually called by its French name, Vinaigrette. It can be made with a great variety of oils, vegetable, olive, hazelnut, walnut and so on, used in varying proportions. The vinegars available are legion – from malt, cider, wine, both red and white, tarragon and other herb vinegars, to raspberry vinegar, and Japanese rice vinegar. Lemon juice can also be used. Almost endless variations can be played on this theme though the basic proportions for the sauce remain the same. Dijon mustard and garlic may also be added.

MAKES about 250 ml/8 fl oz
50 ml/2 fl oz vinegar
Salt

Freshly ground pepper
175-250 ml/6-8 fl oz oil

Combine the vinegar with salt and pepper to taste in a bowl and whisk in the oil in a steady stream until the mixture is well blended.

GARLIC CROUTONS

2 cloves garlic
¼ teaspoon salt

125 ml/4 fl oz olive oil
French or firm white bread

Crush the garlic with the salt and beat into the olive oil. Cut the crusts off slices of bread and cut the slices into enough 0.6 cm/¼ in cubes to make 125 g/4 oz.

In a frying pan, heat the oil and garlic mixture and sauté the bread cubes over low heat until they are browned all over, tossing them frequently. Alternatively they may be sprinkled with the oil and garlic mixture and baked in a preheated, moderate oven (190°C/375°F/gas 5) until browned, about 10 minutes.

FRESH WHITE CHEESE

This is based on Michel Guérard's Fromage Blanc and I have used it very satisfactorily in sauces and in poultry and seafood mousses. It should be heated very gently and never allowed to boil.

375 g/12 oz ricotta cheese
¼ teaspoon salt

4 tablespoons plain yoghurt

In a blender or food processor, combine all the ingredients and process until very smooth. Transfer to a covered container and refrigerate for 12 hours before using.

If a sauce calls for reducing a mixture containing cream, omit this step and simply add fresh white cheese and warm it through without reducing it.

JUNKET CHEESE

This easy-to-make fresh cheese, when made with whole milk, is an admirable substitute for cream in many recipes, with puddings, or added to soups and sauces at the last minute. Made with skim milk, it is an easy and attractive way to reduce the amount of fat in the diet. Anton Mosimann, the famed Maître Chef des Cuisines of London's Dorchester Hotel, and the creator of Cuisine Naturelle, makes a junket cheese that has an exceptionally good texture. He uses skim milk and lets the milk and junket mixture stand for 24 hours instead of the usually much shorter time, which is just until the mixture has set.

MAKES about 350 ml/12 fl oz
1 L/1¾ pt whole or skim milk
Pinch salt

1 junket tablet, or 2 teaspoons rennet essence

In a saucepan, heat the milk with the salt to lukewarm (43°C/110°F). Pour into a bowl. Crush the junket tablet with a little water and stir it quickly into the milk, or stir in the rennet essence. Cover the bowl and let it stand for 24 hours, or until set. Pour carefully into a sieve lined with a double thickness of dampened cheesecloth set over a large, deep bowl and leave until the cheese is firm, about 45 minutes. Pour off and discard the whey. Put the cheese into a container and refrigerate until ready to use. It will keep, refrigerated, for 3–4 days.

YOGHURT CHEESE

This is the easiest of all the fresh cheeses to make. It is attractive with fresh fruit or other desserts instead of cream, perhaps sprinkled with a little sugar.

Makes about 475 ml/16 fl oz
1 L/1¾ pt plain or low-fat yoghurt   Pinch of salt

Line a large sieve with a double layer of dampened cheesecloth and pour in the yoghurt mixed with the salt. Set over a deep bowl and let the whey drain out until the cheese is firm, about 6 hours. Put into a covered container and refrigerate. Will keep for 2–3 days.

TO STABILIZE YOGHURT

1 L/1¾ pt yoghurt   1 tablespoon cornflour
½ teaspoon salt

Pour the yoghurt into a large saucepan and mix with the salt. Mix the cornflour with a little water and stir into the yoghurt. Bring to a simmer, over very low heat, stirring frequently with a wooden spoon. Cook, over the lowest possible heat, uncovered, at below a simmer for about 10 minutes until thickened. If it is at all grainy transfer to a blender or food processor and process for about 30 seconds. The yoghurt can now be used in cooking without curdling. To keep, pour into a container and refrigerate.

TO CLARIFY BUTTER

Clarified butter does not burn at as low a temperature as ordinary butter, and is used whenever high heat is needed. This is useful when the addition of oil to prevent the butter from burning would alter the flavour of a dish. Clarified butter keeps very well and can be stored in the refrigerator.

Cut the butter into pieces and put it into a small, heavy saucepan, over low heat. Skim off the white froth as it rises. When the butter has melted, let it stand for 2–3 minutes. There will be a milky residue on the bottom of the pan. Strain the clear yellow liquid into a bowl. The residue can be added to soups, stews, or sauces to enrich them.

Unsalted or sweet butter is more satisfactory when clarifying butter. The amount of salt in salted butters varies a great deal, making it hard to judge the saltiness of dishes. Unsalted butter has a more delicate flavour and is best used for all cooking.

DUXELLES

MAKES about 125 g/4 oz
250 g/8 oz mushrooms   **Salt**
50 g/2 oz butter   **Freshly ground pepper**
25 g/1 oz finely chopped shallots, or
   spring onions (white part only)

Wipe the mushrooms and chop finely, using both caps and stems. In a small, heavy frying pan, heat the butter and sauté the mushrooms and shallots or spring onions over moderate heat, stirring from time to time, until the mushrooms have given up all their moisture and the mixture is quite dry. Season to taste with salt and pepper and use as directed in recipes.

TO WASH LEEKS

Leeks need thorough washing to remove any dirt or sand between the outer layers of the leaves. To clean leeks, trim the root end and remove any wilted leaves. Trim the tough tops then slit the leeks lengthways in two places almost to the white part. Wash thoroughly under cold running water, pulling the leaves apart to rinse away sand or dirt.

If recipes call for using the white part only, use the green parts for making soups or stocks. The leeks are now ready to be cooked.

SHALLOTS

Shallots (*Allium ascalonicum*) are members of the onion family, small round bulbs with a brownish-purple skin. Their flavour is mild and delicate, reminiscent of both onion and garlic. They are much used in sauces. If they are not obtainable, use the white part of spring onions.

Starters

Starters have always been a favourite course and some of the best and most original dishes of the new chefs come into this category. They have created different flavour affinities and contrasting textures to beguile the palate and whet the appetite without overwhelming it. They also beguile the eye, making unfussy, edible pictures on the plate. Today's chefs use tableware with great flair, borrowing ideas from the Japanese in the use of multi-shaped china to show food off to its best advantage.

Many of the starters, if served in larger portions, make superb lunch or supper main courses, while an array of them makes a fine buffet for a party. A smaller selection is ideal to serve to friends who drop by for drinks.

The new cooking uses ingredients that would have been considered exotic only a few years ago. Beautiful big yellow, red and green sweet peppers are always available, as are mangetout, fresh ginger root, wild mushrooms, a wide range of salad greens including radicchio and lamb's lettuce, and fresh herbs such as coriander and tarragon. The market is expanding all the time.

Today's chefs care about healthy, as well as enjoyable eating. Sauces are no longer thickened with flour but just reduced and lightly thickened with butter and cream. Though their natural love is for fresh cream in sauces, which gives them a rich flavour and delicate texture, chefs serve their sauces in small quantities to balance taste with health. The diet-conscious, cooking at home, should use only as much cream as necessary to give a good texture and then serve the result sparingly. However, many of us today want to avoid even a small amount of cream in cooking, except perhaps for special occasions. I have found that the fresh cheeses, which can substitute for cream, provide an answer. They are more usually known by their French name, *fromage blanc*, since that is where they originated. Anton Mosimann, in his book *Cuisine Naturelle* (recipes without fat or cream), has a good one, junket cheese, that is easy to make with either junket tablets or rennet essence. There is also a simple yoghurt cheese, and stabilized yoghurt that does not curdle when heated and is good in soups. Yet another, and one I find very satisfactory in cooking, is Michel Guérard's version made with ricotta cheese. There are recipes for all of these in the Basic Recipes on page 9. Also available in shops now is a Greek-type strained yoghurt that is especially good with desserts and can be used generally as a substitute for cream.

In the recipes that follow there are some elegant dishes that are worth spending time on for special occasions, others that can be made ahead of time, and still others that are quick and simple to make.

There is also a whole range of salads that have become popular as starters. They use a wide variety of salad greens and may include game, poultry, meat, fish or shellfish. Many of them are served warm. A selection of these can be found in the Vegetables and Salads chapter on page 183.

SMOKED SALMON AND AVOCADO SOUFFLÉ

This inspired yet simple dish comes from the gifted Scots chef, Murdo MacSween, a founding member of Country Chefs Seven. He is now head chef at the country house hotel, Oakley Court near Windsor, where he creates delectable food. Ideal for a summer lunch, the soufflé can be served as a starter or as a main course.

SERVES 8 as a starter, 4 as a main course

3 tablespoons butter, plus butter for soufflé moulds
3 tablespoons plain flour
Salt
Freshly ground pepper
250 ml/8 fl oz boiling milk
4 egg yolks

5 egg whites
75 g/3 oz grated Swiss cheese
125 g/4 oz smoked salmon, chopped
1 medium avocado, pitted, peeled and chopped
1 teaspoon green peppercorns

If serving as a main course, butter a 1.4 L/2½ pt soufflé mould with melted butter or, as a starter, butter eight 175 g/6 oz soufflé moulds. Refrigerate until the butter is set. Heat the rest of the butter in a medium-sized, heavy saucepan and stir in the flour. Cook, over low heat, stirring with a wooden spoon for 2 minutes, without letting the flour colour.

Season to taste with salt and pepper, remove from the heat and pour in the boiling milk, all at once, stirring until the mixture is smooth and well blended. Return to the heat and cook, stirring, for 2 minutes longer.

Off the heat, beat in the egg yolks, one by one. Beat the whites with a pinch of salt until they stand in firm peaks. Stir about one quarter of the whites into the soufflé mixture, then gently but thoroughly stir in the remaining whites, the cheese, smoked salmon, avocado and green peppercorns. Pour the soufflé mixture into the large soufflé dish, or into the eight small ones. Bake in a preheated, moderate oven (180°C/350°F/gas 4), 10 minutes for the small soufflés, 25–30 minutes for the large one.

WINE SUGGESTION: As this dish is created by Murdo MacSween of Oakley Court near Windsor, an English wine made at Hurley is suggested: Chiltern Valley Wine. This is made from a blend of the French grape Madeleine Angevine and Reichsteiner and Bacchus, grown on the Geneva double curtain system.

SMOKED SALMON AND CRAB MOUSSE

Melvin Jordan, head chef of Pool Court Restaurant with Rooms, at Pool-in-Warfedale in West Yorkshire, has devised a most attractive first course in this dish. He trained originally in Switzerland, specializing in pâtisserie, a most exacting art. It may explain his meticulous approach to food, and his talent for creating dishes that look as good as they taste.

SERVES 4

250 g/8 oz fresh crab meat, picked
  over to remove any cartilage
1 tablespoon grated Parmesan cheese
50 ml/2 fl oz double cream
Salt
Freshly ground pepper
⅛ teaspoon cayenne pepper
½ teaspoon paprika
2 tablespoons lemon juice
1 tablespoon mayonnaise (see Basic
  Recipes, page 23) (optional)
1 envelope (1 tablespoon) unflavoured
  gelatine

Butter
250 g/8 oz thinly sliced smoked
  salmon
2 egg whites

For the Garnish:
Lemon wedges
Parsley sprigs
Chicory and hazelnut salad in
  vinaigrette dressing

In a blender or food processor, combine the crab meat, cheese and cream and process to a smooth purée. Season to taste with salt, pepper, cayenne, paprika, lemon juice and mayonnaise, if using. Soften the gelatine in 50 ml/2 fl oz cold water. Pour it into a small saucepan and stir over very low heat until the gelatine has dissolved. Let it cool, then stir it into the crab mixture. Set aside.

Butter four small soufflé dishes or ramekins, 175–250 g/6–8 oz size, and line them with the smoked salmon strips, letting the excess overhang the dishes (see Note). In a bowl, beat the egg whites until they are frothy and fold them into the crab mixture. Spoon the mixture into the ramekins and cover with the overhanging salmon. Refrigerate for at least 3 hours, or until firmly set.

To unmould, stand them in hot water for a few seconds to loosen the salmon, then turn out onto four plates. Garnish with sprigs of parsley and lemon wedges, and serve with a small salad of chicory and hazelnuts.

Note: Lining the moulds can be tricky. If liked omit the smoked salmon until the crab mousse has been unmoulded then carefully cover it with smoked salmon, tucking the ends under. This will take a smaller amount of salmon.

WINE SUGGESTION: A Chardonnay wine.

WATERCRESS MOUSSE

When watercress is at its crisp, fresh green best I like to make this mousse, created by John Hornsby, another of the Country Chefs Seven, when he was head chef at the Castle Hotel in Taunton, Somerset. A farmer's son from Norfolk with a mother who was an excellent cook, John learned from childhood to recognize quality in all types of food. A delicious mousse, it demonstrates this chef's originality and his love of simple, natural ingredients and fresh, clean flavours.

SERVES 6

For the Mousse:
375 g/12 oz watercress
250 ml/8 fl oz double cream
5 large eggs
1 clove garlic, chopped
Salt
Freshly ground pepper
Freshly grated nutmeg to taste
Butter

For the Sauce:
1 small carrot, cut into julienne strips
1 small stalk celery, cut into julienne strips
1 small leek, using white part only, cut into julienne strips
1 tablespoon butter
75 ml/3 fl oz chicken stock (see Basic Recipes page 10)
75 ml/3 fl oz dry white wine
125 ml/4 fl oz double cream
Salt
Freshly ground pepper

Wash the watercress, cut off and discard the stems and any wilted leaves, and purée in a blender or food processor. Add the cream and blend to mix. Transfer the mixture to a bowl and whisk in the eggs, one by one. Add the garlic, salt and pepper to taste, and the nutmeg.

Pour the mixture into six 125 g/4 oz buttered ramekins and bake in a preheated, moderate oven (180°C/350°F/gas 4) for 30 minutes, or until the mousses are puffed and golden and a knife inserted into the centres comes out clean. Stand the ramekins on a rack for 5 minutes.

While the ramekins are baking, make the sauce. In a heavy frying pan, sauté the carrot, celery and leek in the butter over low heat until the vegetables are soft. Transfer the vegetables to a bowl. Pour the chicken stock and wine into the frying pan and reduce the liquid over high heat to half its volume. Add the cream and vegetables and cook, stirring, for a few minutes until the sauce is slightly thickened. Season to taste with salt and pepper. Spoon the sauce onto six warmed plates. Run a knife round the edge of each ramekin and unmould them onto the plates.

WINE SUGGESTION: A Moselle – light but not overpowering.

MOUSSELINE OF MUSHROOMS AND LEEKS WITH FRESH TOMATO SAUCE

Robert Gardiner, head chef at Ardsheal House Hotel, Kentallen of Appin, Argyll, Scotland, came late to cooking but his enthusiasm has overcome his lack of early apprenticeship. He has a very attractive way with fresh, local ingredients producing understated, original and well-flavoured dishes. He values his kitchen staff, especially his closest assistant Isabell Mitchell, and says they all pay great attention to the small things like producing a perfect serving of French beans, sautéeing a steak to the exact degree of rareness, being consistent, and above all else striving to cook well.

This mousseline is a good example of his cooking philosophy. It is simple, light and delicate and depends on the freshest of ingredients cooked with meticulous care. He finds in the work of the great chefs constant inspiration and looks forward to an exciting future in the kitchen.

SERVES 8

375 g/12 oz mushrooms, wiped over and finely chopped
250 g/8 oz leeks, white part only, washed and thinly sliced
4 tablespoons butter
125 ml/4 fl oz dry white wine
375 ml/12 fl oz double cream
1 teaspoon cornflour

Salt
Freshly ground pepper
3 large eggs
3 large egg yolks
Butter for ramekins
½ recipe tomato sauce (see Basic Recipes, page 22)

Cook the mushrooms and leeks in the butter, covered, over very low heat until soft, about 5 minutes. Uncover, turn the heat to moderately high and cook, stirring the mixture, for 2 minutes. Add the wine and continue to cook until the liquid has reduced by half, about 2 minutes. Add half the cream and again cook until the liquid is reduced by half, stirring frequently. Dissolve the cornflour in a little cream or water and add to the mixture. Cook, stirring, for 1 minute until the mixture is thickened. Set aside to cool.

Put half the mushroom-leek mixture into a bowl and set it aside. Transfer the other half to a blender or food processor and process until it is smooth. Add the purée to the mixture in the bowl. In another bowl, lightly beat the eggs and egg yolks together, then whisk in the remaining cream. Fold this mixture into the mushroom-leek mixture, combining thoroughly. Season to taste with salt and pepper.

Butter eight 175 g/6 oz ramekins or small soufflé dishes and fill with the mixture. Put into a baking tin and pour in enough water to come halfway up the ramekins. Bake in a preheated, slow oven (150°C/300°F/gas 2) for about 1 hour or until the mousselines are firm to the touch. Remove from the oven and let them stand for 5 minutes. Run a knife round the inside of the ramekins, then unmould onto heated plates. Run a circle of tomato sauce round each mousseline and serve the rest of the tomato sauce separately.

WINE SUGGESTION: A light Moselle wine.

CHICKEN LIVER PÂTÉ

Chicken livers are infinitely useful, as well as being inexpensive and always available, so I was delighted to find this chicken liver pâté. It is the creation of Brian Prideaux-Brune, the chef at Plumber Manor in Dorset, the seventeenth-century home of the Prideaux-Brune family which they have turned into a Restaurant with Rooms. The pâté is simple to make and has just that touch of originality that makes it different from the usual chicken liver pâté. It is refreshingly uncomplicated.

SERVES 6 to 8

375 g/12 oz unsmoked bacon, sliced
2 teaspoons vegetable oil
1 small onion, very finely chopped
2 cloves garlic, very finely chopped
4 tablespoons butter
625 g/1¼ lb chicken livers, halved
1 tablespoon fresh thyme leaves, chopped
2 teaspoons black peppercorns, crushed
75 ml/3 fl oz brandy
75 ml/3 fl oz dry Madeira
175 ml/6 fl oz double cream
Salt
Clarified butter (see Basic Recipes, page 25)

In a heavy frying pan, sauté the bacon in the vegetable oil until it is crisp. Drain on paper towels and crumble, or chop it finely.

Wipe out the frying pan and sauté the onion and garlic in the butter until the onion is soft. Add the chicken livers and sauté until they are lightly browned on the outside but still pink inside. Add the bacon, thyme and peppercorns to the frying pan, stir to mix then scrape the contents into a food processor or blender and purée coarsely. The mixture should not be smooth. Return the purée to the frying pan, and stir in the brandy, Madeira, cream and salt to taste. Heat the mixture through until it is just under boiling point. Pour into a terrine and cool. Cover with a layer of clarified butter and refrigerate. Serve with toast strips.

WINE SUGGESTION: A full-bodied wine – a Bordeaux, red Burgundy or Côtes-du-Rhône.

CHICKEN LIVER TERRINE WITH MARSALA GLAZE

The versatile chicken liver is used here with great simplicity by Eamonn Webster, who was head chef at Balcraig House, a country house hotel near Scone in Perthshire, Scotland. Eamonn Webster followed his journalist father's footsteps at the start of his career but was lured into food by sheer interest. He found his way into the kitchen of the famed Royal Crescent Hotel in Bath and from there worked with such gifted chefs as Shaun Hill, now at Gidleigh Park. Eamonn believes cooking starts in the sea and the ground, not in the pot, and likes to use as much produce as he can from the Balcraig farm so that he feels at one with nature and the seasons.

The Marsala glaze on this terrine makes an interesting contrast to the smooth richness of the liver pâté, while the mango accompaniment is an unusual and delicious addition. The terrine has an even richer taste when made with duck livers.

SERVES 4
Butter
250 g/8 oz chicken livers*
2 large eggs
Salt
Freshly ground pepper
175 ml/6 fl oz Marsala wine

For the Garnish:
1 large mango, peeled and diced

*Duck livers may also be used for the terrine.

Butter four 7 cm/3 in ramekins or small soufflé dishes and set them aside.

Pat the livers dry and cut them in halves. Put them into a blender or food processor with the eggs, salt and pepper and process to a smooth purée. For a very fine purée, push this mixture through a fine sieve set over a bowl. Spoon the purée into the ramekins or small soufflé dishes and place them in a baking tin with water to come about halfway up the sides of the dishes. Bake in a preheated, slow oven (150°C/300°F/gas 2) for about 1½ hours or until the liver mixture is firm to the touch.

While the livers are baking, pour the Marsala into a small, heavy saucepan and reduce it to coating consistency over moderate heat. Spoon over the ramekins when they are done. Cool, and chill lightly in the refrigerator. Garnish with the mango and serve with fresh wholewheat bread and butter.

WINE SUGGESTION: A big wine such as a full-bodied regional Bordeaux – a St-Emilion, for example, or a red Burgundy or Côtes-du-Rhône, though not one of the great Burgundies or Rhônes.

CHICKEN LIVER PARFAIT WITH GREEN PEPPERCORNS

This is a very luscious way to serve chicken livers. It comes from Allan Garth, the young Master Chef at Gravetye Manor, an elegant sixteenth-century manor house, now a country house hotel, in Sussex. He was born and grew up in Cumbria, England's Lake District, and from a very early age wanted to be a chef. He loves to cook and he studies the recipes of the great chefs of both past and present, gaining ideas and inspiration from them. This parfait is an example of how he works. I think the original inspiration for the dish is a mousse created by one of the great masters, Charles Barrier of Chez-Barrier in Tours, France. The family look is there, but this is clearly something new, and very much Allan's own creation.

SERVES 8 to 10

500 g/1 lb belly of pork, cut into thin strips
250 g/8 oz chicken livers, marinated in milk overnight
125 g/4 oz butter, melted
2 tablespoons dry Madeira
2 tablespoons tawny port
¼ teaspoon green peppercorns

25 g/1 oz sultanas, soaked in the Madeira and port overnight
Salt
Freshly ground pepper
Sprig thyme

For the Garnish:
Lettuce leaves
Parsley or chervil sprigs

Line a 1 L/1¾ pt terrine or soufflé dish with the pork belly strips, letting the excess hang over the edges. Strain the milk from the chicken livers and discard.

Cut the livers in halves and put them into a food processor or blender. Turn on the machine and slowly pour in the melted butter to make a smooth purée. Turn the machine off. Stir in all remaining ingredients except the thyme and pour the mixture into the prepared terrine. Place the sprig of thyme on top, and cover with the overhanging strips of pork belly. Put the terrine into a baking tin with water to come halfway up the side. The water should be hot but not boiling. Bake in a preheated, moderate oven (180°C/350°F/gas 4) for about 1 hour, or until the terrine is firm to the touch.

Remove from the oven and cool at room temperature. Wrap the terrine in foil and chill before serving. Serve garnished with a lettuce leaf or two, or some parsley or chervil sprigs, and accompanied by brioche or plain toast.

WINE SUGGESTION: A St-Emilion, red Burgundy or Côtes-du-Rhône.

VENISON LIVER WITH ORANGE AND JUNIPER BERRY SAUCE

This is a most exciting starter. It is not always easy to find venison liver, so I also tried it with calves' liver and, though it lacks the special flair given it by venison liver, it is very good indeed. The sauce is quite superb. It is the creation of chef John McGeever of Congham Hall, a country house hotel in King's Lynn, Norfolk, who has a special gift for combining foods in new and unusual ways.

SERVES 4

4 seedless oranges, peeled and segmented
75 ml/3 fl oz Mandarin liqueur
125 ml/4 fl oz brandy
625 g/1¼ lb venison or calves' liver, thinly sliced

Plain flour
Salt
Freshly ground pepper
175 g/6 oz butter
1½ teaspoons juniper berries, crushed

In a bowl, combine the orange segments, Mandarin liqueur and brandy and set aside to macerate.

Dip the liver slices in flour seasoned with salt and pepper. In a frying pan, heat 4 tablespoons of the butter and sauté the liver slices over moderately high heat for about 1 minute a side. Transfer to a plate and keep warm.

Lift out the orange segments from the liqueur and brandy and set aside. Pour the liquid into the frying pan, add the juniper berries, and season to taste with salt and pepper. Whisk in the remaining butter, cut into pieces, adding a new piece as the previous one is absorbed into the sauce.

Arrange the liver slices on four warmed plates, garnish with the orange segments and pour the sauce over the liver.

WINE SUGGESTION: A white Loire or a white Côtes-du-Rhône.

SWEET RED PEPPER MOUSSE WITH FRESH TOMATO PURÉE

Raymond Blanc, the brilliant young chef-patron of the Manoir aux Quat' Saisons, an exquisite old Cotswold-stone manor house converted into a country house hotel and elegant restaurant at Great Milton near Oxford, is a chef of quite extraordinary talent. This simplest and freshest of starters is a delight, like all his creations.

SERVES 6

For the Mousse:
375 g/12 oz ripe sweet red peppers
Vegetable oil
125 g/4 oz ripe tomatoes, peeled, seeded and chopped
50 g/2 oz sugar
50 ml/2 fl oz red wine vinegar
½ teaspoon unflavoured gelatine
Salt
Freshly ground pepper
½ teaspoon cayenne pepper

125 ml/4 fl oz double cream, whipped

For the Fresh Tomato Purée:
375 g/12 oz tomatoes, peeled, seeded and chopped
3 tablespoons red wine vinegar
Salt
Freshly ground pepper
1 teaspoon sugar (optional)
3 tablespoons olive oil

Halve the peppers and remove the stems, veins and seeds. Lightly oil a baking sheet and arrange the peppers on it. Bake in a preheated, hot oven (250°C/450°F/gas 8) for 15 minutes. Cool slightly then peel. Chop coarsely and set aside with the tomatoes.

Put the sugar into a small, heavy saucepan over moderate heat, stirring with a wooden spoon from time to time until the sugar caramelizes and is a golden brown. Add the vinegar and continue to cook until the caramel dissolves in the vinegar. Reduce the mixture to half, still over moderate heat. Set aside.

Pour 50 ml/2 fl oz cold water into a small saucepan and sprinkle on the gelatine. When it has softened, dissolve the gelatine over low heat, stirring.

In a blender or food processor, combine the peppers and tomatoes and process to a purée. Pour into a saucepan and simmer over moderate heat to reduce the excess liquid. When the mixture has thickened slightly add the gelatine and the sugar and vinegar mixture. Season with salt, pepper and cayenne and chill lightly. Fold in the cream, transfer to a bowl and refrigerate until set, about 3 hours.

While the mousse is setting, make the fresh tomato purée. In a blender or food processor, combine the tomatoes with the vinegar. Season with salt and pepper, and the sugar if liked, and process until smooth. With the machine running, gradually pour in the oil. Pour the purée over six chilled plates. Using two spoons, shape the pepper mousse into quenelles and place on top of the purée. Do not serve wine with this.

BRIE FAVOURS

Willie MacPherson, when he was head chef at The Feathers Hotel in Woodstock, near Oxford, recalled that Michael Smith, the great expert on traditional English cooking, first suggested this eighteenth-century recipe to him. He has given it his own special touch, turning it into a modern dish and adding the fresh herbs he loves to use. The Favours are delicious with pre-dinner drinks, or as a first course. In the nineteenth century they were served as a savoury at the end of the meal, a course that has now largely disappeared.

SERVES 6

250 g/8 oz wedge ripe Brie, rind left on, cut into 0.6 cm/¼ in cubes

50 ml/2 fl oz olive oil

15 g/½ oz fresh herbs, a mixture of any of the following: parsley, thyme, rosemary, basil, mint, tarragon, chervil

1 clove garlic, crushed

250 g/8 oz puff pastry (see Basic Recipes, page 15)

1 egg yolk

Vegetable oil for deep frying

For the Garnish:

Salad greens

Lemon wedges

In a bowl, combine the cubes of Brie with the oil, herbs and garlic and leave at room temperature, turning them over from time to time with a wooden spoon, for 4 hours.

Roll out the pastry to about 0.3 cm/⅛ in thickness and cut it into 24 rounds, using a 5 cm/2 in cutter. Beat the egg yolk lightly with a teaspoon of water and brush half the pastry circles with the egg wash. Drain the oil from the cheese cubes and distribute them, with any herbs and garlic, among the egg-washed pastry circles. Top with the remaining pastry circles and press to seal the edges firmly. Arrange on a tray or flat dish and refrigerate for 20–30 minutes to rest the pastry.

Deep-fry the pastry circles in the vegetable oil until they are golden brown on both sides and puffed up. Drain on paper towels and serve hot, garnished with salad greens and lemon wedges, two per person as a starter, or serve with pre-dinner drinks on a plate lined with paper napkins.

WINE SUGGESTION: A white Burgundy with the predominance of the Chardonnay grape.

SCRAMBLED QUAIL EGGS WITH TRUFFLES

Michael Croft, who was Michael Quinn's sous-chef at The Ritz in London, and is now head chef at The Royal Cresent Hotel in Bath, matches the luxury of the hotel with his cooking. He has a specially imaginative way with starters. This one would make a late Sunday breakfast into an occasion, or start a celebratory dinner on a festive note. Michael keeps his quails' eggs in a container with 2 or 3 fresh truffles for 24 hours to truffle-scent the eggs before using them, an impractical suggestion for most of us. Even without truffle-scented eggs, or a truffle, the dish has great charm.

SERVES 4

6 tablespoons butter
25 g/1 oz very finely-diced carrot
25 g/1 oz very finely-diced celery
25 g/1 oz very finely-diced onion
1 small fresh truffle, brushed and washed, or 1 small canned truffle (optional)
50 ml/2 fl oz dry Madeira
50 ml/2 fl oz Cognac, or other brandy

475 ml/16 fl oz veal or chicken stock (see Basic Recipes, pages 10, 11)
20 quails' eggs
Salt
Freshly ground pepper
1 tablespoon double cream
4 rectangles cooked puff pastry, each 5 × 7 cm/2 × 3 in (see Basic Recipes, page 15)

In a medium-sized casserole, heat 1 tablespoon of the butter. Add the carrot, celery and onion, cover and cook over very low heat without letting the vegetables colour. Add the truffle, if using, Madeira and Cognac and enough of the stock to barely cover the truffle. Simmer, covered, over low heat for 30 minutes. Lift out the truffle, let it cool and cut it into dice, about 0.6 cm/¼ in. Set aside. Reduce the liquid to half and beat in 3 tablespoons of the butter, cut into pieces, adding each piece as the previous one is incorporated into the sauce. Set aside in a warm place.

Break the quails' eggs into a bowl and season with salt and pepper. Fold in the double cream. Heat the remaining 2 tablespoons of butter in a frying pan, add the egg mixture and gently stir with a wooden spoon or spatula. While they are still soft and runny, fold in the truffle dice and remove from the heat. Have ready the puff pastry rectangles, split horizontally and warmed. Put the bottom halves of the pastry on four warmed dessert-size plates and top with the scrambled quails' eggs. Put the pastry tops on the eggs and pour some of the sauce to one side of each plate.

WINE SUGGESTION: White Burgundy – a Chardonnay or Chablis.

SCALLOPS AND LANGOUSTINE TAILS WITH MUSHROOMS AND CHIVES

When I am feeling self-indulgent I cook this Michael Croft dish just for myself. It is delicate with a lovely mix of flavours. Michael uses wild mushrooms, much more flavourful than cultivated ones, though these will do quite well if wild ones are not available. To serve two people just double the quantities. Dublin Bay prawns are also called langoustines.

SERVES 1

5 tablespoons butter
3 small scallops, halved horizontally
Salt
Freshly ground pepper
4 Dublin Bay prawns, or 4 King prawns
125 g/4 oz wild mushrooms or tiny button mushrooms

25 ml/1 fl oz dry vermouth
125 ml/4 fl oz strong fish stock (see Basic Recipes, page 13)
2 tablespoons reduced shellfish stock (if available)
2 tablespoons chopped chives

Melt 1 tablespoon of the butter in a small frying pan. Season the scallops lightly with salt and pepper and toss them in the butter. Lift out and set aside. Season the prawns and toss in the butter. Add to the scallops. Add the wild mushrooms or tiny button mushrooms to the pan and cook for 3 minutes, over moderately high heat. Add to the scallops. Pour the vermouth into the frying pan, then add the fish stock and shellfish stock, if using. Reduce the mixture to 4 tablespoons. Pour in any liquid that has collected with the shellfish, then whisk in the remaining butter, cut into small pieces. Add the chives and shellfish and warm through on low heat. Arrange on a warmed plate at random.

WINE SUGGESTION: A white Rioja.

TERRINE OF VEGETABLES AND CREAM CHEESE

Philip Burgess grew up in kitchens. His father was chef to the Earl of Morley, and by the time he was six Philip knew he wanted to be a cook. He is now head chef of the Arundell Arms in Lifton, Devon, a favourite hotel with anglers who enjoy fly fishing for trout and salmon. He has an inspired way with simple ingredients. This terrine could not be easier to make and is a perfect first course for an elegant lunch or dinner. I find it also makes a good main course for lunch when accompanied by cold poached salmon or trout, or any seafood such as crab, and a green salad, or sliced tomatoes drizzled with oil and sprinkled with chopped parsley or chervil. I like to serve it with mayonnaise.

SERVES 6

1 recipe crêpes (pancakes, see Basic Recipes, page 19)
3 egg yolks
1 whole egg
125 g/4 oz cream cheese, or fresh white cheese (see Basic Recipes, page 24)
125 ml/4 fl oz double cream
2 teaspoons grated Parmesan cheese
1 clove garlic, crushed
1 tablespoon chopped fresh tarragon, or 1 teaspoon dried
Salt
Freshly ground pepper
12 whole green peppercorns or ½ teaspoon cayenne pepper (optional)

1 small courgette, cut into thin 5 cm/2 in strips
1 medium carrot, scraped and cut into thin 5 cm/2 in strips
1 medium leek, cut into strips 1 × 5 cm/½ × 2 in
125 g/4 oz cauliflower florets
5 tiny Brussels sprouts, left whole, larger ones halved
2 button mushrooms, cut into thick slices
2 tablespoons butter, about

For the Garnish:
Lettuce leaves

Make the crêpes and set aside. In a bowl, combine the egg yolks, egg, cream cheese, cream, Parmesan cheese, garlic, tarragon, and salt and pepper to taste. If liked, add the green peppercorns or cayenne. Whisk the ingredients together until the mixture is smooth.

To assemble the terrine, generously butter a 23 × 12 cm/9 × 5 in loaf tin and line it with the crêpes reserving 2 or 3 to top the terrine. Put half the vegetables into the loaf tin and cover with half the cheese mixture. Top with remaining vegetables and cover with rest of the cheese mixture. Fold the crêpes. Cover with buttered greaseproof and aluminium foil and place in a baking tin with water to come about halfway up the terrine. Bake for 1¾ to 2 hours in a preheated, moderate oven (190°C/375°F/gas 5). Remove from the oven, cool and refrigerate for several hours or overnight.

To unmould, stand the terrine very briefly in warm water. Cut into 6 slices and serve garnished with lettuce leaves.

WINE SUGGESTION: A dry, light white wine such as Muscadet.

SALMON AND PRAWN TERRINE

Sheena Buchanan-Smith, chef-patronne of the Isle of Eriska hotel and restaurant, at Ledaig in Argyll, Scotland, enjoys cooking and enjoys pleasing people with what she cooks. Widely travelled, she has come to believe very strongly that Scots cooks should maintain the tradition of Scottish cooking by using what are some of the very best ingredients in the world. This recipe, wholly delicious, demonstrates her point of view.

SERVES 6

250 g/8 oz smoked salmon, thinly sliced in long strips
250 g/8 oz cooked and peeled medium or small prawns
3 tablespoons lemon juice
Freshly ground pepper
250 ml/8 fl oz mayonnaise (see Basic Recipes, page 23), using lemon juice
250 ml/8 fl oz double cream, or fresh white cheese (see Basic Recipes, page 24)
Salt
1 envelope (1 tablespoon) unflavoured gelatine

For the Garnish:
Lettuce leaves
Lemon wedges

Line an oiled terrine, about 23 × 12 cm/9 × 5 in, with the salmon strips. A long, narrow terrine is best.

In a food processor or blender, combine the prawns, any bits of salmon left over, the lemon juice, pepper and mayonnaise. Process to a smooth purée. Add the cream and process for 30 seconds longer. Taste for seasoning and add a little salt if necessary.

Pour 50 ml/2 fl oz cold water into a small, heavy saucepan. Sprinkle the gelatine on the water to soften. Set the saucepan over the lowest possible heat and stir until the gelatine has dissolved. When it is cool, pour it into the food processor or blender and process just long enough to mix thoroughly. Pour the mixture into the terrine and cover it with the overhanging salmon strips. Cover the terrine with aluminium foil, weight lightly, and refrigerate overnight. To unmould, stand the terrine in hot water for a few seconds to loosen the salmon then invert it onto a flat serving platter. Slice and serve on plates garnished, if liked, with lettuce leaves and lemon wedges.

WINE SUGGESTION: A Sancerre.

STILTON AND PEAR MOUSSE

Sheena Buchanan-Smith has a special talent with appetizers of this kind and I find this as attractive as her salmon and prawn terrine (above). She has an abundance of fresh pears available in the season and invented this dish to take advantage of that abundance.

SERVES 6
Vegetable oil
2 large, very slightly underripe pears
2 envelopes (2 tablespoons) gelatine
125 ml/4 fl oz tawny port
375 g/12 oz Stilton, or other blue
   cheese, coarsely chopped
250 g/8 oz cream cheese, or fresh

white cheese (see Basic Recipes,
   page 24)
250 ml/8 fl oz mayonnaise (see Basic
   Recipes, page 23)
Salt
Freshly ground pepper

Brush a 23 × 12 cm/9 × 5 in terrine with oil and set it aside.

Peel and core the pears. Cut into quarters, and poach in water to cover over low heat for 5 minutes. Drain, cool, and chop coarsely.

Pour 125 ml/4 fl oz cold water into a small, heavy saucepan and sprinkle on the gelatine to soften. When it has softened, place the saucepan over low heat, add the port wine and cook, stirring, until the gelatine has dissolved. Cool.

In a food processor or blender, combine the Stilton, cream cheese and mayonnaise and process to a smooth purée. Pour in the gelatine mixture and process to mix. Transfer to a bowl, season to taste with salt and pepper and stir in the chopped pear. Pour into the oiled terrine and chill until set. Slice and serve with brioche toast or toast as a first course. Or, to serve with drinks, accompanied by cheese biscuits, pour the mixture from the food processor or blender into a serving bowl, add salt and pepper and the chopped pear and refrigerate until set.

WINE SUGGESTION: A Riesling from the Alsace.

TIMBALE DE VOLAILLE AU CRABE

(Chicken Mousse Stuffed with Crab)

While other chefs are writing their menus in English, John Armstrong, head chef at Martin's Restaurant in London, writes his in French 'because it is the language of the kitchen'. Neat poetic terms, he says, become heavy and cumbersome when translated into long phrases in English. His food, however, is English, is poetic, and never cumbersome. Almost all his training has been in England, except for a brief time in France, but that training was his grounding in classic technique. From that basis he creates new dishes which are simple, unpretentious and very good. This recipe calls for a live crab, but like many others I shrink from crab-killing and buy fresh crab ready cooked, or frozen crab meat. Make the crab stock from the shell, or use shellfish stock (see Basic Recipes, page 14). I find this stock so useful that whenever I make it I also freeze some.

SERVES 4

For the Mousse:
1 skinned and boned chicken breast,
    weighing about 125 g/4 oz
1 large egg white
125 ml/4 fl oz double cream
Salt

For the Filling and Sauce:
1 tablespoon vegetable oil
1 tablespoon butter
1 small onion, finely chopped
2 medium carrots, scraped and
    chopped
1 clove garlic, very finely chopped
Bouquet garni of sprig thyme, 2
    sprigs parsley, bay leaf, and sprig
    tarragon

50 ml/2 fl oz brandy
125 g/4 oz tomatoes, peeled, seeded
    and chopped
1 tablespoon tomato purée
250 ml/8 fl oz dry white wine
250 ml/8 fl oz crab stock, or shellfish
    stock (see Basic Recipes, page 14)
125 ml/4 fl oz double cream
250 g/8 oz crab meat, picked over to
    remove any cartilage
Salt
Freshly ground pepper
125 g/4 oz butter

In a blender or food processor, reduce the chicken breast to a purée. Add the egg white and process until the mixture is very smooth. For a very fine, light texture rub the purée through a sieve into a bowl, otherwise just transfer it to a bowl. Refrigerate the purée for at least 15 minutes, then beat in the cream with a whisk, very gradually, until it has all been absorbed. Season with salt. Set aside.

In a heavy saucepan, heat the oil and butter, add the onion and carrots, cover and cook over very low heat for 5 minutes. Add the garlic and bouquet garni, stir to mix and cook for a minute or two longer. Pour in the brandy and reduce to half. Add the tomato, tomato purée, white wine and crab stock. Bring to a boil and simmer until reduced to half. Strain the liquid into a clean saucepan. Add the cream and reduce to 175 ml/6 fl oz. Set aside while assembling the timbales.

Butter six 250 g/8 oz ramekins and line them with some of the chicken mousse. Season the crab meat with salt and pepper and divide between the ramekins, then cover with the rest of the mousse. Cover with buttered aluminium foil. Put in a baking tin with enough water to come about halfway up the sides and bake in a preheated, slow oven (160°C/325°F/gas 3) for 15-20 minutes or until a skewer inserted in the centre comes out clean. Have ready four warmed plates. Beat the butter into the sauce, piece by piece, over low heat until it is thick and creamy, but do not let it boil. Turn the ramekins out onto the plates and mask with the sauce. They may be garnished, if liked, with sprigs of chervil and diced tomato.

WINE SUGGESTION: Pouilly Fuissé or the Rully Aligoté grape for dry flavour.

SEABASS MOUSSE WITH SCAMPI AND CHIVES

Alan Vikops, young head chef at the County Hotel in Canterbury, Kent, says food should be prepared and presented with a feeling that comes from the heart. Expertise is not enough, he says, though he has plenty of that having worked under Anton Mosimann of the Dorchester and Michael Quinn when he was at The Ritz.

SERVES 4

For the Mousse:
250 g/8 oz fillet of striped bass, chilled
125 ml/4 fl oz dry vermouth, preferably Noilly Prat, chilled
Salt
Pinch cayenne pepper
2 chilled egg whites
250 ml/8 fl oz chilled double cream

For the Sauce:
2 tablespoons shallots, finely chopped
250 ml/8 fl oz strong fish stock (see Basic Recipes, page 13)
125 ml/4 fl oz dry vermouth, preferably Noilly Prat

Pinch cayenne pepper
Salt
125 ml/4 fl oz double cream
25 g/1 oz snipped chives
4 tablespoons unsalted butter, cut into pieces
125 g/4 oz peeled cooked scampi, kept warm
4 whole cooked unpeeled scampi or Dublin Bay prawns (optional)

For the Garnish:
4 sprigs chervil

In a blender or food processor, combine the fish, vermouth, salt and cayenne and process to a smooth purée. Add the egg whites and 6 tablespoons of the cream and process for 30 seconds longer. Rub the mixture through a fine sieve into a bowl set in a larger bowl of ice. Whisk the mixture for a few minutes until it stiffens slightly. Gradually beat in the rest of the cream. Taste for seasoning and add salt and cayenne if necessary. Spoon the mixture into four 175 g/6 oz soufflé moulds. Refrigerate for 30 minutes then cover and cook in a preheated, moderate oven (190°C/375°F/gas 5) for about 15 minutes, or until set.

Make the sauce: Put the shallots, fish stock, dry vermouth, pinch cayenne pepper and salt to taste in a small, heavy saucepan and reduce over moderate heat to half. Strain the mixture and return it to the saucepan. Add the cream and simmer until it is slightly reduced. Add the chives and whisk in the butter, piece by piece. Check the seasoning and add salt and cayenne if necessary. Unmould the mousses onto four plates, pour the sauce over, and arrange the peeled scampi round each mousse with the unpeeled, whole scampi or Dublin Bay prawns if using. Garnish with a sprig of chervil.

WINE SUGGESTION: White Burgundy, a Chardonnay.

QUAIL BREASTS WITH HERB DUMPLINGS

This rather grand dish, another creation of Alan Vikops, is not as difficult to make as it sounds. It is, in fact, quite simple as the choux pastry used in the dumplings is the easiest of all pastries to make. The juxtaposition of quail breasts and herb dumplings is deliciously unusual and is the perfect beginning to a meal with fish as the main course, or as the main course of a light meal, lunch or supper.

SERVES 4

4 quail
5 tablespoons butter
1 tablespoon vegetable oil
700 ml/1¼ pt veal or chicken stock (see Basic Recipes, pages 10, 11)
125 ml/4 fl oz dry Madeira

4 tablespoons chopped mixed herbs, chives, parsley, tarragon
½ recipe choux pastry (see Basic Recipes, page 17)
Salt
Freshly ground pepper

Using a small, sharp knife, cut and pull the breasts from the quail, or have your butcher do it. Coarsely chop the carcasses with the legs and wings.

Heat 1 tablespoon of the butter with the oil in a large, heavy frying pan and brown the bones in the fat. Transfer to a saucepan, pour in 350 ml/12 fl oz of the stock and simmer until the liquid is reduced to 125 ml/4 fl oz. Add the Madeira and reduce to 175 ml/6 fl oz. Strain, pressing down hard on the bones to extract all the flavour, season with salt and pepper and set aside.

Pour the remaining stock into a large, shallow saucepan and bring the liquid to a simmer. Mix the herbs into the choux pastry. Using two teaspoons, shape the pastry into quenelles and drop into the stock. When cooked the dumplings will rise to the top of the stock. Lift them out with a slotted spoon and keep them warm. Reserve the stock for another use.

Heat 2 tablespoons of the butter in a frying pan large enough to hold all the quail breasts in a single layer. Add the breasts and sauté over moderate heat until they are lightly browned on both sides, but still pink inside, about 4 minutes.

Heat the reserved sauce in a small saucepan and whisk in the remaining butter, cut into pieces, over moderate heat.

Arrange the quail breasts on four warmed plates. Surround with the herbed dumplings. Pour the sauce over the quail breasts. Serve immediately.

WINE SUGGESTION: A wine from the Rheinhessen or even a Steinwein.

TERRINE OF FRESH CRAB

Baba Hine, chef-patronne of Corse Lawn House, a charming eighteenth-century restaurant in the little village of Corse Lawn in Gloucestershire, has a natural flair for cooking and the sort of feeling for food that is born, not made. She has no formal training but comes from a family that appreciates good food. And she married a Frenchman, Denis Hine of the Cognac family, decidedly a help, not a hindrance as he has a real love of good food and good wine. She is an unfussy cook who likes to create modern dishes, with an emphasis on lighter food.

SERVES 6

Butter

6 × 15 cm/6 in pancakes (crêpes, see Basic Recipes, page 19)

375 g/12 oz monkfish, or similar non-oily white fish

3 egg whites

25 g/1 oz chopped chives

25 g/1 oz chopped parsley

Salt

Freshly ground pepper

⅛ teaspoon grated nutmeg

6 tablespoons double cream

250 g/8 oz each white and brown crab meat, or 500 g/1 lb white crab meat

Beurre blanc (see Basic Recipes, page 22) using tarragon vinegar

For the Garnish (optional):

Fresh herbs

Lightly grease a 23 × 12 cm/9 × 5 in terrine with butter. Line the terrine with the pancakes, letting them hang over the sides of the terrine so they can be folded over the fish and crab meat.

Have the monkfish, egg whites, herbs and double cream thoroughly chilled. In a blender or food processor, process the monkfish to a purée. Add the egg whites and process again until the mixture is light and smooth. Add the herbs, salt, pepper and nutmeg. Process for a few seconds to mix, then slowly pour in the cream with the machine running.

Pour one-third of the mixture into the pancake-lined terrine. Top with the white crab meat, another third of the mixture, the brown crab meat (or white if using all white crab meat), and the remaining third of the mixture. Fold the pancakes over to cover the terrine. Set the terrine in a baking pan with water to come about halfway up the sides, cover and bake in a preheated, hot oven (220°C/425°F/gas 7) for 50 minutes. Allow to cool then refrigerate, weighted, for several hours.

Make 1 recipe of beurre blanc using tarragon vinegar instead of white wine vinegar.

To serve, pour a little beurre blanc onto six plates and top with slices of the terrine. The plate may be garnished, if liked, with sprigs of any fresh herb.

WINE SUGGESTION: A lively white wine – a Sancerre.

CRAB TART

Tim Cumming is chef-patron of The Hole in the Wall Restaurant with Rooms in Bath. Tim had his first job there when trail-blazer George Perry-Smith was running it and starting the British culinary revolution. That was in 1965 and now, twenty-two years later, Tim and his wife Sue, a fine cook who also worked there earlier, are back where they began, still young and very creative. A pleasant homecoming for them.

Tim has created this very richly-flavoured tart which makes a fine beginning to a meal especially when the main course is plainly roasted or grilled meat or poultry. It can also be made as individual tartlets. With a green salad it makes a good main course for four people for lunch.

SERVES 6 as a starter, 4 as a main course

For the Pastry Shells:
1 recipe shortcrust pastry (see Basic
    Recipes, page 17)
Raw rice for weighting shells

For the Filling:
4 tablespoons butter
250 g/8 oz thinly sliced mushrooms
175 ml/6 fl oz tawny port

Salt
Freshly ground pepper
125 ml/4 fl oz double cream
250 g/8 oz fresh crab meat, picked
    over to remove any cartilage
1 recipe béchamel sauce (see Basic
    Recipes, page 20)
50 g/2 oz grated Gruyère cheese

Make the tartlet shells as in the previous recipe, Prawn Tartlets, or make one 20 cm/8 in tart shell. Bake the large tart for 15 minutes, and a further 8 minutes with the rice and greaseproof paper removed. Set the pastry shells aside.

Heat the butter in a saucepan, add the mushrooms and cook over moderately high heat for about 3 minutes. Add the port and simmer until the liquid has reduced to half its volume. Season with salt and pepper, pour in the cream, bring to a boil, remove from the heat and cool. Spread the cooled mixture over the bottom of the large tart shell or the tartlets. Top with the crab meat, finish with the béchamel sauce and sprinkle with the cheese. Bake in a preheated, moderately hot oven (180°C/350°F/gas 4) for 30 minutes for the large tart, 10–15 minutes for the tartlets, or until the cheese is browned and the filling bubbly.

WINE SUGGESTION: Muscadet.

DEVILLED CRAB AND SHRIMPS

This light, attractive starter is a good example of the cooking of Alain Dubois, head chef at The Lygon Arms, a country house hotel in the Cotswold village of Broadway, Worcestershire that began as a coaching inn 450 years ago. It is still a haven for travellers, who today dine or lunch in the Great Hall in an ancient setting with modern comfort. The dish has an interesting mix of texture and flavour.

SERVES 4

2 tablespoons butter
1 sweet red pepper, seeded and finely chopped
1 sweet green pepper, seeded and finely chopped
1 small onion, finely chopped
50 g/2 oz breadcrumbs, made with day-old bread
Salt

Freshly ground pepper
1 teaspoon English dry mustard
2 teaspoons Worcestershire sauce
⅛ teaspoon Tabasco
125 g/4 oz crab meat, picked over and any cartilage removed
125 ml/4 fl oz single cream
125 g/4 oz small shrimps, peeled

In a medium-sized heavy saucepan or casserole, heat the butter and sauté the red and green peppers and the onion until the vegetables are soft. Transfer to a bowl and add the breadcrumbs, salt, pepper, mustard, Worcestershire sauce and Tabasco, tossing lightly to mix. Fold in the crab meat, then stir in the cream.

Butter four 250 g/8 oz ramekins and arrange the shrimps on the bottom. Cover with the crab mixture. Bake in a preheated, moderate oven (180°C/350°F/gas 4) for 15 minutes or until heated through.

WINE SUGGESTION: Muscadet.

LOBSTER MOUSSE

Raymond Duthie, whom I first met when he was head chef at the Royal Crescent Hotel in Bath, is a Scot, trained in French cooking techniques, who also did a two-year stint in pâtisserie under a Swiss chef. He is a perfectionist without being over-fussy.

This dish makes a light and very elegant beginning to a dinner. Raymond serves the mousse on beurre blanc (white butter sauce). I like to vary this using, for example, a fresh tomato sauce. Raymond Duthie also suggests serving the mousses with his Steamed Fish in Butter Sauce (page 118).

SERVES 4

375 g/12 oz cooked lobster meat or lobster tails, coarsely chopped
3 large egg whites
250 ml/8 fl oz double cream, or fresh white cheese (see Basic Recipes, page 24)
Salt
Freshly ground pepper
Butter
1 recipe beurre blanc (white butter sauce, see Basic Recipes, page 22)

In a blender or food processor, reduce the lobster meat to a purée, or pound it in a mortar until the texture is very fine and light. Scrape the purée into a bowl and set it in a larger bowl of ice. Gradually beat in the egg whites, then the cream. Season with salt and pepper.

Spoon the mixture into four 250 g/8 oz buttered ramekins and place them in a baking tin with water to come halfway up the sides. Bake in a preheated, moderate oven (180°C/350°F/gas 4) until puffed and lightly browned, 15-20 minutes. Pour the beurre blanc sauce onto four warmed plates and unmould the mousses on top.

WINE SUGGESTION: A Chardonnay wine.

LANGOUSTINE TAILS WITH STRAWBERRY VINAIGRETTE

Denis Woodtli, head chef at Lochalsh Hotel, Kyle of Lochalsh on Scotland's west coast, likes to use strawberries in an unorthodox way. He feels their tart sweetness makes them ideal with shellfish, and he has created this recipe as proof. Serve as a starter, or in double quantities as a main course. ((Langoustines are also called Dublin Bay prawns.)

SERVES 4

4 small langoustine tails, each weighing about 125 g/4 oz
150 g/5 oz hulled strawberries
Salt
Freshly ground pepper
1 tablespoon red wine vinegar
4 tablespoons olive or vegetable oil
1 large ripe avocado, peeled, pitted and quartered lengthways

For the Garnish (optional):
4 teaspoons caviar

Cook the lobster tails in salted water for 5 minutes. Lift them out of the water and let them cool, then shell them and cut each in quarters, lengthways. In a blender or food processor, purée the strawberries, then sieve to remove the pips. Season with salt and pepper, and return to the blender or food processor. With the machine running, add the vinegar then pour in the oil in a slow, steady stream. Pour the sauce onto four lightly chilled plates. Arrange a slice of avocado on each plate with the sliced lobster tails in a fan round it. Garnish the tails with a little caviar, if using.

WINE SUGGESTION: A crisp, dry wine – a Sauvignon.

MOUSSE OF SMOKED TROUT

Martin Bredda is chef to the Earl and Countess of Normanton at their family seat, Somerley at Ringwood in Hampshire, which they make available for lunch and dinner parties, weekend stays, and banquets and business seminars. Martin has a simple aim in cooking. He wants to cook well, present the food beautifully, and use the best of the good things available to him – the fish and game from the estate especially. The venison dish he gave me (see page 173) is one of the best I have ever had, but it isn't by its nature light, and Martin feels that getting the right balance in a meal is as important as good cooking and presentation. This mousse is a very light and pleasant beginning to a meal.

SERVES 4 to 6

1 smoked trout, weighing about 300 g/10 oz	Salt
⅛ teaspoon grated nutmeg	Freshly ground pepper
Generous pinch saffron powder	125 ml/4 fl oz double cream
1 egg	Butter
1 egg white	Tomato sauce (see Basic Recipes, page 22)

Bone the trout and put it into a food processor or blender with the nutmeg, saffron, egg, egg white and salt and pepper to taste and process until the mixture is smooth. Scrape the mixture out of the food processor or blender and rub it through a fine sieve into a bowl. Beat in the cream with a wooden spoon and pour the mousse into a buttered 850 ml/1½ pt soufflé dish. Bake in a preheated, moderate oven (180°C/350°F/gas 4) for 15–20 minutes or until a knife inserted into the mousse comes out clean. Serve with tomato sauce.

WINE SUGGESTION: A white Burgundy – an Aligoté.

RAINBOW TROUT PÂTÉ

Margaret Brown, chef-patronne of Simonsbath House Hotel in the forest of
Exmoor, Somerset, has created a trout pâté of great delicacy, particularly
appropriate if it is to be followed by highly flavoured food. Margaret, who
originally taught herself to cook from the Time-Life *Foods of the World* series
of cookbooks, is an expert on early English cookery and many of her dishes are
adapted from the past. They tend to be highly flavoured so the pâté makes a
light contrast. If a more definite flavour is needed, use smoked trout.

SERVES 4

Butter

1 whole cleaned rainbow trout

125 ml/4 fl oz dry white wine

125 g/4 oz plus 2 tablespoons butter

1 tablespoon lemon juice, or to taste

50 ml/2 fl oz double cream

Salt

Freshly ground pepper

Generously butter a heavy frying pan large enough to hold the trout
comfortably. Add the trout, pour in the wine and cook, covered, over very
gentle heat, a bare simmer, for 10 minutes, or until done. Uncover, cool, and
lift out the fish. Reduce the liquid in the pan over moderately high heat to
about 1 tablespoon.

While the liquid is reducing, skin and bone the trout and discard the head,
skin and bones. Flake the fish. In a blender or food processor, combine the
trout, cooking liquid, the 125 g/4 oz butter, cut into pieces, and the lemon
juice and process to a purée. With the machine running, add the cream. Season
to taste with salt and pepper and transfer to a bowl. In a small saucepan, melt
the rest of the butter and pour it over the pâté. Chill the pâté for at least 2 hours
before serving. It will keep for about a week refrigerated. Serve with Melba
toast.

WINE SUGGESTION: A dryish Rhine wine – a Moselle.

QUENELLES OF SMOKED HADDOCK
WITH BEURRE BLANC

David Adlard spent years in industry before cooking finally claimed him. He
became a chef because he loves good food, and now has his own restaurant,
Adlard's in Wymondham, Norfolk. His passion is for seasonal food, using
local ingredients wherever he can for their freshness, and often using berries
and wild things growing in hedgerows and meadows. The result is food out of
the ordinary.

SERVES 6
250 g/8 oz smoked haddock fillet
250 g/8 oz fillet of sole or any firm-
  fleshed, non-oily white fish
3 large egg whites
125 ml/4 fl oz double cream
Salt
Freshly ground pepper
Pinch cayenne pepper

Beurre blanc (white butter sauce, see
  Basic Recipes, page 22)

For the Garnish:
Peeled, diced tomato
Sliced raw button mushrooms
Sliced radishes

Purée the haddock and sole in a blender or food processor. With the machine running, add the egg whites and process until well blended. Work the purée through a fine sieve into a bowl and refrigerate for 30 minutes. Set the fish purée in a larger bowl filled with crushed ice and slowly beat in the cream with a wooden spoon. Season to taste with salt, pepper and cayenne.

To shape the quenelles, use two tablespoons dipped in hot water. Scoop out a tablespoon of the fish mixture and smooth it into a neat oval with the other spoon. Slide the quenelles into a saucepan of hot, salted water, or fish stock, and poach gently without letting the liquid boil, for 10 minutes. Lift out carefully with a slotted spoon and arrange two quenelles on each of six warmed plates. Garnish with tomato, mushrooms and radishes and pour the beurre blanc over the fish. If liked this could be served as a main course for 2 perhaps with the addition of boiled new potatoes, tossed in butter and chopped parsley, or mint.

WINE SUGGESTION: Muscadet.

MARINATED SALMON

Scotland has very fine salmon, a challenge to chefs looking for new ways to use it without destroying the integrity of its flavour and texture. I particularly liked two from England, one from Scotland, which show the chefs' ingenuity. They are all different, all good. This recipe is from Kenneth Bell, MBE, a Scot, who devised it when he owned and ran the sixteenth-century Thornbury Castle Restaurant and Hotel, near Bristol. Kenneth is a pioneer of today's good cooking, and this dish is classical in its simplicity.

SERVES 6
750 g/1½ lb centre cut of salmon

For the Marinade:
175 ml/6 fl oz dry white wine
1 tablespoon salt
¼ teaspoon freshly ground pepper

4 tablespoons lemon juice
75 ml/3 fl oz orange juice
1 small onion, finely chopped
1 clove garlic, very finely chopped
4 tablespoons olive oil

Cut the salmon in half horizontally and remove all skin and bones, leaving two fillets. Cut each fillet into three little steaks, each weighing 50–75 g/2–3 oz.

In a bowl, whisk together all the ingredients for the marinade. Add the salmon pieces to the marinade, and refrigerate. Turn the salmon pieces from time to time and make sure they are all covered by the marinade. The salmon is ready after 6 hours but is at its best at 24–48 hours. Serve with a little salad at the side of the plate.

WINE SUGGESTION: A white Burgundy – an Aligoté.

VARIATION 1
Denis Woodtli, head chef at Lochalsh Hotel in the Western Highlands of Scotland, is also a hunter and fisherman. He created this recipe for the salmon he loves to catch.

SERVES 2

250 g/8 oz fresh salmon, skinned and boned, and cut into 0.6 × 1 cm/¼ × ½ in strips
125 ml/4 fl oz lemon juice
2 teaspoons chopped parsley
1 tablespoon green peppercorns*
50 ml/2 fl oz olive oil

Salt
Freshly ground black pepper

*Chef Woodtli sometimes omits the green peppercorns and adds 1 tablespoon chopped shallots and 1 tablespoon freshly grated ginger root.

Combine all the ingredients in a bowl and refrigerate for 4–6 hours. Stir with a wooden spoon from time to time and make sure all the pieces are well covered by the marinade. Serve on a bed of shredded lettuce.

VARIATION 2
Michael Collom, the young head chef at The Priory Hotel in Bath, sees cooks as artists who orchestrate their dishes to create the right harmony of flavours. His marinated salmon is interestingly different from the other two.

SERVES 6

900 g/2 lb piece of fresh salmon from tail section
50 g/2 oz coarse sea salt
Freshly ground pepper
50 g/2 oz coarsely chopped fresh dill
125 ml/4 fl oz brandy

1 teaspoon dry English mustard

For the Garnish:
Mayonnaise (see Basic Recipes, page 23) mixed with chopped chives and dill

Prepare the salmon one day in advance. Ask the fishmonger to skin and fillet the salmon, and remove all the small bones. Sprinkle the salmon fillets with the sea salt. Do not use ordinary salt as this dissolves too quickly. Press the salt firmly into the fish on both sides and wrap in aluminium foil. Refrigerate for 24 hours.

Unwrap the salmon and brush away any salt that has not dissolved. The fish should be firm to the touch. Season generously with pepper then sprinkle with the dill, pressing it down firmly. Sprinkle with the brandy and, using a fine sieve, shake the mustard over the fish. Rewrap in foil, and refrigerate for 3–4 hours before serving. Cut the salmon into thin slices and serve with mayonnaise mixed with a little chopped chives and dill.

BRANDADE OF SMOKED MACKEREL IN PASTRY

George Perry-Smith, whose restaurant The Hole in the Wall in Bath started a revolution in British cooking, had no formal training as a chef. He now runs the Riverside Restaurant with Rooms at Helford in Cornwall where he is chef-patron.

This dish is an interesting putting-together of ideas and demonstrates George Perry-Smith's philosophy of letting ingredients combine as naturally as possible.

SERVES 8

2 recipes puff pastry (see Basic
  Recipes, page 15)
2 large cloves garlic
Salt
250 g/8 oz smoked mackerel, skinned
  and boned

6 tablespoons olive oil, warmed
6 tablespoons warm milk
Freshly ground pepper
2 teaspoons lemon juice
Egg yolk

Make the puff pastry (see Basic Recipes, page 15).

Pound the garlic in a mortar with a little salt. In a food processor or blender, purée the mackerel with the garlic until it is very light, or pound it in a mortar with the garlic. Put the purée in the top of a double boiler over warm water. It is important that the purée should be warm not hot. Pour the oil and milk into 2 small jugs and add them to the mackerel alternately, a little at a time, beating with a wooden spoon. Keep the mixture light and soft, not sloppy. When the mackerel has absorbed all the oil and milk it will take without becoming runny, season it with pepper and lemon juice and a little salt, if necessary. Chill in the refrigerator.

Roll out the pastry fairly thin and cut into twenty four 7 cm/3 in circles. Put a heaped teaspoon of mackerel mixture in the centre of each, fold over and seal. Refrigerate for at least 1 hour.

Mix the egg yolk with 1 teaspoon of cold water and brush the turnovers with it. Bake in a preheated, hot oven (200°C/400°F/gas 6) for about 12 minutes, or until they are puffed and golden. Serve three per serving with a choice of sauces, Dill Cream or Cucumber Sambal (see overleaf).

DILL CREAM:

125 ml/4 fl oz whipping cream
Salt
Freshly ground pepper

1 teaspoon lemon juice
1 tablespoon ground dill seed

Whip the cream until it stands in soft peaks then season with salt, pepper and lemon juice and fold in the dill seed.

CUCUMBER SAMBAL:

1 cucumber, peeled and finely diced
Salt
1 tablespoon finely chopped onion
1 tablespoon finely chopped celery
½ to 1 teaspoon cayenne pepper, according to taste, or 1 fresh hot red chilli, seeded and chopped

Freshly ground pepper
1 tablespoon parsley, or fresh coriander, finely chopped
2 tablespoons oil and vinegar dressing (see Basic Recipes, page 23) made with lemon juice instead of vinegar

Cut the cucumber into a bowl and sprinkle it lightly with salt. Let it stand 15 minutes then rinse and drain thoroughly. Add the onion, celery, cayenne or chilli, pepper and parsley or coriander. Mix well then toss with the oil and lemon juice dressing.

WINE SUGGESTION: A Muscadet or Sancerre.

SOLE AND SCALLOPS WITH SAFFRON SAUCE

Simon Collins, head chef at Bishopstrow House, a lovely Georgian mansion, now an elegant country house hotel, at Warminster in Wiltshire, is a cook of great creativity. His dishes, like this one, are simple and very pure in taste.

SERVES 6
500 g/1 lb fillets of sole or flounder, skinned and boned
250 g/8 oz large scallops, with coral if possible
2 large egg whites
½ teaspoon salt
250 ml/8 fl oz double cream
2 tablespoons lemon juice
Butter

For the Sauce:
250 ml/8 fl oz strong fish stock (see Basic Recipes, page 13)
125 ml/4 fl oz double cream
250 ml/8 fl oz dry white wine
½ teaspoon saffron threads
Salt
Freshly ground pepper

In a blender or food processor, combine the sole, coarsely chopped with the coral from the scallops, the egg whites and salt and process until very smooth and light. Scrape into a bowl and put into a larger bowl filled with ice. Using a wooden spoon, gradually beat in the cream, then the lemon juice. Chill in the refrigerator for at least 30 minutes. Cut the scallops into 0.6 cm/¼ in dice and fold into the chilled sole mixture. Spoon into six 175 g/6 oz buttered soufflé dishes or ramekins, and put into a baking tin. Pour in hot water to come about halfway up the sides and cook covered in a preheated, moderate oven (180°C/350°F/gas 4) for 12–15 minutes or until set.

While the mousses are cooking, make the sauce. Pour the fish stock into a saucepan with the cream, stir to mix and simmer, over moderate heat, until the mixture is reduced to coating consistency. In another saucepan, combine the wine and saffron and simmer until the wine is reduced to half. Pour the reduced saffron-wine mixture into the stock and cream. Taste, and add salt and pepper, if necessary.

Have ready six warmed plates. Run a wet knife round the edge of the moulds and unmould onto the plates. Spoon the sauce round the mousses.

WINE SUGGESTION: A Sauvignon Blanc.

GÂTEAUX OF TOMATOES WITH SCALLOP SAUCE

W. John Dicken, whom I met when he was head chef at Longueville Manor in Jersey (the Channel Islands), never wanted to do anything but cook and now, fully trained but still very young, feels the same way. He is now setting up his own restaurant in St. Saviour. He takes infinite pains, insists on having superb ingredients and in this appetizer has created an unusual and appealing dish.

SERVES 4

For the Gâteaux:
5 tablespoons butter
2 medium onions, finely chopped
1 clove garlic, very finely chopped
500 g/1 lb tomatoes, peeled, seeded and chopped
1 teaspoon chopped fresh basil
2 teaspoons tomato purée
Salt
Freshly ground pepper
2 large eggs and 1 yolk

3 tablespoons double cream

For the Scallop Sauce:
250 ml/8 fl oz fish stock (see Basic Recipes, page 13)
50 ml/2 fl oz dry vermouth, preferably Noilly Prat
8 large scallops, each cut into 3 slices
125 ml/4 fl oz single cream
4 tablespoons butter, cut into pieces

Using 1 tablespoon of the butter, prepare four 125 g/4 oz ramekins or small soufflé dishes. Melt the butter, brush the inside of the ramekins generously and refrigerate them until the butter has set.

Heat the rest of the butter in a medium-sized, heavy saucepan, add the onions and garlic, cover and cook over very low heat for about 10 minutes. Do not let the onion brown. Add the tomatoes, basil, tomato purée and salt and pepper to taste and cook, covered, still over very low heat, for 15 minutes. Pour through a very fine strainer to get rid of surplus liquid, or cook uncovered, for the last 5 minutes of cooking to evaporate the excess. Transfer to a food processor or blender and process until smooth. In a bowl, beat the eggs and egg yolk together, beat in the cream and stir in the tomato mixture. Check the seasoning, and add more salt and pepper if necessary. Pour the mixture into the prepared ramekins. Cover with aluminium foil, put into a baking tin with water to come halfway up the sides, and bake in a preheated, slow oven (150°C/300°F/gas 2) for about 20 minutes, or until the gâteaux are firm to the touch when the foil is removed. Allow to rest for 2-3 minutes before unmoulding. To unmould, slide a knife round the inside edge of the ramekins then invert onto four warmed plates.

While the tomato gâteaux are cooking, make the sauce. In a saucepan, combine the fish stock and vermouth and the scallops. Simmer the scallops for 1-2 minutes, lift out and keep warm. It is important not to overcook them. Over brisk heat, reduce the fish stock mixture to half. Pour in the cream, bring to a simmer and whisk in the pieces of butter, one at a time, adding a new piece as the last one is absorbed.

Garnish the tomato gâteaux with the scallop sauce, pouring it over and around the gâteaux. Make sure each plate gets 6 slices of scallop in the sauce.

WINE SUGGESTION: Moselle or a Hock from the Palatinate.

FRESH CRAB, SORREL AND TOMATO TART

David Harding, head chef at Bodysgallen Hall Hotel in North Wales, has had his training in Wales and the North of England. His point of view is very British, and he also wants his cooking to reflect the atmosphere of Bodysgallen, a great country house, mainly seventeenth century, now a small hotel. The result is exciting. His dishes are all highly original, though based firmly on tradition.

SERVES 4

½ recipe shortcrust pastry (see Basic Recipes, page 17)
125 g/4 oz crab meat, picked over and any cartilage removed
250 ml/8 fl oz double cream
125 g/4 oz tomato, peeled, seeded and chopped
25 g/1 oz sorrel leaves, finely chopped

Salt
Freshly ground pepper
75 ml/3 fl oz hollandaise sauce (see Basic Recipes, page 21)

For the Garnish:
Watercress

Make the shortcrust pastry and refrigerate until ready to use.

In a bowl, combine the crab meat, cream, tomato, sorrel and salt and pepper to taste. Line four 7 cm/3 in soufflé dishes, or ramekins, with shortcrust pastry and fill with the crab mixture. Bake in a preheated, moderate oven (180°C/350°F/gas 4) for about 10 minutes or until lightly set. Pour 2 tablespoons of hollandaise sauce onto each of four warmed plates. Unmould the crab tarts on each and garnish with a little watercress.

WINE SUGGESTION: An Aligoté, Pouilly Fuissé or Rully.

POACHED EGGS AND PRAWNS IN TARTLET SHELLS

David Harding is also the creator of this appetizer, which has a lovely mix of flavours and contrasting textures, crisp pastry in contrast with the unctuous smoothness of egg yolk, and herbs blending with spinach in hollandaise sauce. It is a complicated, though not a difficult dish, and is well worth the trouble. I find this a great luncheon dish if double portions are served. If it is served as a starter, follow it with a very plain main course like grilled lamb chops.

SERVES 8 as a starter, 4 as a main course

For the Prawn Sauce:
175 g/6 oz unpeeled, medium-sized, raw prawns
2 tablespoons butter
250 ml/8 fl oz fish stock (see Basic Recipes, page 13), or water
125 ml/4 fl oz dry white wine
Sprig each thyme and parsley
1 tablespoon plain flour
Salt
Freshly ground pepper
1 teaspoon tomato purée (optional)
1 tablespoon double cream

For the Filling:
250 ml/8 fl oz hollandaise sauce (see Basic Recipes, page 21)

25 g/1 oz fresh mixed herbs such as parsley, tarragon, thyme, basil and marjoram
50 g/2 oz cooked, puréed spinach
8 × 7 cm/3 in shortcrust pastry tart shells (see Basic Recipes, page 17)
½ recipe duxelles (see Basic Recipes, page 26)
8 large poached eggs

For the Garnish:
Watercress sprigs
Peeled chopped tomato

Peel the prawns and set them aside. In a small saucepan, heat 1 tablespoon of the butter and toss the shells in the butter over moderate heat until they turn pink. Pour in the fish stock or water, the dry white wine, and thyme and parsley sprigs and simmer, covered, for 15 minutes. Strain, pressing down hard on the shells to extract all the flavour. Measure and reduce the liquid to 250 ml/8 fl oz over moderately high heat. Pour into a cup and set aside. Rinse out and dry the saucepan. Heat the remaining tablespoon of butter in the pan, stir in the flour and cook, over very low heat, for 2 minutes without letting the mixture colour. Off the heat, gradually stir in the prawn stock until the mixture is smooth, then simmer over low heat until the sauce is reduced to about 125 ml/4 fl oz. Season with salt and pepper. If liked a teaspoon of tomato purée may be added to enhance the colour. Stir in the cream and set the sauce aside.

Pour the hollandaise sauce into another small saucepan and stir in the herbs and puréed spinach. Set the saucepan in a larger pan of warm water to keep it warm without curdling.

Warm the tartlets and half fill them with the duxelles. Put a poached egg into each and spoon the hollandaise sauce over them. Arrange them on a baking sheet and glaze quickly under a grill.

Add the prawns to the prawn sauce and simmer for about 2 minutes to cook the prawns. Pour the sauce over eight warmed plates and place a tartlet on each. Garnish with watercress sprigs and chopped tomato and serve as an appetizer. For a main course arrange 2 tartlets on each of four warmed plates.

WINE SUGGESTION: A Chardonnay.

CRAYFISH TAILS WITH CURRY SPICES

Mark Napper, a young English chef, was in charge of the kitchen at Cromlix House, Dunblane in Perthshire, Scotland when I met him and enjoyed this attractive dish. The curry spices make a reticent appearance in the sauce adding to its subtlety.

SERVES 4

½ sweet red pepper, seeded and cut into thin strips
½ sweet green pepper, seeded and cut into thin strips
Salt
12 crayfish tails, shelled, or 12 king prawns, peeled

250 ml/8 fl oz single cream
1 teaspoon mixed curry spices (turmeric, garam masala, cumin, coriander) or use curry powder with a little extra ground coriander
Salt
Freshly ground pepper

Drop the pepper strips into a large saucepan of briskly boiling, salted water and simmer for 3 minutes. Drain, rinse immediately in cold water, drain and set aside.

Combine the crayfish tails or prawns, cream and curry spices or powder in a medium-sized saucepan and bring to a simmer. Cover and simmer for 2-3 minutes. Take out the crayfish or prawns and keep them warm. Reduce the cream over moderately high heat until it is of coating consistency. Taste for seasoning and add salt and pepper as necessary.

Have ready four warmed plates. Place 3 crayfish tails or prawns on each plate, coat with the sauce and arrange two piles, one red, one green, of pepper strips on each side of the shellfish. Serve immediately.

WINE SUGGESTION: Nothing really goes with curry, but if you must have wine try a white Hermitage.

SCAMPI IN PUFF PASTRY

Paul Vidic, head chef of Michael's Nook in the Lake District, likes uncomplicated presentation without a medley of colours on the plate. This is an exceedingly simple dish which meets that requirement. It tastes wonderful, with an understated balance of flavours. The recipe, doubled, can make a light main course for lunch.

SERVES 4

4 puff pastry rectangles, 7 × 5 cm/3 × 2 in (see Basic Recipes, page 15)
125 ml/4 fl oz strong fish stock (see Basic Recipes, page 13)
250 ml/8 fl oz dry vermouth, preferably Noilly Prat
18 scampi (Dublin Bay prawns), shelled, if frozen thoroughly defrosted
250 ml/8 fl oz whipping cream

½ teaspoon chopped fresh tarragon leaves, or ¼ teaspoon dried, crumbled
Salt
Freshly ground pepper
50 g/2 oz each julienne of leek, celery and carrot
2 tablespoons butter
Squeeze lemon juice

Bake the puff pastry rectangles. Set aside, keeping them warm.

In a small, heavy saucepan, heat the fish stock and the vermouth and simmer for a minute or two. Add the scampi and simmer, covered, for 1 minute. Remove the shellfish from the pan, and keep warm, covered. Over brisk heat, reduce the liquid in the saucepan until syrupy. Add the cream and tarragon, season with salt and pepper and reduce until the sauce coats the back of a spoon.

Meanwhile, cook the vegetables separately in salted water until crisp. Drain, combine, and add to the sauce. Add the butter, shaking the saucepan over moderate heat until the butter has melted. Taste for seasoning, adding salt and pepper if necessary. Add a squeeze of lemon juice. Add the shellfish and cook just long enough to warm them through. Serve immediately on the bottom half of the puff pastry, split in two and topped with the other half.

WINE SUGGESTION: A Sauvignon Blanc.

MOUSSE OF PIKE

Robert Jones was born in Newmarket, Suffolk, son of the famous jockey R. A. (Bobby) Jones who won every classic race except the Derby. Robert took to cookery and is now head chef at Ston Easton Park near Bath, a Palladian mansion of great distinction that was begun in 1739 and is now a country house hotel. Robert is a very modern cook. He believes fervently in healthy food and just as fervently in food that is as good to eat as it is to look at. His cooking is essentially British, brought inventively up to date. When pike is not available, I use any non-oily white fish, preferably sole, and find this works well.

SERVES 8 as a starter, 4 as a main course

500 g/1 lb skinned and boned fillet of pike or other white fish such as sole, flounder or plaice
1 large egg
2 large egg whites
Salt
Freshly ground pepper
Pinch nutmeg
250 ml/8 fl oz double cream, or fresh white cheese (see Basic Recipes, page 24)
Butter for greasing moulds

For the Sauce:
1 small onion, finely diced
125 g/4 oz sliced button mushrooms
125 ml/4 fl oz dry white wine
250 ml/8 fl oz double cream, or fresh white cheese (see Basic Recipes, page 24)
1 teaspoon anchovy essence
Freshly ground pepper
Salt

For the Garnish:
Parsley sprigs

Chop the fish coarsely and purée in a blender or food processor, and process with the egg and egg white until very smooth. Season with salt, pepper and nutmeg. Scrape into a bowl and set in a larger bowl filled with ice. Beat in the cream, or fresh white cheese, a little at a time, using a wooden spoon. Butter eight 250 g/8 oz ramekins or small soufflé dishes and spoon in the mousse mixture. Refrigerate for at least 1 hour.

When ready to cook, put the filled moulds into a shallow baking tin with hot water to come about halfway up the sides. Bake in a preheated, moderate oven (180°C/350°F/gas 4) for about 15 minutes. Lift out of the baking tin and keep warm.

While the mousse is baking, make the sauce. Combine the onion and mushrooms in a saucepan with the white wine and simmer until the liquid is reduced by a third. Pour in three quarters of the cream and simmer until the sauce is thick enough to coat a spoon. Stir in the anchovy essence, season with pepper and a little salt, if necessary. Beat the rest of the cream in a bowl, fold it into the sauce and heat it through. If using fresh white cheese, simply add with the anchovy essence and seasonings and heat gently through.

To serve, turn the moulds out onto eight heated plates and coat with the sauce. Glaze quickly under a preheated grill. Garnish with parsley sprigs.

This makes a light lunch or supper for 4 served with a green salad, cheese and fruit, or a pudding.

WINE SUGGESTION: A Muscadet.

PASTA WITH MIXED MUSHROOMS

This pasta dish is a fine example of Robert Jones' point of view. It is light and unusual.

SERVES 4 as a starter, 2 as a main course

50 g/2 oz morel mushrooms
75 g/3 oz dried Chinese mushrooms
Whiskey (preferably Irish)
1 medium onion, finely chopped
1 tablespoon chopped fresh herbs
   such as parsley, mint, chervil, etc.
2 tablespoons butter
250 g/8 oz sliced mushrooms

250 ml/8 fl oz whipping cream or
   fresh white cheese (see Basic
   Recipes, page 24)
Salt
Freshly ground pepper
250 g/8 oz pasta (fettuccini or
   tagliatelli)

Combine the morels and Chinese mushrooms in a bowl and pour over enough whiskey just to cover. Leave to soak for about an hour or until soft. Lift out and slice. Reserve the soaking liquid.

In a frying pan, sauté the onion and herbs in the butter until the onion is soft. Add the sliced, dried mushrooms and the fresh mushrooms and sauté for 3 or 4 minutes over moderate heat. Add the reserved soaking liquid and the cream and simmer for a few minutes to lightly thicken the sauce. If using fresh white cheese gently heat the sauce through without letting it come to a simmer. Season with salt and pepper and keep warm.

Drop the pasta into a large saucepan of briskly boiling, salted water and boil for about 4 minutes. It should be tender but firm. Fresh pasta will cook in a slightly shorter time. Drain, add the mushroom sauce and heat through. Serve in four shallow bowls.

This makes a hearty lunch for 2 accompanied by a green salad, cheese and fruit.

WINE SUGGESTION: A medium wine - a Hock from the Palatinate.

MOUSSELINE OF CHICKEN AND ASPARAGUS WITH GREEN SAUCE

Campbell Cameron, the young Scots head chef of Culloden House near Inverness, Scotland, has a passion for quality in foods and an equal passion for the good things Scotland produces. When he finds that France produces something better in quality than his native Scotland does, he sends to France for it. However, it amuses him that he can gather fresh chanterelles from the woods around Culloden House. This simple and pleasant dish depends on the freshness of the ingredients used for its best flavour.

SERVES 8

250 g/8 oz cooked, chopped spinach
Salt
Freshly ground pepper
½ teaspoon freshly grated nutmeg
2 tablespoons butter
500 g/1 lb cooked chicken, coarsely
   chopped

350 ml/12 fl oz double cream or
   fresh white cheese (see Basic
   Recipes, page 24)
¼ teaspoon cayenne pepper
375 g/12 oz cooked asparagus tips

Season the spinach with salt, pepper and nutmeg. Heat the butter in a frying pan and toss the spinach in the butter, stirring for 2–3 minutes. Line a 1 L/1¾ pt terrine with the spinach, using about one-third and refrigerate.

In a blender or food processor, reduce the chicken to a purée. Transfer to a bowl and set in a larger bowl of ice. Add the cream gradually, beating constantly. Season with salt, pepper, and the cayenne pepper. Chill for 15 minutes.

Remove the terrine from the refrigerator and spread half of the chicken mousse on top of the spinach, followed by half of the asparagus tips and another third of the spinach. Follow with the rest of the chicken mousse, and the remaining asparagus tips. Top with the rest of the spinach. Chill thoroughly for several hours. Unmould and serve sliced on chilled plates with mayonnaise served separately, if liked.

WINE SUGGESTION: A dry white – a Muscadet.

FANTAIL OF DUCK WITH LEEK AND SPINACH SAUCE

Michael Quinn, the first British chef to be Maître Chef des Cuisines at The Ritz in London, is now head chef at Ettington Park, a luxurious country house near Stratford-upon-Avon. He was one of the founding members of Country Chefs Seven, when he was head chef at Gravetye Manor in Sussex. Michael created this dish as a starter and, like all his dishes, it is brilliantly original, and modern. This is robust enough to make the main course of lunch or dinner.

SERVES 2

4 leeks, using white part only, trimmed and washed
125 g/4 oz leaf spinach
6 tablespoons butter
Salt
Freshly ground pepper
250 ml/8 fl oz chicken stock (see Basic Recipes, page 10)

1 whole duck breast, skinned and boned
8 mangetout
125 ml/4 fl oz double cream
2 tablespoons chives, finely chopped
Slices of truffle (optional)

Coarsely chop the leeks. Wash and chop the spinach and set aside. In a saucepan, heat 2 tablespoons of the butter, add the leek and cook, covered, over very low heat until the leek is softened but not browned, about 4 minutes. Season to taste with salt and pepper, pour in the chicken stock. Cover and simmer for a few minutes longer then add the spinach and simmer for about 3 minutes. Cool and pour the mixture into a blender or food processor. Process to a very smooth purée. For a finer texture, push through a sieve. Set aside.

In a frying pan, heat the remaining butter. Season the duck with salt and pepper and cook in the butter, turning once, until done, about 6–8 minutes. The duck should be pink inside. Slice each breast lengthways into five or six slices. Keep warm.

Drop the mangetout into a saucepan of boiling water and blanch for 1 minute. Lift out and dry. Cut six of the mangetout in half diagonally then slice into a fan shape. Cut the remaining three mangetout into julienne strips.

Return the sauce to the heat, stir in the cream and warm through. Pour the sauce onto two plates. Top the sauce with the duck breast, sprinkle chives round the edge of the plate, garnish the duck with the mangetout fans and sprinkle with the julienne, and truffle slices (if using).

WINE SUGGESTION: White Burgundy – a Chardonnay.

CHICKEN LIVERS WITH MARJORAM

Francis Coulson, chef-patron of Sharrow Bay Hotel in England's Lake District, was one of the pioneers of the renaissance of British cooking. He faced extraordinary difficulties when he arrived at Sharrow with little more than a saucepan and a frying pan, but he had such a zest for cooking, kindled in his youth by the superb cooking of his Lancashire-born mother, that all difficulties were overcome and his small Lakeside hotel, overlooking Lake Ullswater, and his cooking are now world famous. He refuses to take shortcuts in the preparation of his dishes, and serves food that is of a simple nature, created out of the best ingredients, with special touches that give it great interest.

The herb garden at Sharrow Bay provides the kitchen with fresh herbs which add immeasurably to the flavour of this dish. Establishing a herb garden was an early priority for Francis Coulson who feels fresh herbs are very important in cooking. Dried herbs can, of course, be used.

SERVES 4

3 tablespoons bacon fat, or butter
1 medium onion, finely chopped
2 rashers bacon, finely chopped
1 clove garlic, chopped (optional)
250 g/8 oz chicken livers, cut into
   1 cm/½ in pieces
2 tablespoons fresh marjoram leaves,
   chopped, or 1 tablespoon dried,
   crumbled

6 medium-sized mushrooms, thinly
   sliced
1 tablespoon plain flour
125 ml/4 fl oz single cream
75 ml/3 fl oz chicken stock (see Basic
   Recipes, page 10)
Salt
Freshly ground pepper
2 tablespoons finely chopped parsley

Heat the bacon fat or butter in a frying pan and sauté the onion and bacon over moderate heat until the onion is soft. Add the garlic, if liked, and sauté for 1 minute longer. Lift out with a slotted spoon to a bowl and keep warm.

In the fat remaining in the frying pan, adding a little more if necessary, sauté the chicken livers with the marjoram over moderately high heat for about 4 minutes, or until the livers are lightly browned on the outside but still pink inside. Lift out with a slotted spoon and add to the onion and bacon mixture. Add the mushrooms to the pan and sauté, still over moderately high heat, until the mushrooms have given up all their liquid. Add to the other cooked ingredients.

Stir in the flour and cook over low heat, stirring for about 1 minute. Stir in the cream and chicken stock to make a smooth sauce. Season to taste with salt and pepper, stir in all the reserved ingredients and cook just long enough to heat them through. Spoon into small individual dishes and sprinkle with parsley.

WINE SUGGESTION: A white Burgundy – an Aligoté.

TARTE AUX FROMAGES BLANC

(Cheese Flan)

Thérèse A. Boswell, better known as Terry Boswell, is the chef-patronne of Combe House Hotel at Gittisham, in Devon. Her life has involved lots of travel, teaching her much that she has added to her formal training in cooking. She has a simple philosophy in the kitchen, namely that shopping is an art, only the best ingredients are good enough, and that it is a good idea to have a herb garden if you can as fresh herbs add that little extra something to all dishes. And she hates waste in the kitchen.

This is one of her favourite starters. It is a wonderful way to use leftover cheese. She usually has a mixture of Cheddar and Brie with a little Stilton or other blue cheese, but the dish is flexible and any mixture will do, Double Gloucester for Cheddar, Cambazola for Brie and so on. It is very good served with pre-dinner or lunch drinks, or for a buffet.

SERVES 8

1 recipe shortcrust pastry (see Basic Recipes, page 17) with 1 tablespoon paprika added to the flour
500 g/1 lb mixed grated cheeses such as Cheddar, Brie, Stilton or other blue
5 large egg yolks

15 g/½ oz chives or finely chopped spring onion
15 g/½ oz finely chopped parsley
Salt
Freshly ground pepper
⅛ teaspoon freshly grated nutmeg

Make the pastry, adding the paprika to the flour. Line a 20 cm/8 in flan case, fill it half full of dried beans or rice and bake in a preheated, hot oven (220°C/425°F/gas 7) for 8 minutes, baking it half blind. Remove the dried beans or rice and keep them for using again. The flan case should be firm on the bottom. If necessary return it to the oven for 2 or 3 minutes.

In a bowl, mix all the ingredients together, pour the mixture into the flan ring and bake until it is firm to the touch and golden, 30–40 minutes in a preheated, moderate oven (180°C/350°F/gas 4). If the cheese mixture seems at all dry add a tablespoon or two of dry white wine or single cream. Serve warm or cold.

WINE SUGGESTION: A Chardonnay.

HARE PÂTÉ WITH GREENGAGE RELISH

Graham Flanagan, head chef of The Cottage in the Wood, Malvern Wells in Worcestershire, has a great feeling for traditional British cooking which he produces with great flair, always with his own transforming touches. This pâté is good enough to make it worth the trouble of bespeaking a hare from a speciality butcher for a special occasion.

SERVES 8 to 10

For the Pâté:

Young hare, about 1.4 kg/3 lb, boned
  with the bones reserved
Liver of hare, chopped
250 g/8 oz belly of pork, chopped
125 g/4 oz pork liver, chopped
2 medium eggs
2 tablespoons plain flour
2 tablespoons Cognac, or other
  brandy
Salt
Freshly ground pepper
½ teaspoon crumbled thyme

For the Marinade:

475 ml/16 fl oz dry white wine
1 tablespoon white wine vinegar
2 tablespoons olive oil, or vegetable oil
1 medium onion, chopped
1 medium carrot, chopped
1 stalk celery, chopped
1 clove garlic, chopped
1 tablespoon finely chopped parsley
2 cloves
1 teaspoon black peppercorns, lightly
  crushed
½ teaspoon salt
1 bay leaf

To prepare the pâté, there should be about 900 g/2 lb hare meat. Chop the meat coarsely and transfer it to a food processor or blender with the hare liver, belly of pork, and pork liver and process it to a coarse purée. Set it aside and make the marinade.

In a large saucepan, combine the reserved hare bones with the marinade ingredients. Bring to a simmer over low heat, cover and cook for 1 hour. Cool, strain, discarding the bones and solids. Put the pâté into a large bowl and pour the marinade over it. Cover, and refrigerate overnight. Strain, reserving the marinade, and transfer the solids to a large bowl. Combine the solids with the eggs, flour, Cognac or brandy, salt and pepper, thyme and 2 tablespoons of the reserved marinade.

Oil a 1.4 L/2½ pt terrine and spoon in the hare mixture. Cover the terrine with foil, then a lid and bake for 2 hours in a preheated, moderate oven (190°C/375°F/gas 5). Cool, chill lightly and unmould. Serve, sliced, with Greengage Relish (see below).

GREENGAGE RELISH

2 tablespoons salt
1 teaspoon ground cloves
1 teaspoon ground ginger
1 teaspoon ground allspice
550 ml/18 fl oz vinegar, preferably
  malt vinegar
250 g/8 oz Demerara, or brown
  sugar

900 g/2 lb greengages, pitted and
  quartered
250 g/8 oz tart green apples, peeled,
  cored and chopped
3 medium onions, chopped
1 medium carrot, scraped and thinly
  sliced
95 g/3¾ oz seedless raisins

In a small bowl, combine the salt, cloves, ginger, and allspice with enough of the vinegar to make a paste. In a large stainless steel or enamelled saucepan, combine the rest of the vinegar with the sugar and bring it to a boil over low heat. Stir in the spice mixture, the greengages, apples, onions, carrots and raisins and simmer, uncovered, stirring from time to time, until the mixture is well blended and thick, about 45 minutes. Cool, spoon into a glass container and chill lightly until ready to serve.

WINE SUGGESTION: A rich Rhône wine - a White Hermitage.

VENISON PÂTÉ

I very much enjoyed this venison pâté developed by David Moir when he was head chef at Gleddoch House at Langbank, near Glasgow. It is time-consuming to make and I had to search out venison but decided it was worth it. I agree with David that oatcakes with butter are far better than ordinary toast especially since they are very easy to make and they keep well. They are also readily available in most groceries.

SERVES 12

500 g/1 lb venison, finely chopped
1 clove garlic, chopped
50 g/2 oz diced pork fat
1 large egg
Salt
Freshly ground pepper
3 tablespoons tawny port
6 tablespoons butter, melted and cooled
125 ml/4 fl oz single cream
1 large, tart apple, peeled, cored and coarsely chopped

1 tablespoon butter, plus butter for the terrine
½ medium onion, finely chopped
4 mushrooms, sliced
25 g/1 oz shelled and blanched pistachio nuts
95 g/3¾ oz raisins, soaked in warm water for 10 minutes
12 crushed juniper berries
125 ml/4 fl oz aspic jelly, or gelatine dissolved in chicken stock

Put the venison and garlic with the pork fat into a food processor or blender and process until smooth. Add the egg, salt, pepper to taste and the port, and process to mix. With the machine running, slowly pour in the melted butter, and the cream. Transfer the mixture to a large bowl. Mix in the apple. In a small frying pan, heat 1 tablespoon of butter and sauté the onion and mushrooms over moderate heat for 5 minutes. Add the pistachio nuts, raisins and juniper berries, sauté for 1 or 2 minutes then add the mixture to the venison.

Generously butter a 23 × 12 cm/9 × 5 in terrine and pack the venison mixture into it. Cover with foil and place in a baking tin with water to come about halfway up the sides. Bake in a preheated, slow oven (150°C/300°F/gas 2) for about 2 hours or until the terrine is firm to the touch. Remove from the oven and cool.

While the terrine is still slightly warm, pour the melted aspic jelly over it. Cool and refrigerate for at least 12 hours before unmoulding and serving. When sliced the terrine should be marbled with apples, nuts and raisins. Serve sliced, accompanied by oatcakes and butter, and Cumberland Sauce (see below).

WINE SUGGESTION: A Chardonnay.

CUMBERLAND SAUCE

This traditional sauce is served with cold meats, veal and ham pie, ham, venison and venison pâté (see last recipe). Tart yet richly flavoured, it will keep for several weeks refrigerated. This is David Moir's own version of the sauce and one I find particularly appealing

MAKES about 375 ml/12 fl oz

300 g/10 oz redcurrant jelly
50 ml/2 fl oz tawny port
1 teaspoon juice squeezed from fresh
  grated ginger root
50 ml/2 fl oz lemon juice

50 ml/2 fl oz orange juice
Zest of 1 lemon, cut into fine julienne
  strips
Zest of 1 orange, cut into fine julienne
  strips

Combine the redcurrant jelly, port wine, ginger juice, lemon and orange juice in a small saucepan and bring to a simmer over low heat. Add the lemon and orange zest which should be very finely cut, bring back to a simmer, remove from the heat and cool. Pour into a glass container and refrigerate until ready to use.

Soups

Soup, light and delicate, or robust and hearty, is one of the most delightful aspects of the kitchen. It is usually economical and, with blenders and food processors, simple to make. Home-made stocks are very little trouble as they simmer for hours, needing almost no attention. Excellent canned stocks are available when it is impractical to make stock at home, and good stock cubes can be used as enrichments. I was happy to find that today's chefs share my enthusiasm for soup. They delight in inventing new soups and transforming traditional ones.

A lightly-chilled soup makes a perfect beginning to a party dinner or lunch, and since it is made ahead and chilled makes kitchen planning and timing easier. Hot soup takes little more trouble. A really hearty soup is wonderfully restorative for a quick lunch at home, or as the main part of a simple supper. A most versatile dish, it can be elegant or a standby family favourite.

The recipes here have all been given me by chefs and tested by me at home. Any changes that have been made in the recipes are purely practical ones translating a restaurant recipe into a domestic kitchen one. I have also suggested ways to avoid using cream for those who find this desirable.

BEETROOT SOUP WITH TOMATO AND BASIL SORBET

John Hornsby created this soup while at the Castle Hotel in Taunton. Before that he was a sous-chef to Anton Mosimann at The Dorchester. He is now working in the USA but is returning to London to start his own restaurant. He achieves original and fresh-tasting dishes from unexotic, often quite ordinary ingredients, as this soup demonstrates.

SERVES 6

For the Soup:
1.4 L/2½ pt chicken broth
1.4 kg/3 lb raw beetroot, trimmed,
   scrubbed and sliced
1 bay leaf
6 peppercorns
2 egg whites, lightly beaten
2 egg shells, crushed
Salt
2 envelopes (2 tablespoons)
   unflavoured gelatine

For the Sorbet:
175 ml/6 fl oz tomato juice
1 teaspoon Worcestershire sauce
1 teaspoon lemon juice
1 tablespoon fresh basil leaves, finely
   chopped

For the Garnish (optional):
Fresh chervil leaves

In a large saucepan, combine the chicken broth, beetroot, bay leaf and peppercorns, bring to a simmer and cook, covered, for 1½ hours. Strain the mixture through a fine sieve into a bowl. Discard the solids. Measure the liquid and add enough water to bring it up to 1.4 L/2½ pt, if necessary. Return the mixture to the saucepan and add the egg whites and shells. Whisk over very low heat until the liquid comes to a simmer. Simmer without stirring, for 20 minutes. Strain through a fine sieve lined with a double layer of dampened, squeezed-out cheesecloth into a bowl. Rinse out and dry the saucepan and return the soup to it. Season to taste with salt.

Sprinkle the gelatine into 125 ml/4 fl oz water in a small bowl and let it soften, about 5 minutes. Add it to the soup and simmer, whisking, over low heat until the gelatine has dissolved. Cool the soup, then refrigerate it until lightly set, about 2 hours.

To make the sorbet, combine the tomato juice, Worcestershire sauce, lemon juice and fresh basil leaves in a small metal bowl or in an ice cube tray without the dividers. Freeze the mixture, stirring every 15 minutes for 1 hour, or until it is firm but not hard.

Spoon the jellied soup into bowls. Put a spoonful of the sorbet in the centre and decorate the rim of the bowls with chervil leaves, if liked.

JERUSALEM ARTICHOKE SOUP

Jerusalem artichokes are small edible tubers indigenous to North America, and unknown to the Old World until the Pilgrim Fathers arrived. Members of the Daisy Family, they are closely related to the sunflower, another North American indigene. The name is an amusing corruption of *girasole*, the Italian for sunflower. I choose the large tubers, as it is easier to scrape the light brown skin from them, an allowable form of kitchen laziness.

Nicholas Gill, of Country Chefs Seven, the gifted young chef in charge of the kitchen at Hambleton Hall in Rutland, created this as a winter soup. It has an exquisite flavour, is one of the easiest things I know to make, and says a good deal about Nick Gill's special talent. He delights in creating dishes that will give pleasure, some of them elaborate, some simple, but all as near perfection as he can make them. Nick plans to open his own restaurant in London.

I find this soup good even without its butter and cream enrichment.

SERVES 4

500 g/1 lb Jerusalem artichokes, scraped and coarsely chopped
1 L/1¾ pt chicken stock (see Basic Recipes, page 10)
Salt
Freshly ground pepper

1 tablespoon unsalted butter
125 ml/4 fl oz double cream

For the Garnish:
Pinch saffron powder
50 ml/2 fl oz whipping cream

Combine the artichokes and stock in a large saucepan, cover, and simmer over moderate heat until the artichokes are tender, about 20 minutes. Strain the soup through a sieve into a bowl. Rinse out and dry the saucepan and pour in the strained soup. Purée the solids in a blender or food processor then put through a sieve so that any bits of skin from the artichokes can easily be discarded. Season to taste with salt and pepper. Heat the soup and stir in the butter and cream. Pour into four warmed soup bowls.

For the garnish, mix the saffron into the cream and whip the cream. Make a cone with greaseproof paper and fill it with the cream. Pipe a thin spiral of the cream mixture on to the top of the soup, then draw a knife through it to cut into quarters. If this is too difficult or seems too elaborate for family dining, put a small spoonful of cream in the centre of each bowl of soup. The delicate yellow of the saffron in the cream makes an attractive contrast to the creamy white of the soup.

LETTUCE, SORREL, MINT AND YOGHURT SOUP

Eamonn Webster likes to express his philosophy that cooking starts in the sea and the ground, not in the pot, in the dishes he creates. This soup demonstrates that philosophy in a very light and delicious way, lovely for summer.

SERVES 4

1 head of soft lettuce, washed and dried	1 tablespoon lemon juice
	Salt
1 tablespoon fresh mint, finely chopped	Freshly ground pepper
50 g/2 oz sorrel leaves	*For the Garnish:*
600 ml/1 pt plain yoghurt	2 tablespoons chopped chives

Chop the lettuce very finely and put it into a bowl. Add the mint. Wash the sorrel leaves and shake to remove the excess moisture. Cut away and discard the stems and centre veins of the leaves. Stack, roll them up, and slice very finely. Drop the sorrel into a saucepan of briskly boiling, salted water for 30 seconds, drain and plunge into cold water, drain at once. Purée the sorrel in a blender or food processor. It almost purées itself. Add the sorrel purée to the lettuce and mint mixture and stir in the yoghurt. Season with the lemon juice and salt and pepper, mixing well. Thoroughly chill the soup for several hours in the refrigerator.

Serve the soup garnished with chopped chives. Other garnishes may be added, if liked, and shredded carrot, radish, cucumber or diced strawberries may be served in small bowls as accompaniments.

LETTUCE SOUP

This is my favourite lettuce soup. It is simplicity itself, wonderfully fresh and summery. It was given to me by Roy Richards when he and his wife Veronica were running the Lake Isle Restaurant in Uppingham, Leicestershire before they moved to their present restaurant, Manor House at Pickworth, also in Leicestershire. Roy came late to cooking. He taught English in Paris after leaving Cambridge University then, following a stint in the business world in London, he decided he wanted to cook. He trained with the Savoy Group and then went to sixteenth-century Thornbury Castle, now a country house hotel, to work with Kenneth Bell. He has a very decided philosophy, disliking pretention in food above all else. His is family cooking, simple food carefully prepared from the best local ingredients. He will only use exotic ingredients if they belong naturally to a dish.

SERVES 4

3 heads of soft lettuce
4 tablespoons butter
1 small onion, finely chopped
2 tablespoons plain flour
600 ml/1 pt chicken stock (see Basic Recipes, page 10)
125 ml/4 fl oz milk

125 ml/4 fl oz double cream, or fresh white cheese (see Basic Recipes, page 24)
Salt
Freshly ground pepper
Pinch grated nutmeg

Separate the lettuces into leaves, discarding any wilted ones. Rinse, spin dry and chop coarsely. Drop the chopped lettuce into a large saucepan of briskly boiling, salted water and blanch for 5 minutes. Drain thoroughly and purée in a blender or food processor.

Heat the butter in a saucepan and sauté the onion until it is soft. Remove from the heat and stir in the flour. Return to low heat and cook, stirring, for 2 minutes. Gradually stir in the chicken stock and milk. Bring the liquid to a boil, and simmer, stirring, for 5 minutes. Stir in the lettuce purée and the cream. Season to taste with salt, pepper and nutmeg and heat the soup through without letting it boil.

MINT SOUP

I met chef François Huguet when he was head chef at Inverlochy Castle, a very luxurious country house hotel standing among the foothills of Ben Nevis in Scotland, built in 1863 and once the home of the first Lord Abinger. He loved to use fresh ingredients from the herb and kitchen gardens at the Castle when they were at their best. He says mint is best from April to July and certainly this refreshing soup is perfect for spring and summer.

It is also very good served chilled. Yoghurt or sour cream can be used instead of single cream and for the garnish.

SERVES 6

4 tablespoons butter
50 g/2 oz plain flour
1.4 L/2½ pt chicken stock (see Basic
  Recipes, page 10)
125 g/ 4 oz young mint leaves
Salt

Freshly ground pepper
6 tablespoons single cream

For the Garnish:
Whipped cream
Mint sprigs

In a saucepan, heat the butter and stir in the flour. Cook, stirring with a wooden spoon over low heat for about 2 minutes without letting the mixture colour. Off the heat, stir in the chicken stock. Return the saucepan to the heat and simmer, stirring from time to time, for 30 minutes.

Pick over and wash the mint. Chop it coarsely and add it to the saucepan. Simmer for 5 minutes. In a blender or food processor, reduce the mint to a purée, using a little of the soup. Strain it through a fine sieve into the soup. Season to taste with salt and pepper, stir in the cream and heat through. Serve in bouillon cups garnished, if liked, with a teaspoon of whipped cream and a sprig of mint.

VARIATION

Chef Huguet also makes a Rosemary-flavoured Consommé in which sprigs of fresh rosemary are simmered with a very rich clear chicken consommé then strained out and discarded leaving just a delicate rosemary flavour.

TOMATO AND FENNEL SOUP

I was impressed with the cooking of young Scots chef Alan Casey, whom I met when he was at Culloden House in Inverness, Scotland. Now a country house hotel converted from a Jacobean castle, it was once the headquarters of Bonnie Prince Charlie. Alan's aim is to keep the flavours of the foods he cooks as pure and direct as possible and, in the interests of good nutrition, to avoid the pitfalls of too much butter, cream and eggs. He is a naturally inventive cook as this delicious soup shows.

SERVES 6

4 fennel bulbs, trimmed and thinly
  sliced
2 tablespoons butter
50 ml/2 fl oz dry vermouth
900 g/2 lb tomatoes, peeled, seeded
  and chopped
1 small clove garlic, very finely
  chopped
Bouquet garni of sprig parsley, thyme
  and bay leaf
1.1 L/2 pt chicken or veal stock (see
  Basic Recipes, pages 10, 11)

Salt
250 ml/8 fl oz double cream, or fresh
  white cheese (see Basic Recipes,
  page 24)
1 teaspoon Worcestershire sauce

For the Garnish:
Fennel sprigs
Whipped cream (optional)

In a large saucepan, sweat the fennel in the butter, covered, over very low heat for about 10 minutes. Add the vermouth, tomatoes, garlic, bouquet garni, stock, and salt if necessary, and simmer, covered, for 30 minutes, or until the fennel is soft. Remove and discard the bouquet garni. Reduce the solids to a purée in a blender or food processor and return the purée to the liquid. Stir in the cream or fresh white cheese and Worcestershire sauce and heat the soup through. Do not let it boil. Garnish with a sprig of fennel and, if liked, with a teaspoon of whipped cream.

FENNEL AND GREEN PEPPER SOUP

Brian Prideaux-Brune has produced an entirely different fennel soup from Alan Casey's, though both are inspired by the subtle flavour of the vegetable. Brian, whose training has not been formal, is an excitingly original cook, creating new dishes from everyday foods.

SERVES 6 to 8

4 fennel bulbs, trimmed, peeled and
  sliced
4 sweet green peppers, seeded and
  coarsely chopped
2 leeks, trimmed, thoroughly washed
  and coarsely chopped
1 medium potato, peeled and sliced

1.4 L/2½ pt chicken stock (see Basic
  Recipes, page 10)
Salt
Freshly ground pepper
125 ml/4 fl oz double cream
  (optional)

Combine all the vegetables with the chicken stock in a large saucepan and simmer, covered, over moderate heat until the vegetables are tender, about 20 minutes. Remove solids from the soup and purée them in a blender or food processor. Return the purée to the liquid and season to taste with salt and pepper. Stir in the cream if liked, and heat the soup through. If the soup is too thick, add a little more chicken stock.

TURNIP AND FRESH GINGER SOUP

This is a most original soup from young Nigel Lambert, whom I met when he was head chef of The Elms Hotel in Abberley, a Queen Anne country house hotel in the Worcestershire countryside. He describes his cooking as English country cooking with a nouvelle cuisine influence, an intriguing combination. The soup is easy to make and as delicious as it is easy.

SERVES 6

125 g/4 oz butter
500 g/1 lb small white turnips, peeled and diced
50 g/2 oz coarsely grated fresh ginger root
1 small onion, finely chopped
1 clove garlic, crushed
1.1 L/2 pt chicken stock (see Basic Recipes, page 10)
Salt
Freshly ground pepper
125 ml/4 fl oz single cream

Heat the butter in a large saucepan, add the turnips, ginger and onion, cover and cook over very low heat for about 20 minutes. Add the crushed garlic, stir to mix and pour in the stock. Simmer, covered, until the vegetables are tender, about 30 minutes.

In a blender or food processor, reduce the solids to a purée. Return the purée to the saucepan, season to taste with salt and pepper and heat the soup through. Add the cream and cook just long enough to heat the soup without letting it boil.

WATERCRESS SOUP

For years I searched for the perfect watercress soup, now found. Melvin Jordan was equally unsatisfied with the versions he encountered and set about experimenting until he achieved a soup that pleased him. It is typical of his approach to food that he will take so much trouble over a very simple, ordinary-seeming dish.

SERVES 4

2 tablespoons butter
1 medium onion, peeled and chopped
1 small clove garlic, crushed
2 tablespoons mild white vinegar
2 tablespoons dry white wine
1 L/1¼ pt chicken stock (see Basic
   Recipes, page 10)
125 ml/4 fl oz single cream

3 bunches (about 175 g/6 oz)
   watercress, washed and trimmed
2 teaspoons cornflour
Salt
Freshly ground pepper

For the Garnish:
Watercress leaves
4 tablespoons double cream

Melt the butter in a saucepan and sauté the onion and garlic until the onion is soft. Add the vinegar and wine and simmer until the liquid is reduced by half. Add the chicken stock, cover and simmer over low heat for 30 minutes. Stir in the cream and bring the liquid back to a simmer. Add the watercress, stir to mix and immediately remove from the heat. Purée the solids in a blender or food processor then push through a sieve set over a bowl. Return the purée to the saucepan. Mix the cornflour with a little cold water and stir it into the soup. Bring the soup to a simmer over moderate heat, stirring once or twice. Season to taste with salt and pepper. It is important not to cook the soup for long once the watercress has been added as this tends to make the soup bitter. Serve in bowls with a spoonful of cream floated on top, and a watercress leaf placed on top of the cream.

CHILLED AVOCADO SOUP

Chefs move around and I first enjoyed this very attractive soup when chef Alain Dubois was in charge of the kitchen at Huntstrete House near Bath. On another summer day I enjoyed it again when Alain took over the kitchen at The Lygon Arms, in Worcestershire. It could hardly be simpler and it certainly reflects Alain's desire to produce food that is light with all its natural flavour intact.

SERVES 4

2 large, ripe avocados
475 ml/16 fl oz chicken stock,
   skimmed of all fat (see Basic
   Recipes, page 10)
250 ml/8 fl oz single cream
2 tablespoons lemon juice

Salt
Freshly ground white pepper

For the Garnish:
Snipped chives

Cut the avocados in half. Remove the stones and scoop out the flesh. In a food processor or blender, combine the avocados, chicken stock, cream and lemon juice and process until smooth, about 30 seconds; or put the avocados through a sieve set over a bowl. Mix with the stock, lemon juice and cream. Season to taste with salt and pepper. Chill thoroughly. Serve in bouillon cups and garnish with chives.

TOMATO, ORANGE AND GINGER BROTH

Martin Lam, the young chef from Bristol who created this soup, had to struggle for the right to cook. His Welsh mother, a fine cook, had the kitchen all week. On Sundays his father, an importer of fine foods, took over. All the frustrated small boy was allowed to do was make the gravy. Undeterred, he went on to become head chef at L'Escargot in Soho in London, after working at the English House Restaurant, where his special interest in English food was encouraged by co-owner Michael Smith who is the author of fine books on English food. This soup is from his English House period.

SERVES 6

1.1 L/2 pt chicken stock (see Basic
    Recipes, page 10)
250 ml/8 fl oz orange juice
Rind of 1 orange cut into julienne
    strips
2 tablespoons drained ginger in syrup,
    cut into julienne strips
1 tablespoon tomato purée
500 g/1 lb tomatoes, peeled, seeded
    and chopped

Salt
Freshly ground pepper

For the Garnish:
2 tablespoons chopped fresh mint
1 thinly sliced unpeeled orange, seeds
    removed

In a large saucepan, combine the chicken stock, orange juice, orange rind, ginger and tomato purée. Simmer, covered, over low heat for 5 minutes. Add the tomatoes and salt and pepper to taste, bring back to a simmer and cook for 5 minutes longer. Serve in soup bowls with a garnish of mint leaves and orange slices.

CHILLED CUCUMBER SOUP

Chris Pitman, head chef of The George of Stamford, in Lincolnshire, combines ordinary ingredients in an unordinary way. Enlivened by a touch of vinegar and mint, this cucumber soup is not only perfect for summer but makes an attractive beginning to lunch or dinner at any season.

SERVES 6

2 medium-sized cucumbers
3 tablespoons butter
2 medium onions, finely chopped
4 sprigs fresh mint, or 1 teaspoon
    dried mint
25 g/1 oz plain flour
1 L/1¾ pt chicken stock (see Basic
    Recipes, page 10)

475 ml/16 fl oz single cream, or fresh
    white cheese (see Basic Recipes,
    page 24), or strained yoghurt
2 tablespoons mild white vinegar
Salt
Freshly ground white pepper

For the Garnish:
Julienne strips of cucumber peel

Peel and coarsely chop the cucumbers. Cut one quarter of the peel into
julienne strips and set it aside for the garnish. Heat the butter in a large
saucepan, add the cucumber, onions and mint and cook until the onion is soft.
Remove and discard the mint.

Stir in the flour and cook, stirring, for 2 minutes. Off the heat, gradually stir
in the chicken stock. Return the saucepan to the heat and simmer, covered, for
20 minutes. Purée the mixture in a blender or food processor and pour it into
a bowl or jug. When it is cool, stir in the cream, and vinegar. Season to taste
with salt and pepper. Refrigerate the soup until thoroughly chilled, about 4
hours. Serve in soup bowls garnished with julienne strips of cucumber peel.

PARSNIP AND ORANGE SOUP

Young Pierre Chevillard, head chef at Chewton Glen Hotel, once an
eighteenth-century mansion, now a de luxe country house hotel on the fringe
of the New Forest in Hampshire, has been cooking since his apprenticeship at
the age of 15. He has a subtle approach to food, and combines tradition and
his own innovative ideas in this soup with unexpected and delicious results.

SERVES 6

1 small onion, chopped	Salt
1 medium potato, peeled and diced	Freshly ground pepper
1.4 kg/3 lb parsnips, peeled and diced	250 ml/8 fl oz double cream, or fresh
3 tablespoons butter	white cheese (see Basic Recipes,
850 ml/1½ pt chicken stock (see	page 24)
Basic Recipes, page 10)	
175 ml/6 fl oz orange juice	*For the Garnish (optional):*
Rind of 1 orange cut into wide strips	1 orange, peeled and segmented

In a large saucepan, cook the onion, potato and parsnips in 2 tablespoons of
the butter over very low heat, covered, until the vegetables are softened, about
10 minutes. Add the chicken stock, orange juice and rind. Season to taste with
salt and pepper, cover and simmer for 30 minutes. Purée the solids in a blender
or food processor, then push through a sieve for a finer texture. Return the
purée to the saucepan with the liquid. Stir in the cream. Heat through and stir
in the remaining tablespoon of butter. Serve in soup bowls garnished, if liked,
with orange segments.

TOMATO, APPLE AND CELERY SOUP

John Evans, chef-patron of a small hotel and restaurant, Meadowsweet, in
Llanrwst, Gwynedd, Wales, took this traditional soup and created his own
version. It is an example of the inventiveness of today's chefs who not only

create new dishes, but revamp old ones. It is good hot, and makes a refreshing summer soup when served chilled.

SERVES 4 to 6

4 tablespoons butter
1 medium onion, chopped
500 g/1 lb tomatoes, unpeeled, quartered
500 g/1 lb celery, coarsely chopped and using leaves
4 tart green apples, unpeeled, uncored and coarsely chopped
4 tablespoons dry sherry (optional)

1 L/1¾ pt chicken stock (see Basic Recipes, page 10)
Salt
Freshly ground pepper
1 tablespoon lemon juice

For the Garnish:
Chopped chervil

Heat the butter in a saucepan and sauté the onion until it is soft. Add the tomatoes, celery, apples and sherry, if using, cover and cook over very low heat for 5 minutes. Add the chicken stock and simmer, covered, for 45 minutes. Cool. Purée the solids in a food processor or blender then put through a sieve. Return the purée to the saucepan with the stock. Season with salt, pepper and lemon juice. If the soup is to be served hot, heat it through. If it is to be served cold, chill it lightly. Serve garnished with a little finely chopped chervil. The soup may also be garnished with a teaspoon of salted, whipped cream and a little finely chopped apple.

STILTON SOUP, ARDSHEAL HOUSE

Robert Gardiner was encouraged in the kitchen by Bob Taylor, owner of Ardsheal House Hotel, in Scotland, and himself an enthusiastic amateur cook. I was surprised when Robert told me he used a whole pound of Stilton cheese in the soup which I had found light and delicate. He was right as I discovered when I cooked it. If Stilton isn't available, other blue cheeses can be used.

SERVES 6

4 tablespoons butter
1 small onion, finely chopped
1 clove garlic, very finely chopped
500 g/1 lb Stilton cheese, rind removed, coarsely grated, or other blue cheese
50 g/2 oz plain flour
1 L/1¾ pt chicken stock (see Basic Recipes, page 10)
125 ml/4 fl oz dry white wine

1 bay leaf
Salt
Freshly ground pepper
250 ml/8 fl oz double cream, or fresh white cheese (see Basic Recipes, page 24), or strained yoghurt

For the Garnish:
Snipped chives, or black pepper

Heat the butter in a saucepan and cook the onion until it is soft. Add the garlic and cook for about a minute longer. Stir in the cheese and flour and continue to cook, over low heat, until the mixture is well blended, about 3 minutes. Stir in the stock and wine, add the bay leaf and bring to a simmer, whisking constantly. Cook over very low heat, whisking from time to time, for 15 minutes. Remove the bay leaf. Season to taste with salt and pepper. Add the cream and cook just long enough to heat the soup through. Garnish with snipped chives, or a generous grinding of black pepper.

CHILLED STILTON SOUP WITH ALMOND GARNISH

Anthony Blake, Chef de Cuisine at Eastwell Manor, a luxury country house hotel and restaurant at Ashford in Kent, first began cooking at the age of 13 when he opted out of the woodworking class in favour of food – a decision he has never regretted. He created this subtly-flavoured, chilled summer soup. It is smooth and delicate with an interesting garnish.

SERVES 4

For the Soup:
2 stalks celery, finely chopped
½ medium onion, finely chopped
1 leek, well washed, white part only, finely chopped
4 tablespoons butter
Salt
Freshly ground pepper
1 bay leaf
50 ml/2 fl oz dry white wine
50 g/2 oz plain flour

1.1 L/2 pt chicken stock (see Basic Recipes, page 10)
75 g/3 oz grated Stilton cheese or other blue cheese
50 ml/2 fl oz double cream

For the Almond Cream Garnish:
125 ml/4 fl oz double cream
15 g/½ oz ground almonds
⅛ teaspoon almond essence
4 sprigs chervil

In a saucepan, cook the celery, onion and leek in the butter over low heat until the vegetables are soft, 10–15 minutes. Do not let them colour. Season with salt and pepper, add the bay leaf and white wine and simmer for 3–4 minutes. Stir in the flour and cook, stirring, for 5 minutes without letting the flour colour. Off the heat, gradually stir in the chicken stock. The mixture should be smooth. Return the saucepan to low heat, cover and cook at a bare simmer for 1 hour. Remove and discard the bay leaf. Add the Stilton cheese and the cream, stir to mix and add salt and pepper if necessary. Simmer, uncovered, for 6 minutes. Remove from the heat, cool slightly then pour into a blender or food processor and process until very smooth. Transfer to a jug or other container and chill thoroughly in the refrigerator, 2–3 hours.

In a bowl, whip the cream until it stands in peaks. Fold in the almonds and almond essence. When ready to serve, pour the soup into four lightly-chilled bowls. Using 2 teaspoons, make quenelles with the cream and gently place on top of the soup, 2 quenelles to each bowl. Garnish with the chervil sprigs.

BRIE AND SPRING ONION SOUP

This is a rich, delicate and unusual soup created by Campbell Cameron. It makes a fine prelude to a simple main course.

SERVES 6

750 g/1½ lb Brie, coarsely chopped
1 L/1¾ pt chicken stock (see Basic
  Recipes, page 10)
75 g/3 oz spring onions, trimmed
  and using some of the green part,
  finely chopped
475 ml/16 fl oz double cream, or
  fresh white cheese (see Basic
  Recipes, page 24)

6 egg yolks
Salt
Freshly ground white pepper

For the Garnish:
50g/2 oz spring onions, finely
  chopped

Combine the Brie and chicken stock in a saucepan and melt the cheese over very low heat, stirring from time to time. Add the spring onions and cook for 10 minutes, or until they are very soft. Strain the soup through a sieve into a bowl. Return the liquid to the saucepan and purée the solids in a blender or food processor. Add the purée to the liquid.

In another saucepan, bring the cream almost to boiling point. Have the egg yolks in a bowl and whisk the hot cream into them. Reheat the soup and whisk in the egg yolk and cream mixture taking care not to let the soup boil. Season to taste with salt and pepper. Garnish with the spring onions and serve in bouillon cups. If the soup seems too thick, thin with a little hot chicken stock.

BRAZIL NUT AND LEMON SOUP

Joyce Molyneux, the brilliant chef who runs the Carved Angel restaurant in Dartmouth, Devon, created this soup to use up an excess of brazil nuts. It is delicious either hot or cold, and illustrates her creative approach to cooking.

SERVES 4

175 g/ 6 oz chopped onions
2 tablespoons butter
1.1 L/2 pt chicken or veal stock (see
  Basic Recipes, pages 10, 11)
125 g/4 oz shelled brazil nuts, peeled
  and coarsely chopped

Zest of 2 lemons, thinly peeled
Salt
Freshly ground pepper
50 ml/2 fl oz double cream

In a large saucepan, cook the onions in the butter, covered, over very low heat until they are soft. Do not let them brown. Add the stock, nuts, lemon peel, and salt and pepper to taste. Simmer gently, covered, for 20 minutes.

Remove the solids from the soup and purée them in a blender or food processor, using a little of the soup if necessary. The purée should be very smooth. Return the purée to the liquid, stir in the cream and heat through.

CONSOMMÉ OF THE FRUITS OF SEA AND EARTH

Lyn Hall is a perfectionist with a great understanding of the importance of technique. She believes one can never take too much trouble when cooking with love.

SERVES 3 to 4

250 g/8 oz fillet of trout, skinned and boned
250 g/ 8 oz salmon fillet, skinned and boned
250 g/8 oz mixed fresh vegetables, courgettes, carrot, celery stalks, button mushrooms, small white onions, small new potatoes

725 ml/24 fl oz strong fish stock (see Basic Recipes, page 13)
250 ml/8 fl oz dry white wine
Salt
Freshly ground pepper
3 sprigs fresh dill

Cut the fish in 1 cm/½ in cubes and set aside. Cut the courgettes into diagonal slices, slice the carrots and celery into equal-size pieces, and cut the mushrooms into quarters. Peel the onions and scrape the new potatoes. Cook the vegetables, separately, in a large saucepan of briskly boiling, salted water until they are tender. Refresh them quickly under cold water and set aside.

In a saucepan, heat 475 ml/16 fl oz of the stock with the wine. Bring to a boil and simmer for 4 minutes, skimming off any froth from the surface. Cover, reduce the heat as low as possible and keep hot.

Pour the remaining 250 ml/8 fl oz stock into a saucepan. Season the fish with salt and pepper and add it to the stock with the vegetables. Simmer for 1 minute, to cook the fish and heat the vegetables through. Pour into a warmed tureen. Pour the hot stock from the other saucepan into the tureen. Float the dill on top and serve immediately.

CREAM OF SEAFOOD SOUP

This is another of Lyn Hall's fish soups. It has a rich, delicious flavour and looks very pretty with the pink fish and prawns surrounded by the creamy white soup. It makes an elegant beginning to a lunch or dinner.

SERVES 6

12 large unpeeled prawns
1.7 L/3 pt fish stock (see Basic Recipes, page 13)
600 ml/1 pt dry white wine
600 ml/1 pt double cream
250 g/8 oz scallops

125 g/4 oz skinned and boned halibut, cut into 2.5 cm/1 in pieces
125 g/4 oz skinned and boned salmon, cut into 2.5 cm/1 in pieces
Salt
Freshly ground pepper

In a large saucepan, simmer the prawns in the fish stock for 2 minutes. Lift out, allow to cool, shell and set aside.

Pour the wine into the saucepan with the fish stock and reduce over brisk heat to half, just over 1.1 L/2 pt. Pour in the cream and, still over brisk heat, reduce again to just over 1.1 L/2 pt. If the scallops are large, cut them into 2.5 cm/1 in pieces, if small leave whole. Add the halibut, salmon and scallops to the soup and cook for a few seconds. Add the prawns and cook just to reheat them. Season the soup to taste with salt and pepper. Have ready six warmed soup bowls. Lift out the seafood with a slotted spoon and pile it in a mound in the centre of each bowl, putting 2 prawns on top in each bowl. Pour the soup round the seafood and serve immediately.

SCALLOP CHOWDER

This is another of chef Martin Lam's soups, created by him at L'Escargot restaurant in London's Soho. It has his pleasantly innovative touch. When I cook it, I serve double portions and make it a main course because it is so appetizing that I always want more than just a soup serving.

SERVES 6 as a soup, 4 as a main course

250 g/8 oz salt pork
1 medium onion, thinly sliced
1 carrot, scraped and diced
1 small parsnip, peeled and diced
1 medium sweet green pepper, deseeded and cut into julienne strips
2 celery stalks, diced
600 ml/1 pt milk
125 ml/4 fl oz orange juice
Salt
Freshly ground pepper

1 tablespoon plain flour
1 tablespoon butter
500 g/1 lb scallops
2 tablespoons lemon juice
475 ml/16 fl oz fish stock (see Basic Recipes, page 13)

For the Garnish (optional):
4 tablespoons double cream, or fresh white cheese (see Basic Recipes, page 24)
Paprika

Drop the salt pork into boiling water and blanch for a minute or two. Drain, pat dry with paper towels and cut into 5 mm/¼ in dice. Sauté the pork in a saucepan over low heat until the fat runs out. Lift out with a slotted spoon and drain on paper towels. Add the onion to the saucepan and sauté in the pork fat until it is soft. Add the carrot, parsnip, sweet green pepper and celery and stir to mix. Add the milk, orange juice, diced pork, salt and pepper to taste, and simmer, uncovered, until the vegetables are soft.

In a small bowl, mix the flour and butter together with a fork. Set aside.

While the vegetables are cooking, toss the scallops with the lemon juice and let them stand for 5 minutes. If they are large, cut them in quarters, if small leave whole. When the vegetables are soft, add the scallops and any juice to the saucepan with the fish stock. Stir to mix. Stir in the flour and butter mixture (*beurre manie*) piece by piece and simmer just until the soup is lightly thickened. Serve at once. Garnish, if liked, with 2 teaspoons of double cream and a little paprika on each soup bowl.

JOHN DORY AND OYSTER SOUP

John Dory, St. Pierre in France, so-called for the 'thumb prints', dark round marks on each side of the fish, said to have been imprinted by Peter the Fisherman, is no beauty as fish go. However, it has firm, white, bone-free fillets. Either sole or flounder are admirable substitutes. Chris Oakes, formerly head chef at the Castle Hotel, Taunton, and now chef-patron of Oakes restaurant in Stroud, created this very elegant fish soup. It isn't difficult to cook, and though the ingredients list looks rather long, nothing is exotic and only the oysters make this a luxury dish, lovely for a party. The vegetables can just be plainly sliced if preferred.

SERVES 4

16 × 2.5 cm/1 in slices young carrot, trimmed into ovals
16 × 2.5 cm/1 in slices young courgettes, trimmed into ovals
6 tablespoons butter
375 g/12 oz skinned and boned John Dory, or sole, or flounder fillets, cut at an angle into 8 slices
475 ml/16 fl oz fish stock (see Basic Recipes, page 13)
1 small leek, white part only, trimmed, thoroughly washed and cut into julienne strips
2 tablespoons shallots, finely chopped
⅛ teaspoon saffron threads, ground

1 clove garlic, crushed
25 g/1 oz brown lentils, soaked
250 ml/8 fl oz dry white wine
50 g/2 oz peeled, seeded and diced tomato
250 ml/8 fl oz rich chicken stock (see Basic Recipes, page 10)
Salt
Freshly ground pepper
16 oysters *
Fresh thyme leaves, about 8

* If oysters are not available, substitute mussels, cooked just until they open, in a little white wine.

Cook the carrots and courgettes, in separate saucepans, in boiling, salted water until tender but still crisp. Drain and set aside.

Heat 2 tablespoons of the butter in a frying pan and cook the fish, turning once, over low heat for about 1 minute on each side. Add the fish stock and simmer, covered, for 5 minutes. Strain, and reserve fish and stock separately.

Heat the rest of the butter in a saucepan, add the leek and cook for about 3 minutes over low heat. Add the shallots, saffron, garlic and lentils and cook for 5 minutes longer. Add the wine and tomato and cook for 2 minutes longer. Add 350 ml/12 fl oz of the reserved fish stock and the chicken stock. Season to taste with salt and pepper and skim, if necessary. Bring the liquid to a simmer, add the fish, oysters, thyme leaves, carrots and courgettes. Just before the soup comes to a full simmer, remove it from the heat and serve.

HOTPOT OF SCALLOPS, CRAYFISH TAILS AND MUSSELS

Julian Waterer knew from a very early age that he wanted to cook, and was lucky enough to be living near Le Talbooth Restaurant at Dedham, Colchester in Essex. His father was a friend of owner Gerald Milsom and eventually he was allowed, after school, to help with the washing up. Later he worked there as an apprentice under chef-patron Sam Chalmers, rising to sous-chef. I met him when he was the very young head chef at Greywalls, an Edwardian country house designed by Lutyens, and now a country house hotel, at Gullane, near Edinburgh. He is now chef-patron at The Salisbury Restaurant at Old Hatfield in Hertfordshire.

Cooking is not just his profession, it is his passion. He loves to play variations on a theme, this one derived from Paul Bocuse's idea of topping soups with pastry. Julian calls his soups hotpots, and varies the fillings according to the season, and what is best in the market. I have enjoyed two of them. They invite one's own experimentation. Julian suggests sometimes using a 1.1 L/2 pt soufflé dish instead of 6 individual dishes, as the pastry topping looks very impressive brought to the table, a golden dome.

SERVES 6

2 tablespoons shallots, finely chopped
600 ml/1 pt fish stock (see Basic
    Recipes, page 13)
250 ml/8 fl oz dry white wine
475 ml/16 fl oz single cream
1 teaspoon lemon juice
Salt

Freshly ground pepper
12 large scallops
18 mussels
12 crayfish tails or 12 large prawns
700 g/1½ lb puff pastry (see Basic
    Recipes, page 15)
2 egg yolks

In a heavy saucepan, combine the shallots, fish stock and dry white wine and simmer over moderate heat, uncovered, until the liquid is reduced to just over 125 ml/4 fl oz. Add the cream and lemon juice and continue to simmer until the liquid is reduced to 475 ml/16 fl oz. Season this sauce to taste with salt and pepper. Cool it slightly.

Have ready six 250 ml/8 fl oz soufflé dishes, or ramekins, or small oven-proof soup bowls. Slice scallops into thirds, and distribute among the bowls, two to each bowl. Add the mussels and top with the crayfish or large prawns, halved. Cover with the sauce and set aside.

Roll out the pastry about 0.3 cm/⅛ in thick and cut it into six 12 cm/5 in circles. Beat the egg yolks with 1 teaspoon of cold water and brush the rims with the mixture. Drape the circles of puff pastry over the bowls then press the pastry firmly into the sides of the bowls with the hands. Do not press down on the rims. Brush the tops with egg yolk and refrigerate for 20 minutes. Bake in a preheated, hot oven (220°C/425°F/gas 7) for about 15 minutes, or until the pastry is puffed and golden.

Using a spatula, slide the bowls onto plates and serve. To eat, break the crust into the soup.

CABBAGE AND OYSTER SOUP WITH SAFFRON

Paul Gayler, head chef at Inigo Jones Restaurant in London, is a very creative cook. Though his training has been quite formal, his cooking is modern, his dishes light. I love what Paul has done with cabbage soup. He has put together ingredients that do not usually find themselves in the same dish.

SERVES 4

4 tablespoons butter
250 g/8 oz white cabbage, washed and chopped
1 teaspoon cumin seed
⅛ teaspoon saffron threads
1 L/1¾ pt chicken stock (see Basic Recipes, page 10)

4 egg yolks
125 ml/4 fl oz double cream
Salt
Freshly ground pepper
12 fresh oysters and their liquor

Heat 2 tablespoons of the butter in a large saucepan. Add the cabbage, cover and cook over very low heat until the cabbage is soft, about 5 minutes. Do not let it brown. Stir in the cumin seed. Grind the saffron threads in a mortar and add to the chicken stock. Pour the stock into the saucepan with the cabbage, stir, and simmer, covered, over low heat for 15 minutes.

In a bowl, beat the egg yolks into the cream. Pour 125 ml/4 fl oz of the soup into the egg yolk mixture, stirring well, then pour it into the soup and cook over very low heat, stirring, until the soup has thickened lightly. Season to taste with salt and pepper. Strain the oyster liquor and stir it into the soup, then stir in the remaining 2 tablespoons butter. Divide the oysters among four bowls and pour in the hot soup. Serve immediately.

CULLEN SKINK

(Smoked Haddock Soup)

Chef Ken Stott of Kildrummy Castle Hotel, a country house hotel in Aberdeenshire, Scotland, comes from Findochty, a village near Cullen on the Moray Firth in Scotland. Cullen is a fishing village and skink is the old Scots name for broth, and Ken claims he was weaned on this soup. It is a splendid soup, just right for wintry weather, and simple to make in chef Stott's version.

SERVES 6

500 g/1 lb potatoes, peeled and cut
  into 1 cm/½ in dice
1 large onion, finely chopped
500 g/ 1 lb smoked haddock fillets,
  skinned, boned and coarsely
  chopped

475 ml/16 fl oz milk
125 g/4 oz butter, diced
Salt
Freshly ground pepper

Put the potatoes and onion into a large saucepan with 1 L/1¾ pt cold water. Bring to a simmer and cook, covered, over moderate heat until the potatoes are tender, about 10 minutes. Add the haddock, milk and butter, stir to mix and simmer for 5 minutes longer. Add salt, if necessary. Season generously with black pepper.

SMOKED HADDOCK AND LEEK SOUP

Chris Oakes has put together two traditional Scots soups, Cullen Skink (Smoked Haddock) and Cock-a-Leekie (Chicken and Leek with Prunes), to produce an interesting new soup. The prunes add a delicious sweet-sour touch.

SERVES 4 to 6

500 g/1 lb smoked haddock fillets
1 leek, trimmed, thoroughly washed
  and cut into julienne strips
1.1 L/2 pt rich chicken stock (see
  Basic Recipes, page 10)

4 pitted prunes, cut into julienne
  strips
Salt
Freshly ground pepper

Skin and bone the haddock fillets. Combine the haddock, leek and chicken stock in a large saucepan and simmer for 1 minute. Add the prunes and simmer just long enough to heat them through. Season to taste with salt, if necessary, and a generous amount of pepper.

GUINEA FOWL BROTH WITH TARRAGON AND WILD MUSHROOMS

David Miller, head chef of The Ritz Hotel in London, created this rich yet delicate soup. Chef Miller, a Lancastrian born in Liverpool, is only the second British chef to preside over the kitchen of The Ritz. He trained initially in the famed British Transport Hotels, then cooked at Gleneagles in Scotland and the Midland Hotel in Manchester, before coming to London as head chef at the Sheraton Park Tower. He is the English Founding Member of the European Community of Cooks whose French Founding Member is Paul Bocuse.

David Miller is a great believer in good stock slowly simmered and reduced for both soups and sauces. This soup needs little supervision, and can be left to itself on low heat at the back of the stove. Much of the preparation can be done ahead of time. The stock can be made in advance and refrigerated until it is convenient to clarify it. The clarified stock can be refrigerated overnight.

SERVES 6

For the Broth:
2 × 1.1 kg/2½ lb guinea fowl, preferably fresh
Butter for greasing baking tin
900 g/2 lb chicken carcasses, roughly chopped
1 medium onion, roughly chopped
250 g/8 oz carrots, scraped and chopped
125 g/4 oz celery, chopped
125 g /4 oz leeks, trimmed, thoroughly washed and chopped
4.5 L/8 pt water
Bouquet garni: 2 parsley sprigs, sprig thyme or ¼ teaspoon dried thyme, small bay leaf
1 teaspoon white peppercorns, lightly crushed
4 sprigs tarragon

Salt

For Clarifying Broth:
50 g/2 oz tomato purée
125 g/4 oz onions, chopped
125 g/4 oz leeks, trimmed, thoroughly washed and chopped
125 g/4 oz carrots, scraped and chopped
125 g/4 oz celery, chopped
125 g/4 oz wild mushrooms (chanterelles, etc.)
6 stalks tarragon
8 egg whites

For the Garnish:
50 g/2 oz wild mushrooms
Tarragon leaves, fresh, about 12

First make the broth. Cut the meat from the guinea fowl keeping the breast of one of the birds intact. Put all the meat aside in the refrigerator. Coarsely chop the bones.

In a baking tin greased with butter, combine the guinea fowl bones and chicken carcasses with the vegetables and roast in a preheated, moderate oven (190°C/375°F/gas 5), stirring from time to time, for 20–30 minutes, or until browned. Remove the contents to a large saucepan. On top of the stove, pour a little of the water for the broth into the baking tin and stir over moderate heat to scrape up any brown bits. Pour into the saucepan with the rest of the water, the bouquet garni, white peppercorns, tarragon sprigs and a little salt – about ½ teaspoon. Bring to a boil over moderate heat and simmer, removing any scum that rises to the surface, until the liquid is reduced to half. Strain through a fine sieve and set aside in the saucepan.

To clarify the broth, add the tomato purée to the saucepan. Then, in a blender or food processor, mince the guinea fowl meat, except the reserved breast, with the onions, leeks, carrots, celery, mushrooms and tarragon, and scrape into a bowl. Beat the egg whites lightly then beat them into the vegetable mixture. Add this mixture to the broth and whisk until the surface is frothy. Bring to a simmer over moderate heat, reduce the heat to very low and cook at a bare simmer for 1½–2 hours. Do not let the broth boil as this will cloud it. Strain through a sieve lined with dampened muslin set over a bowl, then strain a second time through clean, damp muslin. The broth should then be perfectly clear. Season to taste with salt.

Wrap the reserved guinea fowl breast in foil and roast it in a preheated, hot oven (220°C/425°F/gas 7) for 30 minutes. Remove from the oven, cool, remove the skin and cut the meat into thin pieces. Thinly slice the mushrooms for the garnish and chop the tarragon leaves. Place a little of each into six soup bowls. Reheat the broth and pour it over the garnish. Serve immediately.

MUSHROOM AND MUSTARD SOUP

This is Stephen Frost's version of a traditional English soup. An Englishman from Cambridge, he is head chef at Cromlix House, Dunblane, in Perthshire, Scotland, the family home of the Edens, and now a luxury country house hotel set in a 5000-acre estate which includes a grouse moor. He is also the youngest of the Scottish Master Chefs. Chef Frost, an enthusiast who cherishes simplicity in cooking and dislikes too many contrasting flavours in a dish, seeks to look at food from a new perspective.

This soup is wonderful on a chilly day, and also makes a good beginning to a salad lunch. It is typical of today's young chefs that they not only create new dishes, but recreate old ones.

SERVES 4

2 tablespoons butter
1 medium onion, chopped
1 medium leek, chopped
2 stalks celery, chopped
1 medium carrot, scraped and
   chopped

750 ml/1¼ pt chicken stock, about
   (see Basic Recipes, page 10)
½ teaspoon dry English mustard, or 1
   tablespoon Dijon mustard
Salt
Freshly ground pepper
50 ml/2 fl oz dry sherry

Heat the butter in a saucepan, add the onion, leek, celery, carrot and mushrooms and cook over very low heat until the vegetables are softened, about 5 minutes. Do not let them brown. Add the chicken stock, bring to a simmer, cover and cook until the vegetables are very tender, about 30 minutes. Lift out the solids and transfer to a food processor or blender. Add the mustard and process to a purée, adding a little of the stock if necessary. Return the purée to the saucepan and season with salt and pepper. If the soup seems very thick, add more stock. Pour in the sherry and heat through. If liked, stir in a little cream, or fresh white cheese (see Basic Recipes, page 24), just before serving.

Fish and Shellfish

Today's chefs have come up with wonderfully innovative recipes for the wide range of fish and shellfish that are now available at the fishmongers. Fish is being taken more seriously, and these exciting and original recipes make fish dishes a gastronomic delight, not any longer to be thought of as Friday food, or limited to take-away fish and chips, no matter how good these may be. Fish and shellfish have the great advantage of taking little time to prepare and cook, are appetizing, attractive to look at, and good for us.

POACHED FILLETS OF SOLE WITH ORANGE SAUCE

This is a pleasantly original recipe that turns fillet of sole into something special. It is easy to cook and takes little time. Nigel Lambert, who created the dish, says his aim is to produce unpretentious, honest food that is also original and interesting.

SERVES 4

900 g/2 lb skinned and boned sole or flounder fillets, cut into 8 pieces
Salt
Freshly ground pepper
125 g/4 oz butter, plus butter for pan
1 tablespoon shallot, chopped
250 ml/8 fl oz fresh orange juice
4 tablespoons lemon juice

125 ml/4 fl oz double cream (see Note)
50 ml/2 fl oz Grand Marnier, or other orange liqueur

For the Garnish:
1 orange, peeled and segmented
2 tablespoons chopped parsley
Puff pastry shapes (optional)

Season the fish with salt and pepper and fold the fillets in half. Lightly butter an oven-proof dish large enough to hold the fish in a single layer. Sprinkle with the shallot and arrange the fish on top. Pour in the orange and lemon juice, cover with buttered paper or foil and cook in a preheated, moderate oven (180°C/350°F/gas 4) for about 10 minutes. Lift out the fillets onto a warmed dish, cover and keep warm.

Strain the cooking liquid from the pan into a saucepan and reduce over fairly high heat to about 50 ml/2 fl oz. It should be very concentrated. Pour in the cream and continue to reduce until the sauce reaches coating consistency. Off the heat, stir in the Grand Marnier and beat in the butter, cut in pieces, until it is all incorporated.

Arrange the fish on four warmed plates and coat with the sauce. Garnish with the orange segments and parsley, and the puff pastry shapes if liked.

Note: If I want to cut down on butter and cream, I stir in 125 g/4 oz fresh white cheese, or yoghurt cheese (see Basic Recipes, pages 24, 25) instead of the cream and just heat it through, then stir in the Grand Marnier and leave out the butter.

WINE SUGGESTION: A Chardonnay.

STUFFED POACHED FILLETS OF SOLE

I admire the forthright approach of young John Martin Grimsey of the White Hart Hotel, a hostelry since 1498, in Coggeshall, Essex. He cares deeply for traditional British cooking but recognizes the need for change. He feels this dish meets his requirements, and says of it that he particularly enjoys the subtle blend of flavours and textures. I agree.

SERVES 4

2 large Dover lemon or sand soles
125 g/4 oz unsalted butter
Salt
Freshly ground pepper
4 slices smoked salmon, about 25 g/
    1 oz
1 medium avocado, peeled, pitted and
    sliced

Hollandaise sauce (see Basic Recipes,
    page 21) (optional)

For the Garnish (optional):
Tomato roses
Puff pastry shapes
Fresh chervil or parsley sprigs

Have the fishmonger skin the sole and remove a whole fillet from each side, giving 4 large fillets. Keep the bones for making stock.

Melt the butter in a small saucepan over low heat. Generously brush an oven-proof dish, large enough to hold the fish when folded into envelopes, with the melted butter. Put the fillets on a board and season with salt and pepper. Brush with melted butter and top with the smoked salmon slices. Brush the salmon with melted butter and top with the sliced avocado. Fold the fish over the filling to make an envelope. Brush with butter and press down lightly to seal. Arrange in the buttered dish and bake in a preheated, moderate oven (180°C/350°F/gas 4) for about 15 minutes, or until done.

Arrange the fish on four warmed plates and pour the hollandaise sauce over them, if liked. Garnish, if you wish, with tomato roses, puff pastry cut into tiny fish shapes, or sprigs of fresh chervil or parsley. Serve with new potatoes and any fresh green vegetable, such as green peas, mangetout, courgettes or green beans.

WINE SUGGESTION: A white Burgundy – an Aligoté.

FILETS DE SOLE AU BEURRE D'AVOCAT ET BASILIC

(Fillet of Sole with Avocado and Basil)

John Armstrong cares very much about presentation and even more about flavour. In addition he is a true original. He sees simplicity and unpretentiousness as essential to his cooking style and shuns outrageously expensive garnishes like truffles and foie gras. His extravagance is incorporated into the quality of the dish as a whole. He cooks to please his customers and he hopes to delight the eye as well as the palate. The exciting combination of flavours in this dish should certainly please the palate.

SERVES 6

5 tablespoons butter
4 tablespoons chopped shallots
12 fillets Dover sole, or other sole, each weighing about 125 g/4 oz
Salt
Freshly ground pepper
475 ml/16 fl oz fish stock, about (see Basic Recipes, page 13)
125 ml/4 fl oz double cream

2 large, ripe avocados
1 tablespoon basil leaves, coarsely chopped

For the Garnish:
1 tomato weighing about 175 g/6 oz, seeded and diced
6 small sprigs basil

Using 1 tablespoon of the butter, butter an oven-proof baking dish, about 15 × 23 cm/6 × 9 in. Sprinkle with the chopped shallots. Season the fish with salt and pepper. Lightly flatten the fillets and tie each into a loose knot, or fold over to make triangles. Arrange in the baking dish. Bring the stock to a simmer and pour over the fish. Cover the dish with aluminium foil and bake in a preheated, moderately hot oven (200°C/400°F/gas 6) until firm to the touch, about 8–12 minutes. Lift out the fillets to a warmed dish and keep warm.

Pour the cooking liquid into a saucepan and reduce to 250 ml/8 fl oz over moderately high heat. Add the cream and reduce again to 250 ml/8 fl oz. Pour into a food processor or blender, add one of the avocados, diced, and the basil leaves, and process to a purée. Cut the remaining butter into pieces and add, with the machine running, a piece at a time, until they have all been incorporated. Season to taste with salt and pepper and, for a very fine sauce, put through a strainer. The sauce may be left unstrained.

Peel the remaining avocado and cut into slices. Arrange a fan of avocado on each of six warmed plates. Arrange two fillets on each plate and coat with the sauce. Garnish with tomato dice and basil sprigs.

WINE SUGGESTION: Sauvignon.

FILLET OF SOLE WITH SMOKED SALMON

Ken Stott, head chef of Kildrummy Castle, is himself a Scot who has always worked in the north-east of his own country. He believes in using the produce for which Scotland is famed and adding his own skills and ideas to create appetizing new dishes which will give pleasure to those who eat them. I found this utterly delicious, and the recipe can easily be halved.

SERVES 8

2 teaspoons butter
2 teaspoons plain flour
125 ml/4 fl oz fish stock (see Basic Recipes, page 13)
8 large fillets of sole or plaice, each weighing about 175 g/6 oz
8 slices smoked salmon, about 125 g/ 4 oz

125 ml/4 fl oz dry white wine
125 ml/4 fl oz double cream
2 tablespoons butter, cut in pieces
Salt
Freshly ground pepper

Heat the 2 teaspoons butter in a small saucepan and stir in the flour. Cook, stirring, over low heat for 1 minute. Off the heat, whisk in the fish stock, return the saucepan to the heat and cook, stirring or whisking, until the sauce is smooth and lightly thickened. Set aside.

Put the fillets of sole on a board and flatten them lightly. Top each with a slice of smoked salmon and roll them up. If necessary secure them with a toothpick. Arrange the fish, in a single layer, in a large frying pan that has a lid. Mix the sauce, wine and cream together and pour over the fish. Bring to just under a simmer, cover and poach the fish until done, about 8 minutes. Lift out the fish and keep warm. Reduce the sauce over fairly brisk heat to 250 ml/8 fl oz, lower the heat and whisk in the pieces of butter one by one. Taste for seasoning and add salt and pepper if necessary.

Have ready eight warmed plates. Cut each fillet through the middle and arrange on the plate, cut-side up so that the pink of the salmon can be seen. Pour the sauce round the fish. Serve immediately. Serve with new potatoes and a green vegetable or two, like mangetout or green beans, on small, separate plates.

WINE SUGGESTION: A Chardonnay.

SALMON FILLETS WITH LEEK AND SPINACH SAUCE

I first met Peter Jackson when he was head chef at Bodysgallen Hall Hotel in Wales, and later when he was head chef at Eastwell Manor in Kent.

This attractive, easy to cook dish was given to me by Peter when he was at Bodysgallen Hall. I have cooked it very happily with sea (salmon) trout, and other fish and always enjoy its simple fresh taste. Peter is now chef-patron at The Colonial Restaurant in the heart of old Glasgow – a Scottish chef come home.

SERVES 4

250 g/8 oz fresh spinach leaves, washed and trimmed
4 slices salmon fillet, boned and skinned, each weighing about 150-175 g/5-6 oz
Flour
Salt
Freshly ground pepper
4 tablespoons butter
2 medium leeks, using white part only, thoroughly washed and cut into julienne strips
50 ml/2 fl oz strong fish stock (see Basic Recipes, page 13)
50 ml/2 fl oz dry vermouth
125 ml/4 fl oz double cream

Drop the spinach into a saucepan of briskly boiling water and cook for 4 minutes. Drain, refresh in cold water, then drain thoroughly, pressing out as much water as possible. Rolling the spinach up in a bamboo mat and squeezing it is the easiest way, borrowed from the Japanese. Purée the spinach in a blender or food processor and set aside.

Dredge the salmon with flour, shaking to remove the excess. Season the fish with salt and pepper. Heat half the butter in a frying pan large enough to hold the fish in a single layer and sauté the fillets, turning once, for about 6 minutes, or until done. Lift out of the pan onto a warmed plate, cover, and keep warm.

Add the rest of the butter and the leeks to the pan and cook, stirring, for 2-3 minutes over low heat until the leeks are tender. Add the fish stock and vermouth and simmer, uncovered, until the liquid is reduced to about half. Add the cream and reduce until the sauce is of coating consistency. Stir in the spinach and add salt and pepper if necessary. Spoon the sauce onto four heated plates and put a salmon fillet on top.

WINE SUGGESTION: A Chardonnay.

SALMON WITH WATERCRESS SAUCE

Eduard Hari, when executive chef of the Inn-on-the-Park in London, cared a great deal about the people who came to eat at the Inn's restaurants, and wanted the food to taste and look superb. He likes a little bit of his personality to go into every meal that is served, he says. His aim is to keep natural flavours unspoiled and never to mix flavours that will conflict with each other. Like Shaun Hill of Gidleigh Park in Devon, he dislikes bizarre garnishes that no one can eat. An optimistic and ebullient man, he delights in creating new dishes.

SERVES 2

Puff pastry (see Basic Recipes, page 15)
2 bunches watercress, about 250 g/ 8 oz
2 tablespoons butter
2 tablespoons finely chopped shallots
2 fillets fresh salmon, each weighing about 175 g/6 oz

Salt
White pepper
125 ml/4 fl oz fish stock (see Basic Recipes, page 13)
125 ml/4 fl oz dry white wine
50 ml/2 fl oz double cream

Make half a recipe puff pastry. Roll the pastry out into two 10 × 15 cm/4 × 6 in pieces and bake in a preheated, moderate oven (180°C/350°F/gas 4) until well risen and lightly browned, about 25 minutes. Allow to cool then split each in half. Set aside in the turned-off oven to keep warm.

Wash and pick over the watercress. Discard the stalks. Drop the cress into a saucepan of briskly boiling water and blanch for 1 minute. Drain thoroughly, rinse under cold running water and drain again. Purée in a blender or food processor until very smooth. Divide the purée into two parts and set it aside.

In a frying pan large enough to hold the fish comfortably, heat the butter. Add the shallots and cook over moderate heat until they are softened, about 1 minute. Season the salmon with salt and pepper and cook over low heat, turning once, until the salmon is done, about 5–6 minutes. Lift out onto a plate and keep warm, covered. Pour the fish stock into the pan and reduce it to half over fairly high heat. Add the wine and reduce the liquid in the pan to 125 ml/4 fl oz. Add the cream, bring to a simmer, then stir in half of the watercress purée. Taste for seasoning, adding salt and pepper if necessary. If any juices have collected on the plate with the salmon, add them to the sauce.

To assemble the dish, spread both pieces of each of the pastry cases with the remaining watercress purée. Place the bottom halves on each of two warmed plates and top with the salmon. Spoon the watercress sauce onto the salmon and top with the pastry lid.

WINE SUGGESTION: An Aligoté.

SALMON EN PAPILLOTE WITH SORREL SAUCE

Robert Gardiner created this very attractive dish, the richness of the salmon balanced by the slight acidity of the sorrel sauce. It is very much a party dish.

SERVES 6

900 g/2 lb centre-cut salmon fillet, skinned and boned

250 g/8 oz onions, cut into julienne strips

4 tablespoons butter

250 ml/8 fl oz chicken stock (see Basic Recipes, page 10)

175 g/6 oz carrots, cut into julienne strips

3 tablespoons chives or spring onions, finely chopped

6 tablespoons finely chopped parsley

125 g/4 oz butter, sliced and chilled

150 ml/¼ pt each fish stock (see Basic Recipes, page 13) and dry white wine, mixed

For the Sorrel Sauce:

4 shallots, finely chopped

175 ml/6 fl oz white wine vinegar

175 ml/6 fl oz dry white wine

2 tablespoons heavy cream

250 g/8 oz butter, chilled and cut into pieces

12 medium-sized sorrel leaves, stalks and ribs removed, cut into julienne strips

Salt

Freshly ground pepper

Cut the salmon into 6 slices. In a frying pan, sauté the onions in the butter until they are tender. Pour the chicken stock into a small saucepan, bring to the boil, add the carrots and simmer for 3 minutes. The carrots should be tender, but retain a little crunch. Drain the carrots and refresh in cold water. Drain thoroughly then mix with the onions and set aside.

Lightly oil 6 sheets of parchment or greaseproof paper large enough to wrap the salmon fillets. Put the onion and carrot mixture in the centre of each sheet. Place a slice of salmon on top of the vegetable mixture. Mix the chives or spring onions with the parsley and place on top of the salmon. Put a slice of butter on top of the herbs and moisten with the fish stock and wine mixture. Fold the paper into a half-moon shape, pinching the edges well together. Arrange the packages in an oven-proof dish and bake in a preheated, hot oven (220°C/425°F/gas 7) for 10–12 minutes.

While the salmon is cooking, make the sauce. Combine the shallots, vinegar and wine in a saucepan and simmer over low heat, uncovered, until the liquid is reduced to 3 tablespoons. Add the cream, bring to a boil and remove from the heat. Whisk in the butter piece by piece until it has all been incorporated, on and off the heat, so that the saucepan does not get too hot as this may curdle the sauce. Add the sorrel and season with salt and pepper.

Spoon the sauce onto six warmed plates. Unwrap the salmon and, using a spatula, carefully lift the fish and herbs onto the plates. Serve immediately with new potatoes and some mixed fresh vegetables such as baby carrots, cauliflower sprigs, broccoli sprigs, green peas or beans, on small separate plates.

WINE SUGGESTION: An Aligoté.

SALMON WITH WALNUTS, GRAPES AND SCALLOPS

Chris Oakes of Oakes restaurant has created a medley of flavours that harmonize beautifully in this dish.

SERVES 4

750 g/1½ lb centre-cut salmon fillet, skinned and cut into 4 slices
1 tablespoon fresh tarragon, finely chopped
Salt
Freshly ground pepper
4 tablespoons butter
25 g/1 oz chopped walnuts
50 g/2 oz seedless green grapes, peeled
4 large scallops, sliced
1 tablespoon lemon juice, or to taste

Make a slit in each piece of salmon and stuff each with ¼ teaspoon chopped tarragon. Season the fish with salt and pepper. Heat 2 tablespoons of the butter in a frying pan large enough to hold the salmon in a single layer. Sauté the salmon over moderate heat for 2–3 minutes on each side. It should be firm to the touch. Be careful not to overcook as the fish dries out easily. Transfer the salmon to a warmed plate, cover and keep warm.

Add the rest of the butter to the pan. Add the walnuts, grapes, scallops and lemon juice and toss over moderate heat for about 1 minute, or until the scallops are opaque. Season with salt and pepper and spoon the mixture over the salmon. Sprinkle with the remaining tarragon. Serve immediately.

WINE SUGGESTION: A Chardonnay.

STUFFED ROLLED SALMON

This is the creation of John King, Chef de Cuisine at The Ritz Club in London, and accurately reflects his culinary philosophy. He is a firm believer in chefs having a classical cuisine training which they should use as a springboard to launch themselves into an inventive future, always shunning gimmickry. Born in Kent, the son of a gamekeeper, John grew up in rural surroundings and always wanted to be a chef. He set out at an early age to get the best training possible.

This is a grand dish, but worth the trouble for a special occasion.

SERVES 4

For the Mousse Stuffing:
250 g/8 oz boned and skinned
   salmon
2 egg yolks, plus 2 whole eggs
Salt
Freshly ground pepper
250 ml/8 fl oz double cream

For the Salmon:
750 g/1½ lb centre-cut salmon fillet,
   skinned and cut into 4 slices
Salt
Freshly ground pepper

125 g/4 oz butter plus butter for pan
2 tablespoons shallot, finely chopped
250 ml/8 fl oz dry white wine
250 ml/8 fl oz strong fish stock (see
   Basic Recipes, page 13)
500 g/1 lb mixed wild mushrooms
   such as chanterelles, morels, oyster
   mushrooms
125 ml/4 fl oz double cream

For the Garnish:
Parsley sprigs

To make the mousse, combine the 250 g/8 oz salmon, coarsely chopped, in a blender or food processor with the egg yolks and process to a purée. Add the 2 eggs, salt and pepper and process until smooth. Scrape into a bowl and refrigerate for at least an hour. When the mixture is cold, beat in the cream with a wooden spoon. Taste for seasoning, add more salt and pepper if necessary and refrigerate until needed.

Very lightly flatten the 4 slices of salmon, which should measure about 12 × 10 cm/5 × 4 in. Season them with salt and pepper. Either pipe or spoon the chilled mousse along the short side of the salmon then gently roll the fish up into a fat sausage (see Note). Secure the sausages with toothpicks to stop them unrolling. Butter an oven-proof dish large enough to hold the salmon in a single layer. Sprinkle the dish with the shallots, add the salmon, pour in the wine and stock, cover and cook in a preheated, hot oven (220°C/425°F/gas 7) for about 10 minutes, or until the fish is done. Lift out the salmon onto a warmed plate, cover and keep warm.

Heat 4 tablespoons of the butter in a frying pan and sauté the mushrooms for about 3 minutes. Transfer to a bowl and keep warm. Pour the liquid in which the salmon was cooked into a saucepan and reduce it to half over fairly high heat. Add the cream and reduce to 250 ml/8 fl oz. Cut the butter into pieces and beat it into the sauce. Taste for seasoning. Arrange the salmon fillets on four heated plates and spoon the sauce over them. Sprinkle the salmon with the mushrooms and garnish with a few sprigs of parsley. Serve immediately.

Note: If there is any leftover mousse, make it into quenelles and poach in fish stock. Use to garnish other fish dishes. The uncooked mousse will keep, refrigerated, for 2–3 days.

WINE SUGGESTION: A Chardonnay.

BRAISED SALMON WITH PIKE MOUSSE

The pike mousse in this recipe created by Bernard Rendler, the sous-chef at Gravetye Manor in West Sussex, could not be easier to make. The dish is interestingly different from Martin Bredda's Haddock and Salmon Surprise (see page 114) though the ingredients are very much the same. It demonstrates the creative originality of the chefs. When I find pike hard to get I substitute a non-oily white fish and I have also substituted sea (salmon) trout for the salmon with great success.

SERVES 4

For the Mousse:
250 g/8 oz skinned and boned pike, or other non-oily white fish
Salt
Freshly ground pepper
1 large egg
250 ml/8 fl oz double cream

For the Fish and Sauce:
Butter
475 ml/16 fl oz fish stock, plus 125 ml/4 fl oz (see Basic Recipes, page 13)

4 slices salmon fillet, each weighing about 150 g/5 oz
125 ml/4 fl oz dry white wine
2 tablespoons finely chopped shallots
4 medium-sized mushrooms, sliced
2 medium tomatoes, peeled and chopped
125 ml/4 fl oz double cream
Salt
Freshly ground pepper

For the Garnish:
2 tablespoons chopped chives

In a food processor or blender, purée the pike or other fish until it is very light and smooth. Season with salt and pepper. Add the egg and process until thoroughly mixed. For a very fine, light texture rub the mixture through a sieve into a bowl, or simply scrape the mixture from the food processor into a bowl. Set the bowl in a larger bowl filled with ice and very slowly beat in the cream with a wooden spoon.

Butter a shallow, flameproof dish large enough to hold the fish fillets in a single layer. Pour in the 475 ml/16 fl oz fish stock and bring it to a simmer. Remove from the heat. Carefully spread the mousse over the fish. Arrange the fish in the baking dish and cook in a preheated, hot oven (220°C/425°F/gas 7) for 15 minutes. Run under a grill to glaze.

While the fish is cooking, make the sauce. Pour the 125 ml/4 fl oz fish stock and the white wine into a saucepan. Add the shallots, mushrooms and tomatoes and simmer, uncovered, until the liquid is reduced to 125 ml/4 fl oz. Add the cream and continue to simmer until the sauce reaches coating consistency. Season to taste with salt and pepper.

Pour the sauce onto four heated plates. Top with a salmon fillet and sprinkle with chives. Serve immediately.

WINE SUGGESTION: Muscadet.

SALMON AND ASPARAGUS TERRINE

Andreas Antona, whose work I knew when he was sous-chef under Michael Quinn at The Ritz in London, and before that when he was with Anton Mosimann at The Dorchester Hotel, is now head chef at The Elms Hotel in Abberley, near Worcester, a Queen Anne mansion built in 1710 and now a country house hotel. He typifies the new young chefs who have brought about a peaceful revolution in our cooking. Trained at Ealing Technical College, he worked in Switzerland and Germany for experience before returning to London. He is now working out his own ideas. In this recipe he uses wild Scottish salmon and Evesham asparagus. It works very well with any fresh salmon and fresh asparagus and makes a delectable summer main course, light yet satisfying.

SERVES 6 as a main course. To serve as a starter, slice more thinly for 8 to 12

750 g/1½ lb salmon fillet

2 L/3½ pt clarified (strong) fish stock (see Basic Recipes, page 13)

300 ml/½ pt Pouilly Fuissé, or other dry white wine

750 g/1½ lb fresh green asparagus

2½ envelopes (2½ tablespoons) unflavoured gelatine

Salt

Freshly ground pepper

3 tablespoons finely chopped mixed fresh herbs such as chervil, coriander, parsley, tarragon, basil

Measure the salmon at its thickest part and cook it for 10 minutes to the 2.5 cm/1 in. Put it into a fish kettle or a casserole large enough to hold it comfortably. Pour in the fish stock and half the wine, bring to a simmer and cook, covered, over very low heat for the time required. Cool in the stock.

Meanwhile, prepare the asparagus. Using a small, sharp knife, peel away the tough part of the lower end of the spears. Trim them so that all the spear is edible. Choose a casserole large enough to hold the asparagus comfortably, and fill it with salted water. Bring the water to a rolling boil and add the asparagus spears, tied with kitchen string into loose bundles. Cook the asparagus, uncovered, until it is tender but still crisp, about 10 minutes. Lift out the bundles, drain and remove the string. Let them cool.

Remove the salmon from the stock to a chopping board. Add the rest of the wine to the stock and bring the mixture to a simmer. Pour 125 ml/4 fl oz cold water into a small bowl and sprinkle the gelatine over it. When it has softened, stir it into the fish stock, then stir to dissolve. Strain through a fine sieve lined with a double layer of dampened cheesecloth. Cool, season to taste with salt and pepper and stir in the herbs.

Choose a terrine, or other deep dish, that will fit two layers of the salmon neatly, and cut the salmon in half to fit. Ladle a thin layer of aspic into the terrine, and chill in the refrigerator to set. Arrange half the salmon on top of the jelly and ladle enough aspic over it to cover. If the remaining aspic jelly has set, warm it just a little to liquify. Chill again until set and cover with a layer of half the asparagus and more aspic. Chill again. Repeat with the rest of the salmon and asparagus and finish with a layer of aspic. Chill in the refrigerator for at least 4 hours, or until firmly set.

To serve, run a knife rinsed in hot water round the edge of the terrine, or dip the terrine very quickly into hot water, and unmould onto a serving platter. Using a very sharp knife, cut into slices and serve with mayonnaise or, for a lighter dressing, mayonnaise mixed with an equal amount of plain yoghurt.

WINE SUGGESTION: Pouilly Fuissé, or other dry white wine or Champagne.

COLD POACHED SALMON WITH SORREL MAYONNAISE

Peter Jackson is a passionate believer in fresh, natural food, but he does not believe in undercooking or combining ingredients that will quarrel with each other in the mouth; foods and flavours should complement each other. I enjoyed his salmon one brilliant summer day and feel his cooking lives up to his philosophy.

SERVES 8

1½ recipes fish stock (see Basic Recipes, page 13)
1 tablespoon green peppercorns
1 × 2.3 kg/5 lb whole salmon, unskinned with head and tail left on
1 recipe mayonnaise (see Basic Recipes, page 23), made with lemon juice

2 teaspoons dry vermouth, preferably Noilly Prat
25 g/1 oz sorrel, stems and ribs removed and very finely shredded

In a fish kettle large enough to hold the salmon comfortably, bring the fish stock to a boil with the green peppercorns. Wrap the salmon in cheesecloth and lower it gently into the briskly boiling liquid. Bring the liquid back to a boil over high heat, cover, turn off the heat and allow to cool. The fish will be perfectly cooked, moist and tender. Lift it out onto a large serving platter and carefully skin it. Leave head and tail intact. Mix the mayonnaise with the vermouth and stir in the sorrel. Serve with the salmon.

If liked the salmon may be garnished with lemon slices, or cucumber slices and cherry tomatoes. It may be accompanied by cucumber salad, green salad or potato salad.

WINE SUGGESTION: Chardonnay.

SALMON IN RED WINE

This was cooked for me by Alan Casey when he was head chef at Culloden House. It is extremely simple and very flavourful. There are not a great many fish recipes using red wine, and this has become one of my favourites.

SERVES 4

4 × 175 g/6 oz slices salmon fillet, cut
    on the slant
Salt
Freshly ground pepper
Flour
4 tablespoons butter
12 peeled white onions, about
    2.5 cm/1 in in diameter
12 button mushrooms

475 ml/16 fl oz dry red wine such as
    a Beaujolais or Côtes de Provence
1 bay leaf
½ teaspoon thyme
125 ml/4 fl oz double cream
1 teaspoon lemon juice
½ teaspoon Worcestershire sauce
2 tablespoons finely chopped parsley

Season the salmon with salt and pepper and dredge with flour, shaking to remove the excess. Heat the butter in a frying pan that has a lid and seal the salmon steaks quickly on both sides. Lift out and set aside, covered. In the butter remaining in the pan, lightly brown the onions and mushrooms. Pour in the wine, add the bay leaf and thyme and bring to a simmer. Return the salmon, and any juices that may have collected, to the pan, cover and simmer just until the salmon is tender, about 10 minutes. Remove the fish to a warmed serving dish and keep warm.

Remove and discard the bay leaf and thyme. Add the cream and reduce to coating consistency over fairly high heat. Add the lemon juice and Worcestershire sauce. Pour the sauce over the salmon and sprinkle with the parsley. Serve with boiled new potatoes.

WINE SUGGESTION: Drink the same wine as used for cooking the fish, a light, young, red wine, Beaujolais or Côtes de Provence.

TURBOT AND SALMON WITH
A CHAMPAGNE SAUCE

Simon Collins is brilliantly inventive. He has a talent for putting together quite ordinary ingredients in a way that transforms them into something very special. Instead of dry Champagne, use a dry white wine from the Champagne region, or any dry white wine.

SERVES 4

25 g/1 oz carrot, cut into julienne strips
25 g/1 oz celery, cut into julienne strips
25 g/1 oz white part of leek, cut into julienne strips
25 g/1 oz mixed sweet red and green peppers, cut into julienne strips
Butter
Salt
Freshly ground pepper
4 × 75 g/3 oz slices of turbot, or similar fish, cut on a slant
4 × 75 g/3 oz slices of salmon fillet, cut on a slant
1 bay leaf

A little fish stock (see Basic Recipes, page 13)

For the Sauce:
475 ml/16 fl oz dry white wine
475 ml/16 fl oz strong fish stock (see Basic Recipes, page 13)
½ teaspoon chopped fresh tarragon, or ¼ teaspoon dried
Pinch ground saffron
Freshly ground pepper
250 ml/8 fl oz double cream
Salt

For the Garnish (optional):
Fresh tarragon sprigs

Combine the julienne strips of carrot, celery, leek, and peppers in a saucepan of briskly boiling water and blanch for 2 minutes. Drain and refresh under cold water. Drain thoroughly.

Cut four 25 cm/10 in circles of aluminium foil, or greaseproof or parchment paper and butter generously. Season all the fish with salt and pepper and place a slice of turbot on each circle of foil. Top each with the vegetable julienne, a little piece of bay leaf and a teaspoon or so of fish stock. Top with the salmon slices and seal the paper or foil by folding it securely. Arrange the fish in an oven-proof baking dish and bake in a preheated, hot oven (220°C/425°F/gas 7) for 6 minutes.

Meanwhile, make the sauce. Pour the wine into a saucepan and reduce it over high heat to 250 ml/8 fl oz. Add the fish stock, tarragon, saffron and a few grinds of black pepper and reduce the liquid again, over high heat, to 250 ml/8 fl oz. Add the cream and continue to reduce, still over high heat, until the sauce reaches coating consistency. Season to taste with salt and pepper, strain and warm through. Pour the sauce onto four warmed plates. Take the fish out of the foil or paper and serve on top of the sauce. Garnish, if liked, with a sprig of fresh tarragon.

WINE SUGGESTION: Still Champagne.

FILLET OF TURBOT IN SORREL

Martin Rowbotham, head chef at Hunstrete House Hotel, Bath, an eighteenth-century country manor house, now a country house hotel, was not immediately captivated by cooking. It took some time before the art captured him, and now he hopes to achieve much.

Here he combines three flavours in a pleasantly understated way, no one flavour dominant, the rich turbot, delicate mushrooms, and slightly acid sorrel enhanced by the creamy sauce. He says that the blending of ingredients is like the creation of a symphony. He enjoys cooking immensely and is eager to learn all he can from books and from other chefs.

SERVES 4

500 g/1 lb mushrooms, finely
   chopped
2 medium onions, finely chopped
½ clove garlic, crushed
Salt
Freshly ground pepper
4 fillets of turbot, or similar fish,
   skinned and weighing 175–250 g/
   6–8 oz each

Large sorrel leaves, about 12
125 g/4 oz butter, cut into pieces,
   plus butter for frying pan
250 ml/8 fl oz dry vermouth
125 ml/4 fl oz double cream
1 tablespoon lemon juice

Combine the mushrooms, onion and garlic in a heavy frying pan and cook over moderate heat until the mushrooms have given up all their liquid. Shake, or stir, the contents of the pan so that they do not burn. Season with salt and pepper and set aside.

Season the fish with salt and pepper and cover with the reserved mushroom mixture. Wrap each fillet in sorrel leaves. Butter the frying pan and arrange the fish in it. Pour in the vermouth, bring to a simmer, cover and poach for about 10 minutes or until the fish is done. Remove the fish and keep warm.

Reduce the liquid in the pan to half over moderately high heat. Add the cream and reduce until the sauce coats a spoon. Add the lemon juice, then whisk in the butter, over low heat, piece by piece until the sauce is light and creamy. Taste for seasoning, add salt and pepper if necessary. Pour the sauce onto four warmed plates and arrange a package of fish on each. Serve the rest of the sauce separately.

WINE SUGGESTION: Muscadet.

TURBOT FILLET 'LAMBERT'

This is another of Denis Woodtli's interestingly different fish dishes. The recipe can easily be doubled but it does make a lovely self-indulgent meal when one is dining alone and is not content to dine less than well.

SERVES 1

1 turbot or halibut fillet, weighing 150-175 g/5-6 oz
2 Dublin Bay prawns, or large prawns, whole, unpeeled
2 large scallops
2 tablespoons butter
½ medium onion, finely chopped
125 ml/4 fl oz medium dry white wine

125 ml/4 fl oz strong fish stock (see Basic Recipes, page 13)
2 tablespoons tomato purée
50 ml/2 fl oz brandy
125 ml/4 fl oz double cream (see Note)
Salt
Freshly ground pepper

Lightly flatten the fish fillet. Shell one of the prawns and place it, with one of the scallops, on the fish. Roll it up and secure with a toothpick. Generously butter a small frying pan, add the onion, white wine, fish stock and stuffed fish. Bring to a simmer, cover and cook for 5-6 minutes, or until done.

In another frying pan, heat a little butter and toss the other prawn, unshelled, in the pan over moderately high heat for 1-2 minutes. Add the tomato purée and stir, then pour in the brandy and, when it is warm, light it. Add half the cream and cook until the sauce reaches coating consistency. Add salt and pepper to taste.

Lift the fish out of the first frying pan and put it on a heated plate. Cover and keep warm. Reduce the liquid in the frying pan to half its volume, add the remaining cream, and the scallop and reduce the sauce to coating consistency. Season with salt and pepper.

Pour the white wine sauce onto one half of the fish and plate, and the tomato purée sauce onto the other half. Put the scallop on the tomato sauce, and the whole prawn on the white wine sauce. The finished dish looks very attractive and tastes wonderful. It is worth the trouble. Serve with a green salad.

Note: If I want to avoid cream, I stir in fresh white cheese (see Basic Recipes, page 24) and warm it through. It will be quite heavy enough and the scallop only needs minimal cooking.

WINE SUGGESTION: A dry Moselle as turbot is a light fish.

FILLETS OF TURBOT WITH LEEKS AND WILD MUSHROOMS

This is a delectable dish, not difficult, but requiring attention to detail. Don't be put off by the long list of ingredients. Many of them are ordinary kitchen items. Created by Raymond Blanc, I find I can do no better than describe it in his own words: 'the colour effect is magnificent, the textures so different and the taste will fulfil the enchantment of this still life'. Raymond has a deep respect for tradition, believing innovation springs from a desire to perfect dishes from the past. He is in love with cooking and this dish shows it.

SERVES 6

175 g/6 oz butter
2 tablespoons finely chopped shallots
400 ml/14 fl oz Gewurtztraminer, or
     other dry white wine
50 g/2 oz mushrooms, finely chopped
6 turbot or halibut fillets, each
     weighing about 150 g/5 oz
Salt
Freshly ground pepper
2 tablespoons lemon juice
2 tablespoons whipping cream

1 tablespoon finely chopped chives
12 baby leeks, trimmed, washed, tied
     up and blanched for 3-4 minutes
     then cut into 1 cm/½ in pieces
250 g/8 oz mixed wild mushrooms
     such as chanterelles (girolles),
     morels, etc.
2 tablespoons dry Madeira
2 tablespoons truffle juice (optional)
500 g/1 lb freshly cooked small new
     potatoes, kept warm

Set a flameproof dish, large enough to hold the fish in a single layer, over low heat. Melt ½ tablespoon of the butter in the dish, add the shallots and cook until the shallots are soft but not brown. Add the wine and simmer for 1 minute. Add the chopped mushrooms. Season the fish with salt and pepper. In a small saucepan, melt 2 tablespoons of the butter and mix it with 1 tablespoon of the lemon juice. Arrange the fish on top of the shallot-mushroom mixture and brush with the lemon-flavoured butter. Cover the dish and cook in a preheated, moderately hot oven (200°C/400°F/gas 6) for 3-5 minutes. Strain the juices from the pan through a sieve into a saucepan. Cover the fish and keep warm in a turned-off oven.

Reduce the juices over fairly brisk heat by about one-third. Add the cream, then whisk in all but 4 tablespoons of the butter cut in pieces. Add the chives, season to taste with salt and pepper and add a little lemon juice, if liked. Set aside and keep warm.

Meanwhile, warm the leeks in a frying pan with hot water and a little butter, about 1 tablespoon. Drain and keep warm.

Melt a tablespoon of the remaining butter in a small frying pan and sauté the wild mushrooms with a little of the remaining lemon juice for about 4 minutes. Lift out the mushrooms with a slotted spoon onto a warm plate, cover and keep them warm. Add the Madeira to the pan and reduce it to half.

Add the truffle juice, if using. Whisk in the remaining 2 tablespoons of the butter, cut in pieces. Cover and keep warm.

To assemble the dish, have ready six warmed plates. Put a fish fillet in the middle of each plate and garnish the plate with alternate mounds of leeks and wild mushrooms. If necessary return the plates, covered with buttered paper, to the oven for 2 minutes to heat through. Pour the butter sauce over the fish, and the Madeira sauce over the mushrooms. Add the new potatoes and serve.

WINE SUGGESTION: A Chardonnay.

HALIBUT FILLETS WITH GREEN GRAPES

Roy Richards uses Pineau des Charentes, a sweet fortified wine of the Cognac region, in this recipe. It is a very pleasant apéritif but not easy to buy outside France or even outside the Cognac region. I have used a demi-sec white wine successfully in place of the Pineau. A teaspoon of brandy added to the wine is an advantage.

SERVES 6
Butter
6 halibut fillets, each weighing about
   250 g/8 oz
Salt
Freshly ground pepper

250 g/8 oz seedless green grapes
125 ml/4 fl oz semi-sweet white wine
1 teaspoon brandy
125 ml/4 fl oz double cream

Generously butter an oven-proof baking dish large enough to hold the fish in a single layer. Season the fish with salt and pepper and arrange it in the dish. Scatter the grapes over the fish, pour in the white wine mixed with the brandy and the double cream. There should be enough liquid to barely cover the fish, but it should not be swimming in it. Bake in a preheated, hot oven (220°C/425°F/gas 7) basting frequently until the fish is done, 10–15 minutes. The sauce should be golden and glistening, with a creamy sweetness in contrast with the slight acidity of the grapes.

WINE SUGGESTION: A Muscadet from the Loire.

MONKFISH AND TURBOT IN CHIVE SAUCE

This interesting combination of fish comes from Alan Vikops. Though classically trained, his personal preference is for lighter, healthier foods with sauces that are distinctively flavoured but which do not overpower the dishes they accompany. He also likes his dishes to look attractive, pleasing both eye and palate. I think he succeeds very well in this simple recipe.

SERVES 4

8 pieces skinned and boned monkfish, each weighing about 50 g/2 oz (500 g/1 lb total weight)
4 pieces skinned and boned turbot each weighing about 75 g/3 oz (375 g/12 oz total weight)
Salt
Freshly ground pepper

4 tablespoons sweet paprika
175 ml/6 fl oz dry vermouth, preferably Noilly Prat
175 ml/6 fl oz strong fish stock (see Basic Recipes, page 13)
125 g/4 oz butter, cut into pieces
25 g/1 oz chopped chives

Season the fish with salt and pepper then roll the pieces in the paprika. Put the fish into a frying pan large enough to hold them in a single layer. Pour in half the dry vermouth, bring to a simmer, cover and cook over very low heat until the fish is done, about 3–4 minutes. Transfer the fish to a warmed plate, cover and keep warm.

Pour the rest of the vermouth and the fish stock into the frying pan and reduce it over high heat to half. Whisk in the butter and the chives. Arrange the fish on four heated plates and pour the sauce round them. The reddish-brown of the fish, coloured by the paprika, will make an attractive contrast to the sauce, white, flecked with green.

WINE SUGGESTION: An Aligoté.

MONKFISH WITH LIME AND GARLIC

Aidan McCormack, the young Welsh head chef at Middlethorpe Hall, a lovingly-restored Queen Anne mansion, now a small hotel in York, has a forthright philosophy of cooking: what is on the plate is to eat, and over-decoration with fussy garnishes gives good cooking a bad name. He believes in the virtues of simplicity and true flavour, and the use of the nose – a sauce is right when it smells right. I enjoyed this dish, the recipe for which bears out his philosophy. If lime juice is not available, use lemon juice.

SERVES 4

4 slices boned and skinned monkfish,
  each weighing about 175 g/6 oz
300 g/10 oz peeled, seeded and
  chopped tomatoes
3 tablespoons shallots, finely chopped
2 cloves garlic, chopped

3 tablespoons chopped parsley
250 ml/8 fl oz dry white wine
125 ml/4 fl oz mayonnaise (see Basic
  Recipes, page 23) made with lime
  juice

In a frying pan large enough to hold the fish in a single layer, combine the fish, tomatoes, shallots, garlic, parsley and wine. Bring to a simmer and cook, covered, for about 3 minutes, or until the fish is done. Lift the fish out onto a warmed dish, cover and keep warm.

Reduce the liquid in the frying pan over moderately high heat to about one quarter. Pour in any liquid that has collected on the plate with the fish, bring to a simmer, remove from the heat and whisk in the mayonnaise. Arrange the fish on four heated plates and mask with the sauce. Serve immediately.

WINE SUGGESTION: A Muscadet.

MONKFISH WITH GINGER AND SPRING VEGETABLES

This creation from Kenneth Bell is both original and delicious.

SERVES 4

2 medium carrots, scraped and cut
  into cork shapes
2 small turnips, peeled and cut into
  cork shapes
2 tablespoons butter
900 g/2 lb monkfish, skinned, boned
  and cut into 2 cm/¾ in pieces
1 tablespoon drained, finely sliced
  stem ginger in syrup

2 medium stalks celery, diced
475 ml/16 fl oz dry white wine
Salt
Freshly ground pepper
250 ml/8 fl oz double cream
25 g/1 oz chopped parsley, dill or
  chervil

Blanch the carrots and turnips in briskly boiling, salted water for 5 minutes. Drain and set aside.

In a large frying pan, heat the butter and add the fish, the ginger, celery, carrots, turnips and the wine. Season with salt and pepper, and simmer for 10 minutes.

Lift out the fish and arrange it on a warmed serving dish. Cover and keep warm. Add the cream to the sauce and simmer for 5 minutes longer, uncovered. Taste for seasoning. Reduce it over moderately high heat if it is too thin. It should be almost of coating consistency. Taste the sauce and add salt and pepper if necessary. Pour the sauce over the fish and sprinkle with the herbs. Serve immediately with new potatoes and a green salad.

WINE SUGGESTION: A strong wine such as a White Hermitage.

HADDOCK AND SALMON TROUT SURPRISE

Martin Bredda uses pike from the estate at Somerley in this recipe. If it is not available, substitute a non-oily white fish like sole or flounder.

SERVES 8

500 g/1 lb pike, or sole or flounder, or similar white fish
Salt
Freshly ground pepper
4 egg whites
175 ml/6 fl oz double cream
Butter
5 haddock fillets, each weighing 75–125 g/3–4 oz
5 sea (salmon) trout fillets, each weighing 75–125 g/3–4 oz

250 ml/8 fl oz single cream, or fresh white or junket cheese (see Basic Recipes, page 24)
375 g/12 oz shelled, medium-sized prawns
2 tablespoons tomato purée
2 tablespoons melted butter (optional)

Chop the pike, or substitute fish, coarsely. Season with salt and pepper and put into a blender or food processor. Process to a purée. With the machine running, add the egg whites, one by one, until the whites are thoroughly incorporated and the mixture is light and fluffy. Scrape the purée into a bowl. Put the bowl into a larger bowl filled with ice and refrigerate for 1 hour. Remove from the refrigerator and beat in half the double cream, using a wooden spoon. Return the mousse to the refrigerator for 15 minutes, then beat in the rest of the cream. Refrigerate the mousse until ready to use.

Butter a ring mould. Season the haddock and sea trout fillets with salt and pepper and, using each type of fish alternately, line the mould, letting the ends of the fillets hang over the sides. Spoon the mousse into the mould, fold the ends of the fillets over the mousse and press them lightly in place. Cover the mould with aluminium foil or parchment paper and place in a baking tin with hot water to come about halfway up the side. Bake in a preheated, moderate oven (180°C/350°F/gas 4) for 35 minutes, or until the fillets are firm to the touch. Remove the mould from the pan and allow it to rest.

While the mould is resting, make the sauce. In a medium-sized saucepan, combine the cream, prawns and tomato purée. Cook just long enough to warm through and cook the prawns. Unmould the salmon and haddock mousse onto a warmed, circular dish. Brush it with the melted butter if liked and serve the sauce separately.

WINE SUGGESTION: An Aligoté.

STUFFED FILLET OF PINK TROUT

This recipe was created by David Nicholls, head chef of Walton's in London whom I first met when he was head chef at The Old Lodge, Limpsfield in Surrey, and I found his enthusiasm infectious. His first job was as a footman to H.M. The Queen at Buckingham Palace, but cooking soon claimed him and at 18 he became the youngest *chef de partie* the London Waldorf had ever had.

This dish makes a superb lunch or dinner for two. When pink trout is not available I use sea (salmon) trout.

SERVES 2

250 ml/8 fl oz single cream
¼ clove garlic, crushed
1 teaspoon butter, plus butter for
   greasing pan
25 g/1 oz carrots, celery and leek, cut
   into julienne strips
Salt
Freshly ground pepper
Skinned and boned fillets from a
   500–625 g/1–1¼ lb pink trout

125 ml/4 fl oz dry vermouth,
   preferably Noilly Prat
125 ml/4 fl oz dry white wine
50 ml/2 fl oz strong fish stock (see
   Basic Recipes, page 13)
50 g/2 oz tomatoes, peeled, seeded
   and chopped

For the Garnish:
Dill sprigs

In a small saucepan, combine 50 ml/2 fl oz of the cream, the crushed garlic clove, the teaspoon of butter and the julienne of vegetables, and simmer until the cream is thick and the vegetables tender, about 5 minutes. Season with salt and pepper. Cool.

Place the fish fillets on a board and season with salt and pepper. Put half the cream and vegetable mixture on the fish about one-third way up from the tail end. Fold the tail end over the vegetables then fold the other end over. Fasten with toothpicks. Lightly butter a frying pan big enough to hold the two fillets comfortably. Arrange the fish in the pan, pour in the vermouth and dry white wine, cover and poach until the fish is cooked, about 8 minutes. Lift out onto a warmed plate, cover and keep warm. Add the fish stock to the pan and bring to a boil. Add the remaining cream and simmer until the sauce reaches coating consistency. Season to taste with salt and pepper. Add the tomato and cook for 1 minute longer. Spoon the sauce onto two heated plates and arrange a stuffed fillet on each plate. Garnish with the sprigs of dill. Serve with new potatoes or noodles, and a green salad.

WINE SUGGESTION: A fairly fat wine to cope with trout: a Chardonnay.

BAKED FILLETS OF STRIPED BASS WITH CHIVE AND LEMON SAUCE

Nothing could be simpler than Chris Oakes' recipe for bass. Chris has a strong feeling for cooking methods that preserve the fresh taste of foods. Striped bass is such a delicate fish that this recipe is perfect for it. The chive and lemon sauce is an attractive and equally simple accompaniment.

SERVES 2

2 tablespoons butter
2 striped bass fillets, each weighing
    about 175-200 g/6-7 oz
Salt
Freshly ground pepper
250 ml/8 fl oz dry white wine

For the Sauce:
1 large lemon

50 ml/2 fl oz white wine vinegar
250 ml/8 fl oz olive oil
Salt
Freshly ground pepper
1/8 teaspoon sugar
25 g/1 oz chives, very finely chopped

Butter a flameproof baking dish large enough to hold the fillets comfortably. Season the fish with salt and pepper and arrange in the dish. Pour the wine over it, dot with the rest of the butter, cover with aluminium foil and bring the liquid to a simmer on top of the stove. Bake in a preheated, moderate oven (180°C/350°F/gas 4) for 5 minutes, or until the fish is springy to the touch.

While the fish is cooking, make the sauce. Remove the zest from the lemon and cut it into very fine julienne strips. Squeeze the juice from the lemon. In a bowl, combine the julienne strips and lemon juice. Stir in the vinegar, then whisk in the oil a little at a time until the mixture is thick. Season to taste with salt, pepper and sugar. Add the chives.

Arrange the fish on two heated plates and spoon the sauce over them.

WINE SUGGESTION: Sauvignon Blanc.

BRILL À LA BREVEL

Tim Cumming is an instinctive cook. He does not analyze the reasons why he cooks as he does but believes the answer lies in his background and training, as he was deeply influenced by Elizabeth David's work, and by George Perry-Smith and Joyce Molyneux who taught him to cook. He does not look backward however and just tries to apply what he has learned to our much expanded national larder. His watchword is enjoyment. If there is no happiness in executing a dish, he feels there is no satisfaction for either chef or diner. His wife Sue, a fine cook, agrees.

SERVES 2

Butter for greasing dish, plus 1
   tablespoon
1 tablespoon finely chopped shallots
2 brill fillets, each weighing
   175–250 g/6–8 oz
250 g/8 oz tomatoes, peeled, seeded
   and chopped

4 medium-sized mushrooms, thinly
   sliced
Salt
Freshly ground pepper
¼ teaspoon thyme
125 ml/4 fl oz dry white wine
2 tablespoons double cream (see Note)

Generously butter an oven-proof dish large enough to hold the fish in a single layer. Scatter the shallots over the bottom of the dish, add the fillets, top with the tomatoes and mushrooms, and season with salt, pepper, and thyme. Cut the tablespoon of butter into pieces and dot the fish with it. Pour in the wine. Cover and bake in a preheated, moderate oven (180°C/350°F/gas 4) for 12–15 minutes, or until done. Carefully remove the fish and keep warm.

Pour the juices from the oven-proof dish into a small saucepan and reduce them over fairly high heat to 125 ml/4 fl oz. Lower the heat and stir in the cream and heat through. Taste for seasoning and pour half the sauce over each fish fillet. Serve with new potatoes, or rice and a green salad.

Note: The sauce can be finished, if liked, with fresh white, junket, or yoghurt cheese (see Basic Recipes, pages 24, 25) instead of cream.

WINE SUGGESTION: Muscadet.

SKATE WINGS BRAISED IN CIDER

Paul Gayler likes cooking with fish, especially as he has a supplier who brings it to him fresh daily and lets him choose just what he wants. He also likes to put together ingredients that do not usually find themselves in the same dish, and does this with impeccable good taste. In this recipe he combines tomatoes, apple, wine, cider, calvados, mustard and tarragon with skate wings with great felicity, the disparate ingredients, which at first glance look incompatible, blending into a complex of flavour at once both forthright and subtle.

SERVES 4

4 tablespoons butter, plus butter for
   greasing dish
1 tablespoon finely chopped shallot
250 g/8 oz tomatoes, peeled, seeded
   and diced
1 large, tart, cooking apple, peeled,
   cored and diced
4 medium-sized skate wings
Salt
Freshly ground pepper

125 ml/4 fl oz dry cider
50 ml/2 fl oz dry white wine
250 ml/8 fl oz fish stock (see Basic
   Recipes, page 13)
125 ml/4 fl oz single cream
1 teaspoon Dijon mustard
50 ml/2 fl oz Calvados
2 tablespoons fresh tarragon leaves,
   chopped

Butter a flameproof dish large enough to hold the skate wings. Add the shallot, tomato and apple. Season the fish with salt and pepper and arrange on top of the shallot mixture. Pour in half the cider, the wine and the fish stock. On top of the stove, bring the cooking liquid to a simmer. Cover the dish with buttered, greaseproof paper and bake in a preheated, moderate oven (180°C/350°F/gas 4) for 10–15 minutes, or until the skate is cooked. Remove the fish to four warmed plates and keep warm.

Pour the liquid into a saucepan, add the cream and reduce over moderately high heat until it coats a spoon. Beat in the butter, cut into pieces, the mustard, the rest of the cider and the Calvados. Taste for seasoning and add salt and pepper if necessary. Spoon the sauce over the fish and sprinkle with the chopped tarragon. Serve immediately with new potatoes.

WINE SUGGESTION: A white Bordeaux – Sauvignon Blanc.

STEAMED FISH IN BUTTER SAUCE

Raymond Duthie has decided ideas about food. He believes in following traditional methods of preparation, but at the same time wants the dishes he prepares to be clean-tasting, crisp, uncomplicated and eye catching. His food is subtle and delicious, as this fish dish shows.

SERVES 4

900 g/2 lb assorted fish fillets from 4 varieties if possible, including striped bass, John Dory, striped mullet, red porgy or similar fish, filleted and cut into 2.5 cm/1 in pieces
Salt
Freshly ground pepper
1 medium onion, chopped

1 medium carrot, scraped and chopped
Sprig thyme
1 teaspoon black peppercorns, lightly crushed
Seaweed, if available
1 recipe beurre blanc (white butter sauce, see Basic Recipes, page 22)

Season the fish with salt and pepper and set aside. In the bottom part of a steamer, combine the onion, carrot, thyme, peppercorns and a generous amount of salt, with water to cover.

Line the basket of the steamer with seaweed, if available, and arrange the pieces of fish on top. Cover, and steam until the fish is cooked, about 6 minutes.

Have ready the butter sauce and pour it onto four warm, not hot, plates. Arrange the pieces of fish on top of the sauce. Serve any extra sauce separately.

WINE SUGGESTION: A Pouilly Fuissé or Rully Aligoté.

PANACHE OF FISH

Shaun Hill, head chef at Gidleigh Park, Chagford, a secluded Edwardian manor, now a charming country house hotel on the edge of Dartmoor, Devon, started cooking as an enthusiastic amateur, a classics scholar with no notion of cooking as more than a hobby. Cooking won the battle with classics, and he acquired some training but found himself quite quickly promoted to head chef at prestigious restaurants. His enthusiasm survives and his recipes reflect his philosophy that cooking should celebrate the qualities and flavours of the ingredients the cook is using. This is a delicious dish, pretty to look at and worthy of its name as it is a kind of flourish. It is not half as complicated as it looks, and the results are more than worth the effort. Any combination of fish and shellfish can be used according to what is best at the market.

SERVES 4

For the Butter Sauce with Tomato:
125 ml/4 fl oz strong fish stock (see
   Basic Recipes, page 13)
1 tablespoon tomato purée
125 g/4 oz butter, cut into pieces
Salt
Freshly ground pepper

For the Butter Sauce with Broccoli:
125 ml/4 fl oz dry white wine
1 tablespoon cooked puréed broccoli

125 g/4 oz butter, cut into pieces
Salt
Freshly ground pepper

375 g/12 oz fresh salmon fillet, cut
   into 4 slices
375 g/12 oz turbot or halibut fillet,
   cut into 4 slices
4 large scallops, with coral if possible
8 large prawns, peeled, or scampi

To make the Butter Sauce with Tomato, pour the fish stock into a small, heavy saucepan, add the tomato purée and reduce, over moderately high heat, until only about 1 tablespoon of liquid remains. Reduce the heat to low, then whisk in the butter, piece by piece, to make a smooth sauce. Taste for seasoning, add salt and pepper to taste, and set aside in a warm place until needed.

In another small saucepan, combine the wine and broccoli purée and reduce over moderately high heat until only about 1 tablespoon of liquid remains. Reduce the heat to low, then whisk in the butter, piece by piece, to make a smooth sauce. Season to taste with salt and pepper, remove from the heat and set aside in a warm place until needed.

Arrange the fish and shellfish in a steamer over boiling water and steam until cooked, about 4 minutes. Be careful not to overcook. Have ready four warmed plates. Arrange the fish and shellfish in the centre of each plate and pour the sauces over them so that each sauce covers half of the fish and shellfish, or pour the sauces separately onto each side of the plates. The effect is very pretty with the brilliant red and green sauces, pink and white fish, pink prawns and white scallop with its pink coral.

WINE SUGGESTION: A Chardonnay.

SCALLOPS AND MUSSELS WITH SCALLOP MOUSSELINE

Sonia Blech, chef-patronne of Mijanou restaurant in London, experiments with dishes, seeking the ideal combination of flavour, texture and taste. This simple, and beautiful to look at dish achieves that aim. It is not difficult to make, but is very impressive both to see and eat, though not for everyday cooking.

SERVES 2

12 large scallops with coral
1 whole egg
325 ml/11 fl oz double cream
1 teaspoon lemon juice
1 teaspoon Cognac, or other brandy
Salt
Freshly ground pepper
Butter

For the Scallops and Mussels:
12 mussels, thoroughly scrubbed,
   cleaned and soaked

125 ml/4 fl oz dry white wine
1 tablespoon finely chopped shallots
175 ml/6 fl oz veal or chicken stock
   (see Basic Recipes, pages 10, 11)
Salt
Freshly ground pepper
50 ml/2 fl oz double cream
1 teaspoon Cognac or other brandy
12 medium-sized prawns, shelled

Carefully remove the pink coral from the scallops and put the corals into a blender or food processor. Add the egg and process to a purée. Scrape out of the blender or food processor into a bowl and chill thoroughly. Return the mixture to the blender or food processor and, with the machine running, gradually pour in the cream. Season with the lemon juice and Cognac, and salt and pepper to taste. Butter two ramekins or small soufflé moulds and fill with the mixture. Set in a baking tin with water to come about halfway up the sides.

Bake in a preheated, moderate oven (180°C/350°F/gas 4) for 15–20 minutes or until done. Unmould, cover and keep warm.

While the mousseline is cooking, put the mussels into a shallow pan with a tight-fitting lid. Add the wine and shallots, cover and cook over moderately high heat for 5 minutes or until the mussels have opened. Discard any that do not open. Lift out the mussels and discard the top shell. Strain the liquid in the pan and pour it into a saucepan. Add the veal or chicken stock and simmer until the liquid is reduced to half. Season with salt and pepper if necessary, pour in the cream and simmer for 1 or 2 minutes. Add the Cognac. Pour the sauce into a frying pan. Add the mussels in their half shells, the scallops and the prawns. Cover and simmer for about 1 minute or until the scallops and prawns are cooked and the mussels warmed.

To serve, pour the sauce onto two heated plates. Place the mousseline in the centre of each plate and surround it with the mussels and scallops alternately. Place a prawn above each scallop.

WINE SUGGESTION: A white Bordeaux – Sauvignon Blanc.

SCALLOPS WITH AVOCADO SAUCE

The delicate flavour of avocado complements the equally delicate flavour of the scallops in this elegantly simple and lovely to look at dish created by Allan Garth of Gravetye Manor. It takes only a very brief time to prepare, and requires only a very few ingredients, ideal for the cook in a hurry who wants to make something special.

SERVES 4

250 ml/8 fl oz fish stock (see Basic Recipes, page 13)
475 ml/16 fl oz single cream
1 large ripe avocado
Salt

Freshly ground pepper
20 large scallops, with coral if possible
175 g/6 oz wild rice, or long grain rice, freshly cooked

Pour the stock and cream into a saucepan, simmer over moderate heat, uncovered, until reduced to 350 ml/12 fl oz. Peel and pit the avocado. Mash with a fork until smooth. Stir it into the reduced fish stock and cream mixture. Season with salt and pepper and warm through. Keep warm, not hot.

Steam the scallops for 2-4 minutes or until they have lost their opaque look. Be careful not to overcook. Spoon the cooked, hot wild rice or long grain rice onto four heated plates. Divide the scallops among the plates and spoon the sauce over them.

WINE SUGGESTION: A Chardonnay.

RISOTTO OF MUSSELS WITH SAFFRON

This is an extremely simple, entirely delicious dish created by Simon Hopkinson of Hilaire restaurant in London. It is perfect, accompanied by a green salad and plenty of wine, for entertaining friends at an informal weekend supper.

SERVES 6

1.1 L/2 pt mussels, cleaned
125 ml/4 fl oz dry white wine
6 tablespoons butter
6 tablespoons shallots, finely chopped
375 g/12 oz Arborio (Italian risotto) rice

475 ml/16 fl oz chicken stock (see Basic Recipes, page 10)
Salt
Freshly ground pepper
1 teaspoon saffron threads, ground
25 g/1 oz parsley, finely chopped

Put the mussels into a large, shallow pan with a lid. Pour in the wine, cover and simmer for 5 minutes. Lift out and reserve the mussels. Discard the shells. Discard any unopened mussels. Strain the liquid in the pan through a sieve lined with a double layer of dampened cheesecloth and measure it. There should be about 475 ml/16 fl oz. Make up the quantity, if necessary, with equal amounts of chicken stock and dry white wine.

In a large, heavy saucepan, melt the butter. Add the shallots and sauté until they are soft, about 5 minutes. Add the rice to the pan, stirring over low heat until all the rice is coated with the butter but not browned. Pour in the chicken stock and the mussel liquor. Season with salt and pepper and stir in the ground saffron threads. Bring to a simmer over moderate heat, stir and cook, covered, over very low heat until the rice is almost tender, about 20 minutes. Add the reserved mussels and the parsley, stir to mix and cook just long enough to heat the mussels through and finish cooking the rice. Serve with a green salad.

WINE SUGGESTION: A Sancerre.

SHELLFISH RAGOÛT CROWNED WITH AN OYSTER SOUFFLÉ

This invention of head chef David Miller, of The Ritz in London, is for a special occasion, designed to give great pleasure to friends and/or family. In a grand dinner it could be served as a fish course, but it is so richly flavoured and satisfying that I find it suitable as a main course, especially if preceded by Chef Miller's Guinea Fowl Broth (page 90) and followed, after cheese and salad, by a fresh fruit dessert. The ingredients list may seem rather long but many are kitchen staples, and much of the dish can be prepared ahead making it easy to put together at the last minute. Ask your fishmonger for broken crab and lobster claws and prawns for the Ragoût Sauce.

SERVES 6

For the Ragoût Sauce:
1 tablespoon salad oil
500 g/1 lb raw prawns, crab and lobster claw bits, coarsely chopped
50 ml/2 fl oz brandy
125 ml/4 fl oz dry white wine
25 g/1 oz each onion, carrot, leek and celery, chopped
½ tablespoon tomato purée
25 g/1 oz plain flour
1.1 L/2 pt fish stock (see Basic Recipes, page 13)
Bouquet garni (2 parsley sprigs, sprig thyme or ¼ teaspoon dried thyme, 1 bay leaf)
Salt
Freshly ground pepper
25 g/1 oz unsalted butter

For the Oyster Soufflé:
Butter and finely grated Cheddar cheese for 6 small soufflé moulds and grated cheese for sprinkling on soufflé
75 g/3 oz unsalted butter
75 g/3 oz plain flour
450 ml/15 fl oz warm milk

6 large egg yolks
9 oysters, preferably natives
Pinch paprika
Dash Tabasco
Salt
6 large egg whites
25 ml/1 fl oz lemon juice

For the Ragoût Filling:
15 g/½ oz butter
6 large raw prawns, peeled
6 raw scallops, halved crosswise
6 scampi
1 lobster tail cut into 6 medallions
25 ml/1 fl oz brandy

For the Champagne Sauce:
40 g/1½ oz very finely chopped mushrooms
1 bay leaf
10 white peppercorns, crushed
150 ml/¼ pt dry Champagne
50 ml/2 fl oz dry white wine
150 ml/¼ pt fish stock (see Basic Recipes, page 13)
300 ml/½ pt double cream
Salt

Make the ragoût sauce, ahead of time if liked. Heat the oil in a heavy saucepan, add the shellfish and sauté over moderate heat until the shells change colour, a few minutes. Flame with the brandy, add the white wine, vegetables, tomato purée and flour and stir vigorously for 2 minutes. Add the fish stock, bouquet garni and bring to a simmer. Over low heat, reduce the liquid to half, being careful not to let it burn. Season to taste with salt and pepper. Strain the sauce through a fine sieve pressing down hard on the solids to extract all the flavour. Stir in the butter. Set aside until ready to use. If the sauce is made ahead of time and refrigerated, let it come to room temperature before using.

Make the oyster soufflé. Prepare six small (individual) soufflé dishes. Coat with butter and sprinkle with the finely grated Cheddar cheese, shaking out the excess. Set the dishes aside.

In a saucepan, melt the butter, stir in the flour with a wooden spoon and cook over low heat until the roux shrinks away from the side of the pan. Do not let it colour. Off the heat, stir in the milk, a little at a time, until the mixture is smooth. Return to the heat and cook for 2–3 minutes. Off the heat, add the egg yolks, one at a time, mixing thoroughly. Drop the oysters into a small pan of boiling water and blanch for 30 seconds. Drain and purée in a food processor or blender. Stir into the soufflé mixture and season with the paprika, Tabasco and salt to taste. The soufflé can be prepared ahead of time to this point. Dot the surface with a little butter and set aside while you make the ragoût filling.

In a non-stick pan, heat the butter, and sauté the shellfish for about 1 minute. Flame with the brandy, remove from the heat and allow the ragoût filling to cool.

To assemble the dish, heat the soufflé mixture to lukewarm. Beat the egg whites with a pinch of salt and the lemon juice until they stand in firm peaks. Stir a heaped tablespoon of the whites into the soufflé mix, then gently fold in the rest of the whites.

Divide the ragoût filling among the six soufflé dishes and top with the ragoût sauce. Top with the soufflé mixture and sprinkle with a little grated cheese. Bake in a preheated, moderately hot oven (200°C/400°F/gas 6) for 10–12 minutes or until puffed and lightly browned.

While the soufflés are baking, make the Champagne sauce, or make it ahead of time. In a saucepan, combine the mushrooms, bay leaf, peppercorns, Champagne, white wine and fish stock. Bring to a simmer over moderate heat and cook, uncovered, until reduced by two-thirds. Stir in the cream and reduce to half. Season to taste with salt, strain through a fine sieve and keep warm until ready to serve.

Serve the soufflés straight from the oven accompanied by the Champagne sauce.

WINE SUGGESTION: Drink a Condrieu or other Côtes-du-Rhône dry white wine.

Poultry and Feathered Game

Poultry is always, and deservedly, popular. It is versatile, inexpensive and readily available, as well as being nutritionally desirable these health-conscious days. Our chefs have met the challenge to create new dishes for poultry with enthusiasm. They have developed delectable recipes for both chicken and duckling, some elegant and suitable for parties, some very simple and quick to cook for put-together-in-a-hurry meals. Game has always been a great favourite and chefs have created new and attractive recipes for pigeon, grouse, quail and pheasant.

CHICKEN WITH AVOCADO

Sam Chalmers, formerly chef-patron of Le Talbooth Restaurant in Dedham, Essex, and now chef-patron of Chimneys Restaurant at Long Melford, Suffolk, constantly comes up with attractively simple variations on classical dishes, transforming the well-known into something new. Nothing could be simpler than this subtly-flavoured chicken dish which takes little more than half an hour to cook.

SERVES 4

4 chicken breasts, skinned and boned	4 tablespoons butter
Salt	1 large, ripe avocado
Freshly ground pepper	2 tablespoons dry sherry
4 tablespoons finely chopped shallot	50 ml/2 fl oz double cream

Season the chicken breasts with salt and pepper. Sauté the shallots in a medium-sized frying pan in 2 tablespoons of the butter. Add the chicken breasts, cover and sauté over low heat, turning once, until the chicken is tender, but not browned, about 8 minutes.

While the chicken is cooking, peel and halve the avocado. Remove and discard the stone. Slice one half thinly. In a bowl, mash the other half.

When the chicken breasts are cooked, remove from the pan, cover and keep warm. Pour the sherry into the pan, bring to a simmer, stirring, add the cream, simmer for 1 or 2 minutes, season with salt and pepper and stir in the avocado purée. Beat in the remaining butter. Remove from the heat.

Arrange the chicken breasts on four heated plates, mask with the avocado sauce and garnish with slices of avocado.

WINE SUGGESTION: Claret.

MELON RAJ

Michael Collom likes to experience the cooking of other countries and is sometimes inspired by what he finds. He calls this Melon Raj because of the curry powder but the real inspiration is his own.

SERVES 4

2 small ripe melons such as honeydew
  or Ogen
2 skinned and boned, cooked chicken
  breasts
125 ml/4 fl oz mayonnaise (see Basic
  Recipes, page 23)
Pinch curry powder, or to taste
125 g/4 oz black grapes, halved and
  pitted

125 g/4 oz seedless white grapes,
  halved

For the Garnish:
Crushed ice
Parsley sprigs

Halve the melons and scrape out the seeds. Trim the bases so that they sit firmly. Cut the chicken into 1 cm/½ in cubes and fill the melon halves with the chicken. Mix the mayonnaise with the curry powder and coat the chicken with it. Alternate the black and white grapes round the edge of each melon half and place a sprig of parsley in the middle. Serve on a bed of crushed ice, if liked.

WINE SUGGESTION: Côtes-du-Rhône.

CHICKEN AND VEGETABLE TERRINE

Kenneth Bell has created the perfect summer luncheon dish in this terrine. It is delicious.

SERVES 6 to 8

500 g/1 lb skinned and boned
  chicken breasts
850 ml/1½ pt double cream, chilled
Salt
Freshly ground white pepper
Butter
250 g/8 oz young courgettes,
  trimmed and cut into lengthways
  strips

250 g/8 oz baby carrots, scraped and
  cut into lengthways strips
250 g/8 oz calabrese, trimmed and
  separated into small sprigs
50 g/2 oz mangetout, trimmed
125 g/4 oz thin, small green beans,
  trimmed

Coarsely chop the chicken breasts and purée in a blender or food processor. Gradually pour in the cream with the machine running and blend for 30 seconds, or long enough to mix thoroughly. Transfer to a bowl and season to taste with salt and pepper. Chill in the refrigerator for about 15 minutes.

Butter the bottom and sides of a terrine about 25 cm/10 in long by 10 cm/4 in wide and put a thin layer of the chicken mixture on the bottom. Cook the vegetables separately in briskly boiling, salted water, the time will depend on the vegetables. They should be tender but still crunchy. Strain, refresh in cold water and strain again thoroughly, chilling them for a few minutes if necessary.

Make a layer of the courgettes on top of the chicken, cover with a layer of chicken mixture, top with the carrot strips, cover with chicken mixture and top with the calabrese sprigs. Cover the calabrese with chicken and top with mangetout, add more chicken and cover with the beans. Finish with a layer of chicken mixture. Put the terrine into a baking tin and pour in hot water to come about halfway up the terrine. Cover the terrine with aluminium foil and cook in a preheated, moderate oven (180°C/350°F/gas 4) for 35-45 minutes. It will feel firm to the touch when cooked. Cool, then chill in the refrigerator for at least 4 hours. Unmould and slice. Serve with a light, chilled tomato sauce (see below).

TOMATO SAUCE:

500 g/1 lb tomatoes, peeled, seeded   Freshly ground pepper
   and chopped   1 tablespoon tomato purée
Salt

Purée the tomatoes in a food processor or blender with salt and pepper to taste, and the tomato purée. Pour into a bowl and chill. Serve with the sliced Chicken and Vegetable Terrine, above.

WINE SUGGESTION: Claret.

BREAST OF CHICKEN WITH MANGO, GINGER AND CORIANDER SAUCE

Stanley Matthews, the young head chef at the Feathers Hotel in Woodstock, Oxfordshire, always wanted to be a chef. His earliest memories of learning to cook are of licking his mother's wooden spoons to find out what things tasted like. He has asked questions ever since. He loves his work and is dedicated to the idea of giving his guests, for that is how he thinks of them, well-balanced, nutritious and exciting food. This chicken breast dish meets his requirements, and is also extremely simple to cook.

SERVES 2
2 chicken breasts, skinned and boned   250 g/8 oz thinly sliced or coarsely
Salt   chopped fresh mango
Freshly ground pepper   1 tablespoon fresh coriander, coarsely
2 tablespoons butter   chopped
1 teaspoon fresh ginger root, grated   4 tablespoons double cream

Season the chicken breasts with salt and pepper. Heat the butter in a flameproof casserole, add the chicken breasts, turning them in the butter. Bake in a preheated, moderately hot oven (200°C/400°F/gas 6) for about 10 minutes, or until they are springy to the touch. Remove the breasts from the casserole, cover and keep warm. Pour away any excess fat from the casserole, add the ginger, mango and coriander, stir to mix and simmer, on top of the stove, for a minute. Add the cream, stir and cook for a minute or so longer to slightly reduce the sauce and blend the flavours. Serve with boiled new potatoes and broccoli or green beans.

WINE SUGGESTION: A Beaujolais.

CHICKEN BREASTS 'FRANÇOIS' WITH JUNIPER BERRY SAUCE

Francis Coulson, one of the forerunners of the renaissance of British cooking, is continuingly inventive. This dish makes a splendid main course that can be prepared ahead of time with little fuss. It does not keep the cook in the kitchen after the guests arrive, making it very special for entertaining.

SERVES 6

8 chicken breasts, skinned and boned
2 large egg whites
Salt
Freshly ground pepper
250 ml/8 fl oz double cream, or fresh white cheese (see Basic Recipes, page 24)
2 tablespoons finely chopped mixed fresh herbs such as chervil, mint, thyme, marjoram, tarragon, parsley
750 g/1½ lb puff pastry (see Basic Recipes, page 15)
1 egg yolk

For the Sauce:
30 g/1¼ oz juniper berries

3 tablespoons butter
3 tablespoons plain flour
475 ml/16 fl oz chicken stock (see Basic Recipes, page 10)
125 ml/4 fl oz dry cider
125 ml/4 fl oz double cream, or fresh white cheese (see Basic Recipes, page 24)
Salt
Freshly ground pepper

For the Garnish:
250 g/ 8 oz seedless white grapes

Set aside 6 of the breasts. Coarsely chop the remaining 2 breasts and purée them in a blender or food processor. Add the egg whites and process until thoroughly mixed and smooth. Season with salt and pepper. Add the cream or fresh white cheese gradually with the machine running and process for 30 seconds longer. Add the herbs and process only long enough to mix. Transfer the mousseline to a bowl and chill in the refrigerator for 30 minutes.

Using a sharp, pointed knife, cut a lengthways pocket in each of the 6 breasts and stuff with the mousseline. Chill again in the refrigerator.

Roll out the pastry to about 0.3 cm/⅛ in and cut into 6 rectangles large enough to enclose the chicken breasts. Place a breast on each of the pieces of pastry. Beat the egg yolk with 1 teaspoon water and, using a pastry brush, paint the edges of the pastry then fold it over to cover the breast, sealing well. Use a knife or the fingers to decorate the edge and, if necessary, trim it neatly. Brush the tops with the egg wash. The pastry can be refrigerated until ready to bake. When ready to cook arrange the pastry on a lightly oiled baking sheet and bake on the middle shelf of a preheated, moderate oven (180°C/350°F/gas 4) for 35 minutes, or until golden.

While the pastry is baking make the sauce, or make it ahead of time. In a spice, nut or coffee grinder, pulverize the juniper berries and put them into a small bowl.

In a medium-sized saucepan, heat the butter. Stir in the flour and cook, stirring with a wooden spoon, for 1 minute over low heat without letting the mixture colour. Off the heat, stir in the chicken stock and cider, until the mixture is smooth. Return to the heat and cook for 10 minutes, stirring from time to time. Stir in the juniper berries and simmer for 5 minutes longer. Strain through a fine sieve into a bowl. Rinse out and dry the saucepan. Return the sauce to the pan, add the cream or fresh white cheese, season to taste with salt and pepper and heat the sauce through.

To serve, pour the sauce on each of six warmed plates and put a chicken breast on top. Garnish with a few of the seedless green grapes halved, and serve with a green salad.

WINE SUGGESTION: A Burgundy - Côte de Nuits.

STUFFED CHICKEN BREAST WITH TARRAGON AND SAFFRON SAUCE

Baba Hine has an attractively original version of chicken with tarragon. It would make a very elegant dish for a party.

SERVES 4

5 chicken breasts, skinned and boned
3 large egg whites
Salt
Freshly ground pepper
⅛ teaspoon freshly grated nutmeg
75 ml/3 fl oz double cream
4 sheets aluminium foil 20 × 20 cm/8
    × 8 in
Vegetable oil

125 ml/4 fl oz dry white wine
125 ml/4 fl oz chicken stock (see
    Basic Recipes, page 10)

For the Sauce:
75 ml/3 fl oz double cream
⅛ teaspoon saffron threads, crumbled
1 tablespoon fresh tarragon leaves,
    chopped

Set aside 4 of the chicken breasts. Coarsely chop the remaining breast and purée it in a blender or food processor. With the machine running, add the egg whites and process until smooth. Season with salt and pepper and nutmeg.

Add the cream and process for 30 seconds longer. Chill in the refrigerator for 15 minutes.

With a sharp knife, cut a lengthways pocket in each of the 4 chicken breasts and fill it with the mousseline. Lightly brush the sheets of aluminium foil with the vegetable oil and place a chicken breast in the centre of each one. Pour 2 tablespoons each of wine and stock over the chicken. Wrap the breasts in the foil, twisting it to seal it thoroughly. Place the packages on a lightly oiled baking sheet and bake in a preheated, moderately hot oven (200°C/400°F/gas 6) for 20 minutes.

Unwrap the packages and lift the chicken breasts onto a dish. Cover and keep warm in the turned-off oven with the door slightly ajar. Carefully pour the liquid in the packages into a saucepan. Add the cream, saffron and tarragon and reduce over brisk heat until the sauce coats a spoon. Pour the sauce onto each of four heated plates, and put a chicken breast on each plate. Serve immediately with rice, noodles, or new potatoes and a green vegetable, or a green salad.

WINE SUGGESTION: Côtes-du-Rhône.

CHICKEN BREASTS STUFFED WITH CRAB

This recipe, developed by Christopher Grist, could hardly be less like the recipes of Francis Coulson or Baba Hine but is just as easy to cook and just as delicious to eat. Christopher is now Executive Chef at Grims Dyke Hotel, Harrow Weald, a country house hotel, formerly the home of Sir W. S. Gilbert.

SERVES 6

6 chicken breasts, skinned and boned
375 g/12 oz fresh or frozen crab
  meat, picked over to remove any
  cartilage
Salt
Freshly ground pepper
3 tablespoons butter

1 recipe Béarnaise Sauce (see Basic
  Recipes, page 21)

For the Garnish:
Watercress sprigs
12 asparagus tips (optional)

Trim the chicken breasts and remove the small fillet. Set the fillets aside for another use. Flatten the breasts and top with the crab meat but without going to the edge of the breasts. Season with salt and pepper and roll up gently. Secure with toothpicks. In a large, heavy frying pan that will hold all the chicken breasts comfortably, melt the butter, add the stuffed chicken breasts, turning to coat them with the butter. Cook over low heat, turning once or twice until the chicken is done, about 8 minutes, without letting them colour. Lift out the chicken breasts onto the tray of a grill, mask with the Béarnaise sauce and glaze quickly under the preheated grill until they are golden brown. Garnish with watercress sprigs and, if liked, the asparagus tips, and serve with a green salad.

WINE SUGGESTION: A Beaujolais.

CHICKEN BREASTS WITH GINGER STUFFING AND ORANGE SAUCE

David Adlard is a most unusual cook whose dishes are never routine or ordinary. He serves pickled marsh samphire and pickled elderberries with pâtés and terrines, and when he can't find what he wants locally, like special salad greens, he grows them himself. He says he does not fit into any particular category of chef but cooks as he likes in the way he likes and knows, and hopes others will enjoy the results. He is a great enthusiast. This is a simple dish changed into something special by the combination of fresh ginger and oranges.

SERVES 6

250 g/8 oz finely chopped
  mushrooms
1 tablespoon shallots, finely chopped
1 tablespoon fresh ginger root, very
  finely chopped
Salt
Freshly ground pepper
6 chicken breasts, skinned and boned

For the Sauce:
Grated peel of 2 oranges
150 ml/¼ pt orange juice
1 tablespoon sugar
3 tablespoons white wine vinegar

475 ml/16 fl oz chicken stock (see
  Basic Recipes, page 10)
250 ml/8 fl oz double cream, or fresh
  white cheese (see Basic Recipes,
  page 24)
Salt
Freshly ground pepper

For the Chicken Breasts:
250 ml/8 fl oz chicken stock

For the Garnish:
1 orange, peeled and segmented

Put the mushrooms into a non-stick frying pan and cook over low heat until the moisture has evaporated. Take out and set aside in a bowl. Add the shallot and cook for 2 minutes. Add the ginger and cook 2 minutes longer. Return the mushrooms to the frying pan, stir to mix and season with salt and pepper. Cool. When the mixture has cooled, cut a slit in each of the chicken breasts and stuff with the mixture. Fasten with a toothpick.

Put the grated orange peel into a heavy pan with the orange juice and the sugar and simmer until it has reduced to a light caramel syrup. Add the vinegar and simmer until the caramel has dissolved and the mixture is syrupy. Stir in the chicken stock and simmer, uncovered, until reduced to 250 ml/8 fl oz. Add the cream, season to taste with salt and pepper and simmer over very low heat for 10 minutes. If using fresh white cheese just heat through.

Pour the 250 ml/8 fl oz of chicken stock into a large baking tin that will hold the chicken breasts comfortably. Bring to a simmer. Arrange the breasts, seasoned with salt and pepper, in the pan, cover and bake in a preheated, moderate oven (180°C/350°F/gas 4) for 10-12 minutes, or until done. Drain, arrange 1 breast on each of six heated plates and cover with the sauce. Garnish with the orange segments, and serve with rice.

WINE SUGGESTION: A Beaujolais.

CHICKEN BREASTS 'DUICH'

Denis Woodtli, head chef at Lochalsh Hotel on the Kyle of Lochalsh in Scotland, gets magnificent langoustines (Dublin Bay prawns, scampi) as well as other shellfish and fish. This combination of chicken breast and shellfish is delicious.

SERVES 2

4 Dublin Bay prawns (scampi) or 4
   large, uncooked prawns
2 chicken breasts, skinned and boned
250 g/8 oz butter
4 tablespoons tomato purée
50 ml/2 fl oz brandy
250 ml/8 fl oz double cream, or fresh
   white cheese (see Basic Recipes,
   page 24)

Salt
Freshly ground pepper
50 g/2 oz sliced mushrooms
125 ml/4 fl oz medium dry sherry

For the Garnish:
Parsley sprigs

Shell the Dublin Bay prawns or prawns and set the heads aside. Cut a pocket in the chicken breasts and stuff with the shellfish. In a frying pan, heat half the butter, add the shellfish heads and sauté over moderately high heat for 1 or 2 minutes. Add the tomato purée, stir, then add the brandy and flame. Add half the cream immediately and simmer over low heat until it has thickened. If using fresh white cheese, just heat it through. Season to taste with salt and pepper. Strain the sauce into a bowl pressing down on the shellfish heads to extract all the flavour.

Heat the rest of the butter in a frying pan and sauté the chicken breasts over moderate heat, turning 2 or 3 times until they are cooked through but not browned, about 8 minutes. Remove the chicken breasts, cover and keep warm. Add the mushrooms and sherry to the pan and cook for 3 or 4 minutes. Add the remaining cream, season with salt and pepper and simmer until the sauce is thickened. If using fresh white cheese, just heat it through.

To serve, warm the prawn sauce and pour it onto each of two heated plates. Place a chicken breast on each plate and cover with the mushroom sauce. Garnish with a parsley sprig.

WINE SUGGESTION: A Burgundy – a Côte Chalonnaise.

CHICKEN BREASTS, JACQUELINE

Allan Holland has created a lovely contrast of flavours in this dish. The delicate chicken breast contrasts with the richness of duckling mousse which can be prepared ahead of time, and the whole dish assembled quite quickly as the chicken breasts take only about 10 minutes. The sauce is also quickly made. It is worth the effort for a delectable meal.

SERVES 6

250 g/8 oz raw, skinless and boneless duckling meat
1 large egg white, lightly beaten
250 ml/8 fl oz chilled whipping cream, lightly whipped
Salt
Freshly ground white pepper
6 skinned and boned chicken breasts, each weighing 175-200 g/6-7 oz
Butter
475 ml/16 fl oz chicken stock (see Basic Recipes, page 10)

For the Sauce:
125 ml/4 fl oz tawny port

250 ml/8 fl oz double cream, or fresh white cheese (see Basic Recipes, page 24)
Lemon juice
Salt
Freshly ground pepper
2 tablespoons butter, cut into pieces
50 g/2 oz toasted flaked almonds

For the Garnish:
6 thin slices truffle (optional)
Sprigs of fresh chervil or parsley

To make the mousse, chop the duckling meat coarsely and purée it in a blender or food processor. With the machine running, slowly pour in the egg white and process until the mixture is smooth and well blended. Scrape the mixture into a bowl and refrigerate for 1 hour. Set the bowl into a larger bowl filled with ice and, using a wooden spoon, gradually beat in the whipped cream. Season with salt and pepper and return the mousse to the refrigerator.

Using a very sharp knife, make a lengthways slit in the chicken breasts to make a pocket. Fill with the duck mousse. Do not overfill as the mousse expands during cooking. Place the stuffed chicken breasts in a buttered frying pan, large enough to hold them all in a single layer. Pour in the chicken stock. Cover the pan and simmer over low heat for 8–10 minutes, or until the breasts are just cooked. Remove the breasts from the frying pan to a dish, cover and keep warm while making the sauce. Pour the port into the frying pan and boil it over high heat until the port and stock are very reduced and syrupy. Add the cream and continue to simmer, over low heat, until the sauce has a coating consistency. Remove from the heat and add lemon juice to taste, and salt and pepper. Beat in the butter. Keep the sauce warm.

Arrange the chicken breasts on six heated plates and coat with the sauce. Sprinkle with almonds and garnish with truffle, if using. Surround with sprigs of chervil or parsley.

WINE SUGGESTION: A refined Bordeaux – a Margaux.

BREAST OF DUCK WITH ORANGES IN A HONEY SAUCE

This is one of the dishes I enjoyed when Willie MacPherson was head chef at The Feathers in Woodstock. It makes a very attractive dinner for two and takes little time to cook as the duck breast can be removed from the carcass of the duck and boned ahead of time.

SERVES 2

1 whole duck breast, boned and halved	125 ml/4 fl oz orange juice
Salt	250 ml/8 fl oz demi-glace (see Basic Recipes, page 12)
Freshly ground pepper	1 orange, peeled and segmented
Flour	25 g/1 oz sliced and toasted almonds*
2 tablespoons butter	
1 tablespoon vegetable oil	*To toast the almonds, put them in a
1 shallot, finely chopped	baking tin in a preheated, moderate
1 tablespoon brandy	oven (180°C/350°F/gas 4) for 10
1 tablespoon clear honey	minutes.

Season the 2 duck breasts with salt and pepper and dredge lightly with flour, shaking to remove the excess. Heat the butter and oil in a heavy frying pan and sauté the breasts until they are tender, but still pink inside, about 4 minutes a side, or longer if well-cooked duck is preferred. Lift out of the frying pan onto a warm plate, cover and keep warm.

Add the shallots to the frying pan and sauté until they are soft but not browned. Add the brandy and flame. Add the honey, orange juice and demi-glace and simmer until the sauce reduces to coating consistency. Season with salt and pepper. Add the orange segments in the last few minutes of cooking.

To serve, cut each duck breast diagonally into 4 slices and arrange on two heated plates. Lift out the orange segments and arrange round the duck breast, then pour the sauce over and around them and sprinkle with the almonds. Serve with rice and a green salad.

WINE SUGGESTION: Michael Harris would not drink wine with this dish. However, I would drink an Alsation wine such as a Gewürtztraminer or a slightly chilled Provençal rosé.

DUCKLING BREAST WITH BRUSSELS SPROUT PURÉE

Michael Croft has a natural elegance in the way he deals with food, which is appropriate for the head chef of The Royal Crescent Hotel in Bath, itself the very essence of modern Georgian elegance. All the same, I was pleasantly surprised by the flavour of the Brussels sprout purée. The vegetable emerges transformed.

SERVES 2

1 whole duckling breast, boned and halved with skin left on, each half weighing about 175 g/6 oz

For the Marinade:
1 medium carrot, finely chopped
1 medium onion, finely chopped
3 tablespoons chopped shallots
1 sprig parsley
1 sprig thyme
1 bay leaf
1 teaspoon black peppercorns
4 tablespoons white wine vinegar
175 ml/6 fl oz dry white wine
4 tablespoons olive or vegetable oil
½ teaspoon salt

For the Duckling:
2 tablespoons butter
250 ml/8 fl oz game stock, or duck or chicken stock (see Basic Recipes, pages 10, 12)
2 or 3 tablespoons butter, cut into pieces
Salt
Freshly ground pepper

For the Brussels Sprout Purée:
2 shortcrust tartlet shells
500 g/1lb Brussels sprouts, trimmed
2 tablespoons double cream
1 tablespoon butter
Salt
Freshly ground pepper

Put the duckling breasts in a bowl large enough to hold them comfortably. Combine all the ingredients for the marinade and pour them over the duckling breasts. Refrigerate for 24 hours, turning once or twice. When ready to cook, lift the breasts out of the marinade and pat them dry with paper towels. Reserve the marinade. In a heavy frying pan, heat the 2 tablespoons of butter and sauté the breasts over moderate heat turning once, until they are springy to the touch but still pink inside, about 8 minutes in all. Pour off and discard the excess fat from the frying pan. Put the breasts on a plate, and keep warm.

Pour 250 ml/8 fl oz of the marinade, including vegetables, into the pan and simmer, uncovered, until it is reduced to 25 ml/1 fl oz. Add the game stock and bring to a boil. Simmer to reduce by half. Skim and strain. Return the sauce to the pan and beat in the butter, piece by piece. Taste for seasoning, add salt and pepper if necessary, and keep warm.

For the Brussels sprout purée, have ready a large saucepan filled with briskly boiling, salted water. Add the sprouts, bring back to a boil over fairly high heat, then reduce the heat and cook the sprouts, uncovered, at a gentle simmer for 10-12 minutes, or until tender. If the sprouts are very small they will take only about 8 minutes. Drain and put into a blender or food processor with the cream and butter and purée until smooth. Transfer to a small saucepan, season with salt and pepper and heat through. Have ready the tartlet shells. Fill them with the purée and keep warm.

To serve, remove the skin from the duck breasts and cut it into very fine julienne strips. Crisp it under a preheated grill and set it aside. If preferred, discard the skin, or leave it on the duckling and crisp it under the grill. Cut the breasts into slices and arrange them, in a fan shape, on two heated plates, or leave whole. Surround with the sauce and garnish with a tartlet of the sprout purée. If using the julienne of duck skin, garnish the breast with it.

WINE SUGGESTION: A Côte de Beaune.

BREAST OF DUCK WITH BLACKBERRIES, AND DUCK LIVER TARTLET

There is just enough tartness in the blackberries to make a contrast with the rich duck flavour while the garnish of duck liver tartlet provides another sort of contrast. Chris Oakes puts it all together in a felicitous manner.

SERVES 2

1 × 2-2.3 kg/4½-5 lb duckling	1 egg yolk
Salt	1 tablespoon double cream
Freshly ground pepper	2 shortcrust tartlet shells, baked blind
2 tablespoons butter	475 ml/16 fl oz duck stock
250 g/8 oz fresh ripe blackberries	2 sprigs lemon thyme, or any fresh
Sugar, if necessary	herb
Liver from duck	

Remove the breast from the duckling and skin and bone it, or have the butcher do it. Cut the breast in two. Reserve the rest of the duck for another meal. Season the breasts with salt and pepper. Heat the butter in a frying pan just large enough to hold the breasts and sauté them for 3-4 minutes on each side.

They should remain pink. Remove the breasts from the frying pan to a heated plate, cover and keep warm.

Put the blackberries into a small saucepan with a little water. If they are very tart, add a little sugar. Warm them through over low heat, about 3-4 minutes. Drain and keep warm.

Coarsely chop the duck liver and put into a blender or food processor with the egg yolk, cream and seasoning and reduce to a purée. Pour the mixture into the 2 tartlet shells and bake in a preheated, moderately hot oven (200°C/400°F/gas 6) for 3-4 minutes, or until lightly set. Pour the duck stock into a small saucepan, bring it to a boil over fairly brisk heat and simmer until the stock is reduced by half.

Pour the reduced duck stock onto two heated plates. Slice each breast into four lengthways and arrange on the plate in the shape of a fan, or leave in one piece if preferred. Arrange the blackberries round the duck and put the tartlets at the bottom of each plate. Put a sprig of lemon thyme, or other herb at the top.

WINE SUGGESTION: A Chianti.

TWO DUCKLINGS WITH TWO SAUCES

This is another of the poultry recipes created by Francis Coulson. It is simple to cook but is a little time-consuming, not suitable for the cook in a hurry but very worth cooking for a special occasion.

SERVES 4

2 × 1.5 kg/3½ lb ducklings
Salt
Freshly ground pepper
125 g/4 oz mixed chopped celery,
  carrots and leeks
Peel from 1 orange, chopped
Peel from 1 lemon, chopped
1.7 L/3 pt chicken stock (see Basic
  Recipes, page 10)
1 tablespoon honey
2 large egg whites
125 ml/4 fl oz double cream
2 tablespoons butter

For the First Sauce:
1 tablespoon flour
125 ml/4 fl oz tawny port, or dry red
  wine

Salt
Freshly ground pepper
125 g/4 oz chopped orange
  segments, or chopped pineapple, or
  redcurrants (optional)

For the Second Sauce:
5 tablespoons butter
½ medium onion, finely chopped
20 g/¾ oz plain flour
125 ml/4 fl oz dry white wine
50 g/2 oz peeled hazelnuts (filberts),
  pulverized
2 bay leaves
Salt
Freshly ground pepper
250 ml/8 fl oz double cream

Remove the legs from the ducklings and set them aside. Season the rest of the duckling with salt and pepper and put into a baking tin with the mixed vegetables, orange and lemon peel and 250 ml/8 fl oz of the chicken stock. Roast in a preheated, moderate oven (180°C/350°F/gas 4) for 1 hour and 15-20 minutes.

While the duckling breasts are roasting, bone the legs, chop the meat coarsely then purée in a blender or food processor. With the machine running, add the egg whites and process until the mixture is very light and smooth. Scrape the mixture into a bowl and chill for 15 minutes. Set it over a bowl of ice and gradually beat in the 125 ml/4 fl oz of double cream. Butter four 250 g/8 oz soufflé or similar moulds and fill with the mixture. Put into a baking tin filled with hot water, cover with foil and bake in a preheated, moderate oven (180°C/350°F/gas 4) for about 15 minutes, or until firm. Keep warm.

When the ducklings are cooked, remove from the oven and drizzle the honey over the duckling breasts. Return to the oven for 5 minutes, taking care it does not burn. Remove the ducklings from the oven and let stand for a few minutes. Remove the breasts, cover and keep warm. Reserve the rest of the carcass for stock.

To make the first sauce, pour off the excess fat from the baking tin and stir in the flour. Stir and cook on top of the stove for 1 or 2 minutes then add the tawny port or dry red wine and 250 ml/8 fl oz of the chicken stock. Simmer over low heat until the sauce has reduced to 250 ml/8 fl oz. Season with salt and pepper and strain into a small saucepan. Stir in the chopped fruit, if liked, and set aside.

Make the second sauce. In a saucepan, heat 5 tablespoons of the butter and sauté the onion until it is soft, but not browned. Stir in the flour and cook, stirring, over low heat for 2–3 minutes without letting the mixture colour. Stir in the wine and 1 L/1¾ pt of chicken stock, off the heat. Return the mixture to the heat and add the ground nuts and bay leaves. Simmer over low heat for 15 minutes. Strain and return to the saucepan. Season to taste with salt and pepper and add the cream. If the sauce is too thin, simmer, uncovered, to reduce it a little.

To serve, place 1 duckling breast on each of four heated plates and mask with the first sauce. Unmould the mousses and coat with the second sauce. Serve with green vegetables and, if liked, a mixed fruit compote.

WINE SUGGESTION: A Côte de Beaune.

ROAST DUCKLING IN TWO SERVINGS

Pierre Chevillard presents his ducklings in two separate servings with different garnishes, unusual and very appetizing.

SERVES 4

2 × 1.1 kg/2½ lb ducklings
Salt
Freshly ground pepper
6 tablespoons butter
2 medium carrots, scraped and cut into julienne strips
1 leek, using white part only, well washed, and cut into julienne strips
125 ml/4 fl oz Grand Marnier, or other orange-flavoured liqueur
125 ml/4 fl oz double cream

4 potatoes, peeled and cut into balls
1 onion, thinly sliced
125 ml/4 fl oz dry white wine
475 ml/16 fl oz veal or beef stock (see Basic Recipes, page 11)
1 soft lettuce, separated into leaves
125 g/4 oz canned hearts of palm, rinsed and diced
125 ml/4 fl oz oil and vinegar dressing (see Basic Recipes, page 23)

Pull away the excess fat from the cavities of the ducklings. Season the birds with salt and pepper and roast on a rack in a baking tin in a preheated, hot oven (220°C/425°F/gas 7) for 45 minutes.

Heat 2 tablespoons of the butter in a saucepan and cook the carrots and leek until the vegetables are soft. Add the liqueur and cream and simmer for 5 minutes, uncovered. Cover and set aside.

Heat 2 more tablespoons of the butter in a frying pan and sauté the potato balls until they are tender and golden brown, about 10 minutes. Season with salt and pepper. Keep them warm.

When the ducklings are cooked, remove them from the baking tin to a platter, and keep warm. Pour off the fat from the tin, add the onion, wine and stock and simmer until the onion is very soft and the liquid slightly thickened. Strain the sauce through a fine sieve into a saucepan and stir in the remaining

2 tablespoons of butter, cut into pieces. Season with salt and pepper if necessary, cover and keep warm.

For the first serving, cut the duckling breasts into thin slices. Arrange the leek and carrot mixture on four heated plates and top with the sliced duckling. Spoon the sauce over the breasts and arrange the potatoes on the plates.

For the second serving, toss the lettuce and hearts of palm with the oil and vinegar dressing in a salad bowl. Arrange the duckling legs on four plates and garnish with the salad.

WINE SUGGESTION: A Côte de Beaune.

CONFIT OF DUCK

Simon Hopkinson says of this dish that it is simple and completely effortless and is one of his favourites. It is also a favourite of mine and I like to serve it as a simple meal for friends on a Sunday night. It is easier to prepare than the classical confit.

SERVES 6

6 legs and thighs from 3 ducklings each weighing about 2.7 kg/6 lb	1 bay leaf
6 tablespoons salt, preferably coarse sea salt	500 g/1 lb duck or goose fat or lard
Freshly ground pepper	900 g/2 lb potatoes, peeled and sliced
1 teaspoon fresh thyme, finely chopped or $\frac{1}{2}$ teaspoon dried	2 or 3 cloves garlic, finely chopped
	50 g/2 oz finely chopped parsley

Put the duck pieces in a large bowl with the salt, pepper, thyme and bay leaf. Mix all together, cover and refrigerate overnight, turning once or twice. The next day, wipe off the excess salt and herbs with kitchen towels and place the duck pieces in a large baking tin. It is important to have a tin big enough so that the pieces do not overlap. Use 2 baking tins if necessary. Melt the duck or goose fat, or lard, and pour over the duck. There should be enough to cover the duck completely. Add more if necessary. Bake in a preheated, moderate oven (180°C/350°F/gas 4) for 2 hours, or until the duck is very tender. Take out of the baking tin and put into a container, pour the fat over and store in the refrigerator, or in a cool place, for 1 week.

To serve, sauté the duckling in a nonstick frying pan, or in a heavy frying pan with a little of the fat, until the duck skin is crisp. In a separate pan, sauté the potatoes with the garlic. Pile the duck and potatoes onto a large, heated platter and sprinkle with the parsley.

WINE SUGGESTION: A rich Bordeaux – a St-Emilion.

DUCKLING BREAST WITH WILD MUSHROOM SAUCE

John Webber, whom I met when he was head chef at Gidleigh Park in Devon, dislikes the tendency in modern cooking to be dependent on fashion, nor does he like presentation so complex as to take hours, and be overpowering to the eye of the diner. In his view, flavour is the most important factor. Birmingham-born, he has an interesting background as he went straight into the Birmingham College of Food and Domestic Arts with no thought other than of becoming a chef. He was sous-chef to Anton Mosimann at The Dorchester before moving to Devon where he had a chance to develop his individual talent. He is now at Cliveden, Taplow in Buckinghamshire.

SERVES 4

For the Sauce:
15 g/½ oz dried cèpes
15 g/½ oz dried morels
125 ml/4 fl oz dry white wine
125 ml/4 fl oz chicken consommé
475 ml/16 fl oz veal or chicken stock
  (see Basic Recipes, pages 10, 11)
1 teaspoon tomato purée
½ teaspoon arrowroot
Salt

Freshly ground pepper

For the Duckling:
2 ducklings, each about 2.3 kg/5 lb
250 ml/8 fl oz veal or chicken stock
1 tablespoon honey
1 teaspoon dry English mustard

For the Garnish:
125 g/4 oz fresh wild mushrooms

To make the sauce, start, if possible, the night before. Put the dried mushrooms, wine and consommé in a saucepan and bring to a boil. Remove from the heat and allow to stand for at least 2 hours, overnight is better.

When ready to cook, strain the sauce and remove and discard the soaked mushrooms or add them to the stockpot to enrich the flavour. Return the liquid to the saucepan, add the veal stock, simmer and reduce by one-third. Whisk in the tomato purée. Mix the arrowroot with a little water and stir it into the sauce to thicken. Remove from the heat as soon as the sauce is thickened. Season with salt and pepper and keep warm.

Remove the breasts from the ducklings and cut off the wings but do not bone or skin them. Keep the rest of the ducklings for another meal. Make a glaze. Pour the veal stock into a small saucepan and reduce it by three-quarters over fairly high heat. Whisk in the honey. Mix the mustard with a little water and stir it in.

Put the duckling breasts, skin-side down, in a baking tin and roast in a preheated, hot oven (220°C/425°F/gas 7) for 10 minutes. Turn the breasts over and brush the skin with the glaze. Cook for another 12 minutes, brushing every 4 minutes with the glaze.

Add the garnish of fresh wild mushrooms to the sauce and simmer over very low heat for 5 minutes. Remove the duckling breasts from the bone and slice with the skin on. Brush with the glaze. Arrange the breasts on four heated plates and pour the mushroom sauce around each one. Serve vegetables like new potatoes and green peas separately.

WINE SUGGESTION: A St-Emilion.

ROAST MALLARD DUCK WITH GINGER AND PORT SAUCE

This is a gala way to prepare wild duck, and merits a special occasion. It was created by Julian Waterer, when he was head chef of Greywalls Hotel.

SERVES 8

1 tablespoon vegetable oil
4 mallard ducks
Salt
Freshly ground pepper
1 tablespoon syrup from stem ginger in syrup
475 ml/12 fl oz game stock, or use rich chicken stock (see Basic Recipes, pages 10, 12)

125 ml/4 fl oz tawny port
1 tablespoon finely chopped shallot
4 pieces stem ginger, chopped
2 teaspoons grated fresh ginger root
2 teaspoons lemon juice
175 ml/6 fl oz double cream
2 pink grapefruit, peeled and separated into segments

Heat the oil in a baking tin. Season the ducks with salt and pepper and seal on all sides in the oil. Roast in a preheated, hot oven (230°C/450°F/gas 8) for 20-25 minutes. Remove from the tin to a dish and allow to rest in a warm place while the sauce is made.

In a heavy saucepan, combine the ginger syrup, game stock, port and shallots and reduce to half. Add the chopped ginger, grated ginger and lemon juice. Continue to reduce over moderate heat until the sauce is almost syrupy. Add the cream and continue to simmer until the sauce reaches coating consistency. Season to taste with salt and pepper, strain and keep warm.

Cut the legs from the ducks and remove the breasts. Reserve the carcasses for making stock. If liked, cut the breasts into 3 or 4 slices, or leave whole. Arrange the duck pieces on a large dish and put the grapefruit segments neatly over the duck. Put into the hot oven for 5 minutes, then serve at once with the sauce separate. Serve with new potatoes, broccoli and carrot purée, flavoured with a little dry sherry.

WINE SUGGESTION: My suggestion for this is a full red wine such as a Burgundy, a Côtes-du-Rhône or Châteauneuf-du-Pape.

POT-ROASTED GROUSE WITH HONEY

Anton Mosimann, Maître Chef des Cuisines at The Dorchester Hotel, in London, is a chef of infinite creativity. His pot-roasted grouse is uncomplicated, needing little time in the kitchen. The end result is a subtly-flavoured, elegant main course for four people.

SERVES 4
125 g/4 oz butter
170 g/6 oz mixed carrot, leek and
    celery, finely chopped
½ teaspoon fresh thyme, chopped
4 young grouse
2 tablespoons honey, heather honey
    preferably
250 ml/8 fl oz dry cider

350 ml/12 fl oz game or rich chicken
    stock thickened with 2 teaspoons
    arrowroot (see Basic Recipes, pages
    10, 12)
125 ml/4 fl oz double cream
Salt
Freshly ground pepper

In a heavy casserole, heat half the butter. Add the vegetables and thyme and cook over low heat until they are soft. Add the grouse, spoon the honey over the breasts, cover and cook in a preheated, slow oven (160°C/325°F/gas 3) for 1 hour. Remove the birds from the casserole and keep them warm.

Pour the cider and stock into the casserole on top of the stove and deglaze over high heat, stirring to scrape up any brown bits. Simmer, uncovered, over moderate heat until the sauce is reduced to 250 ml/8 fl oz. Strain through a fine sieve and return the sauce to the casserole. Warm it through over low heat, stir in the cream, taste for seasoning and simmer just until the sauce is slightly thickened. Beat in the remaining butter, cut into pieces. Taste and, if liked, add a little more honey. Arrange the grouse on four heated plates and serve the sauce separately.

WINE SUGGESTION: My suggestion is a chilled white Burgundy or Graves, or a light red such as a Beaujolais or Médoc.

BREAST OF GROUSE WITH PORT JELLY

This is another of Anton Mosimann's inspired recipes for grouse. It makes a lovely lunch or summer evening dinner. When I can't get grouse I use chicken breasts, or any game breasts for this.

SERVES 4

1 envelope (1 tablespoon) unflavoured gelatine
250 ml/8 fl oz clear game or chicken stock (see Basic Recipes, pages 10, 12)
125 ml/4 fl oz tawny port
4 breasts of grouse, or other game, or chicken
Salt
Freshly ground pepper
3 tablespoons butter

For the Salad:
500 g/1 lb diced fruits such as seeded orange or tangerine segments; sliced bananas; peeled, cored and chopped apples; black or white grapes seeded and halved; sliced, peeled kiwi fruits; strawberries, etc.
125 ml/4 fl oz soured cream or to taste
4 or more large lettuce leaves
2 tablespoons chopped chives

Sprinkle the gelatine over 50 ml/2 fl oz cold water in a small bowl to soften. In a saucepan, combine the stock and port wine. Stir in the softened gelatine, simmer over low heat, stirring, until the gelatine has dissolved. Set aside until ready to use.

Season the grouse breasts with salt and pepper. Heat the butter in a casserole, add the grouse, cover with buttered greaseproof paper and the lid and cook in a preheated, moderately hot oven (200°C/400°F/gas 6) for about 8 minutes or until they are springy to the touch. Remove from the oven, lift out and cool. If liked, the breasts may be poached in game or chicken stock barely to cover, on top of the stove for about 8 minutes. Lift out and cool.

Chill the gelatine mixture until it is syrupy. Put the breasts on a wire rack and mask with the aspic. Any aspic that runs off may be returned to the saucepan and warmed until liquid enough to use to make a thicker coat of jelly. Refrigerate the breasts until the jelly is set and trim neatly.

For the salad, combine the fruits in a bowl with the soured cream and spoon into the lettuce leaves. Sprinkle with the chives.

Serve the grouse breasts on slightly chilled plates with the salad in a lettuce leaf alongside.

WINE SUGGESTION: Michael suggests port. A suitable wine would be any full-bodied red such as a good Burgundy.

PIGEON BREASTS WITH PRUNES IN ARMAGNAC

The cooking of Stephen Ross, chef-patron of Homewood Park Hotel and Restaurant at Hinton Charterhouse, Bath in Avon, is a blend of traditional and new. Homewood Park won the 1986 'Hotel of the Year' award from Egon Ronay. This is a rich-tasting, luscious but not difficult dish.

SERVES 8

500 g/1 lb pitted prunes
125 ml/4 fl oz Armagnac, or other brandy
8 pigeons
Salt

Freshly ground pepper
475 ml/16 fl oz dry red wine
125 ml/4 fl oz dry Madeira
2 tablespoons redcurrant jelly

Put the prunes in a bowl, pour in the Armagnac or other brandy and leave to soak overnight, turning once or twice.

Season the pigeons with salt and pepper and arrange in a baking tin. Roast in a preheated, hot oven (220°C/425°F/gas 7) for 20 minutes. They should be kept pink. Remove from the oven and rest for 15 minutes. While the birds are resting, pour the red wine into the baking tin and bring to a simmer on top of the stove, scraping with a wooden spoon to take up any brown bits. Add the Madeira and the redcurrant jelly and simmer until the sauce is reduced to a dark, rich consistency. Add the prunes and the Armagnac in which they have soaked.

Remove the breasts from the pigeons and carve them into thin slices. Arrange on eight heated plates and spoon the sauce over them. Serve with new potatoes, or noodles, and a green vegetable.

WINE SUGGESTION: Armagnac. However, I would prefer a Bordeaux-Médoc.

PHEASANT BREASTS IN GINGER AND WHISKY SAUCE

Julian Waterer, who is one of the most brilliantly original chefs I have ever met, has a special way with game, using ginger to point up its rich flavour. His recipes are seldom complicated and can be cooked in little time, coming to the table with their flavours fresh and vivid. This is a quite luxurious dish as pheasants are not everyday fare. Chicken breasts, though less robust in taste, can be used instead.

SERVES 6

6 young pheasant breasts, boned
Salt
Freshly ground pepper
6 tablespoons butter
125 ml/4 fl oz Scotch whisky
1 tablespoon syrup from stem ginger
  in syrup
½ teaspoon fresh ginger root, grated
1 tablespoon shallot, finely chopped

475 ml/16 fl oz game stock (see Basic
  Recipes, page 12)
½ teaspoon lemon juice
125 ml/4 fl oz double cream
2 pieces stem ginger in syrup, drained
  and chopped
250 g/8 oz courgettes, trimmed and
  cut into thin strips

Season the pheasant breasts with salt and pepper. Heat 3 tablespoons of the butter in a casserole large enough to hold the breasts comfortably. Add the breasts, skin-side down, and sauté over moderate heat for 1 minute. Turn, cover with the lid, and cook in a preheated, moderate oven (190°C/375°F/ gas 5) for 8–10 minutes. The breasts should be pink inside. Remove from the casserole to a warmed platter and keep warm while making the sauce.

In a saucepan, combine the whisky, ginger syrup, grated ginger and shallot and boil over moderate to high heat for 1 minute. Add the stock and lemon juice and simmer, over moderate heat, until the mixture is thickened. Add the cream and simmer for 3 minutes longer. Season to taste with salt and pepper and strain. Return to the saucepan, add the chopped ginger and heat through.

Add the remaining butter to a frying pan and sauté the courgettes quickly over moderately high heat, a few minutes. They should be slightly crisp. Pour the sauce onto six heated plates and arrange a pheasant breast on each one. Surround with the fried courgette strips. If liked, slice the pheasant breasts into 6 slices and place on top of a bed of courgettes arranged over the sauce.

WINE SUGGESTION: Michael suggests whisky. A suitable wine would be a medium Claret (red Bordeaux), or a Chianti Classico.

VARIATION

Graham Flanagan has a simple and attractive variation on Julian Waterer's more sophisticated dish. Four boned pheasant breasts are sautéed in a little butter and oil, removed from the pan and kept warm. The fat is discarded and 125 ml/4 fl oz tawny port is added to the pan and reduced, over moderate heat, to 50 ml/2 fl oz. Next, 350 ml/12 fl oz of double cream or fresh white cheese (see Basic Recipes, page 24) is added to the pan and simmered until slightly thickened. If using fresh white cheese, simply heat it through gently. The sauce is seasoned with salt and pepper and the pheasant breasts are returned to the sauce to heat through. The breasts are served with the sauce and are garnished with sprigs of watercress. Straw potatoes are good with this. Serves 4.

ROAST PHEASANT WITH FRUIT GARNISH

Chris Pitman enjoys game dishes and has turned this pheasant into something very special. The slight tartness of the fruit contrasts agreeably with the rich flavour of the pheasant.

SERVES 2

1 young pheasant, weighing about 900 g/2 lb
6 tablespoons butter
4 rashers bacon, halved
6 small, peeled, white onions
6 button mushrooms
2 rashers bacon, blanched, rind removed, and cut into 0.3 cm/⅛ in strips, crosswise
25 g/1 oz croutons (see Basic Recipes, page 24)

10 seedless white grapes, halved
10 black grapes, peeled, halved and pitted
1 orange, peeled and segmented
10 fresh cranberries
4 whole cooked chestnuts
2 tablespoons brandy
2 tablespoons chopped parsley

Spread the breast of the pheasant with 4 tablespoons of the butter softened at room temperature. Cover with the bacon slices. Place on its side on a rack in a roasting tin and roast in a preheated, hot oven (230°C/450°F/gas 8) for 25–30 minutes, turning the bird onto its other side halfway through the cooking. During the last 5 minutes of cooking, remove the bacon and turn the bird breast-side up to brown the breast. Remove the bird from the oven and turn it breast-side down for 5 minutes to let the juices return to the breast. Turn it right-side up, transfer to a platter, halve the bird, put on two heated plates and keep warm.

In a medium-sized, heavy frying pan, heat the remaining 2 tablespoons of butter and sauté the onions, mushrooms and bacon pieces over moderate heat until the onions are tender. Add the croutons, white and black grapes, orange segments, cranberries and chestnuts and sauté for about 1 minute longer. Add the brandy, flame and pour over the pheasant halves. Sprinkle with chopped parsley.

WINE SUGGESTION: A Côtes-du-Rhône.

Meats
and Game

The innovative chefs who are changing food in Britain hold our beef in high esteem and have created new dishes that do justice to the fine flavour of the meat. They use fillet steaks a great deal as these are very practical in restaurants, always tender, quickly cooked, and uniform in size. The home cook can use other steaks that are less expensive and just as suitable for the chefs' sauces and garnishes. They are not everyday dishes, with the exception of Braised Oxtail, but they can make a dinner party for special friends doubly special.

Lamb is exceptionally fine and chefs make fine use of it. They delight in this lean and succulent meat that they feel is both appetizing and healthful. But the Welsh chef does claim that Welsh lamb surpasses all other lamb; the Scots chef knows better, as Scots lamb is pre-eminent; while the English quite smugly know that nothing beats the best English lamb. It is fortunate that lamb is good enough to support all their claims while the home cook often buys New Zealand lamb, especially later in the year, as the New Zealand lambing season is the reverse of ours.

Another favourite meat is venison which is gaining in popularity with chefs, perhaps because it is another lean meat. Chefs have come up with some really splendid venison recipes that would appeal to even the most jaded palates.

Good veal is not easy to get but when it is, chefs have created some very imaginative recipes to take full advantage of the goodness. They have also devised tempting recipes for organ meats (offal) and for pork and rabbit dishes. Today's chefs very well understand the needs of the meat lover.

BEEF FAN WITH ROQUEFORT CHEESE

This unusual and richly-flavoured steak dish comes from Vaughan Archer, whom I met when he was head chef at the very beautiful 90 Park Lane restaurant in London. It is one of those luxurious dishes that can be got together in very little time, a great comfort to those who like to eat well but have minutes rather than hours available to spend in the kitchen.

SERVES 4

475 ml/16 fl oz dry red wine	6 tablespoons butter
250 ml/8 fl oz beef stock (see Basic Recipes, page 11)	4 tablespoons Roquefort cheese, or other blue cheese
Salt	2 tablespoons finely chopped chives
Freshly ground pepper	25 g/1 oz finely chopped mushrooms
4 × 175 g/6 oz fillet steaks, about 2.5 cm/1 in thick	

Combine 250 ml/8 fl oz of the wine with the beef stock in a small saucepan and reduce to 250 ml/8 fl oz over moderately high heat. Set aside.

Salt and pepper the steaks. Heat half the butter in a heavy frying pan and sauté the steaks for 3–4 minutes on each side for medium rare. Lift out the steaks and keep warm. Pour off any fat from the pan and add the remaining 250 ml/8 fl oz of wine to the pan juices. Reduce over high heat until syrupy. Add the reserved wine and beef stock and the Roquefort cheese mashed with the rest of the butter. Season to taste with salt and pepper, if necessary. Stir in the chives and mushrooms and keep warm.

Cut the steaks into lengthways slices. Pour the sauce onto four warmed plates and arrange the steak in a fan on each plate. If preferred, the steak may, of course, be served unsliced. Serve with Stuffed Potato (see page 190).

WINE SUGGESTION: A full-bodied wine – a red Rioja.

SIRLOIN STEAK WITH STILTON CHEESE

This recipe from Philip Burgess takes even less kitchen time than Vaughan Archer's Beef Fan with Roquefort Cheese (see previous recipe). It pleases both beef and cheese lovers as well as the economy-minded, as leftovers from a whole Stilton cheese can be used.

SERVES 4

250 ml/8 fl oz dry red wine
250 ml/8 fl oz beef stock (see Basic
  Recipes, page 11)
250 g/8 oz Stilton cheese
2 tablespoons butter
1 tablespoon vegetable oil

4 × 250 g/8 oz sirloin steaks
Salt
Freshly ground pepper

For the Garnish:
Watercress sprigs

Combine the red wine and beef stock in a saucepan and reduce over moderately high heat to 250 ml/8 fl oz. Set aside.

Mash the Stilton cheese with 1 tablespoon of the butter and set aside.

In a heavy frying pan, heat the oil and the remaining tablespoon of the butter. Season the steaks with salt and pepper and sauté over fairly high heat for 2 minutes on each side, longer if better done steak is preferred. Spread the steaks with the Stilton cheese mixture and grill until the cheese has melted. Serve garnished with watercress and accompanied by green vegetables and potatoes.

WINE SUGGESTION: A red Rioja.

SIRLOIN STEAK WITH FOUR PEPPERS

It isn't easy to come up with a new way of presenting sirloin steak but this creation of famed chef Anton Mosimann looks like becoming a classic. It exemplifies the chef's philosophy: Make it simple, but make it perfect.

SERVES 4

4 × 2.5 cm/1 in thick sirloin steaks, each weighing about 175 g/6 oz
2 tablespoons each crushed black and white peppercorns
Salt
4 tablespoons vegetable oil
50 ml/2 fl oz Cognac, or other brandy

250 ml/8 fl oz veal or beef stock (see Basic Recipes, page 11)
125 ml/4 fl oz double cream
3 tablespoons butter, cut into pieces
Freshly ground pepper
1 teaspoon each pink and green peppercorns

Season the steaks on both sides with the black and white peppercorns and salt. Heat the oil in a heavy frying pan and sauté the steaks for 3–4 minutes on each side for medium rare meat. Transfer the steaks to a platter and keep them warm. Pour off and discard any fat in the pan. Pour in the Cognac and flame it. Add the stock. Reduce it to half over moderately high heat. Add the cream and reduce the sauce until it is lightly thickened. Whisk in the butter, piece by piece. Taste for seasoning and add salt and pepper as liked. Stir in the pink and green peppercorns, cover the steaks with the sauce and serve immediately.

WINE SUGGESTION: My suggestion is a Côte de Nuits, or other red Burgundy.

FILLET OF BEEF WITH TWO PEPPERCORNS

John Mann, head chef at The Old Lodge in Limpsfield, Surrey, is a chef of exceptional brilliance. His creations are always gratifying to the palate but, alas, are seldom sensible dishes for the home cook. This beef dish is part of a far more elaborate dish but since it is splendid by itself, is not complicated, and takes little time to cook, I have taken the liberty of abstracting it.

SERVES 4

1½ tablespoons black peppercorns
1½ tablespoons white peppercorns
Salt
4 × 125 g/4 oz fillet steaks, about 2.5 cm/1 in thick
½ tablespoon vegetable oil

1 tablespoon butter
1 tablespoon brandy
350 ml/12 fl oz veal stock, or use rich chicken stock (see Basic Recipes, pages 10, 11)

Mix the peppercorns together and crush coarsely with ½ teaspoon salt. Season the steaks with the peppercorn mixture, pressing it in firmly. Heat the oil and butter in a frying pan and sauté the steaks for 3–4 minutes on each side for medium rare meat. Transfer the steaks to a platter and keep them warm.

Pour away any fat from the frying pan, leaving only the pan juices. Flame with the brandy then add the veal stock and reduce over moderately high heat until it is slightly thickened. Add any meat juices that may have collected on the platter and season the sauce to taste with salt.

Serve the steaks on four warmed plates with the sauce spooned over them. There will not be a great deal of sauce. Garnish the plate with boiled potatoes, young carrots and baby turnips cut into olive shapes, mangetout and some straw potatoes, if liked.

WINE SUGGESTION: A Côte de Nuits.

FILLET STEAKS WITH ASPARAGUS TIPS

Michael Collom has come up with a way of lifting fillet steaks into a new dimension. If I have the time and energy I make the Béarnaise sauce which adds a touch of luxury to the dish, otherwise I make this as one of my cook-in-a-hurry dishes, quickly cooked, quickly assembled and very appetizing. (Nicholas Knight serves a delicious sauce with his steaks, see overleaf.)

SERVES 6

125 ml/4 fl oz Béarnaise Sauce (optional) (see Basic Recipes, page 21)
6 fillet steaks, cut 2.5 cm/1 in thick, each weighing about 125 g/4 oz
Salt
Freshly ground pepper
2 tablespoons butter
1 tablespoon vegetable oil

12 asparagus tips, white or green, cooked
250 ml/8 fl oz veal or beef stock (see Basic Recipes, page 11)
250 ml/8 fl oz dry Madeira

For the Garnish:
Watercress sprigs
Straw potatoes

Make the Béarnaise sauce, if using, and set it aside.

Season the steaks with salt and pepper. In a frying pan large enough to hold all the steaks comfortably, heat 1 tablespoon of the butter, and the oil and sauté the steaks over moderately high heat for 3–4 minutes on each side. Remove from the pan and keep warm. Warm the asparagus tips.

Discard any fat from the frying pan and pour any juices into a small saucepan. Pour in the stock and reduce it to half over brisk heat. Add the Madeira, bring to a simmer. Continue to simmer the sauce over very low heat.

With a very sharp knife, cut a diagonal pocket into each of the steaks and stuff with the asparagus tips. Garnish the asparagus with a spoonful of Béarnaise sauce, if using. Stir the remaining tablespoon of butter into the sauce which should have reduced to a slightly syrupy consistency. Put a steak onto each of six heated plates, pour the sauce round the steaks and garnish with the watercress sprigs and straw potatoes.

WINE SUGGESTION: A Côte de Beaune.

VARIATION

Another attractive and inventive way of serving fillet or other steaks comes from Nicholas Knight, the head chef at Master's Restaurant. He masks steaks with a carrot and green peppercorn sauce which is light and delicious, the sweetness of the carrot sharpened by the bite of green peppercorns (see page 190).

FILLET OF BEEF WITH PICKLED WALNUT SAUCE

Peter Jackson created this prize-winning dish when he was head chef at Bodysgallen Hall Hotel in North Wales, and was named North Wales Chef of the Year (1981) and was runner-up British Chef of the Year, 1982. Winning awards seems to come naturally to him as he's been doing it since 1978 when he was a very young man at the beginning of his career.

Though there is quite a lot of preparation ahead of time, the actual dish takes very little cooking time which makes it ideal for an important dinner.

SERVES 4

500 g/1 lb beef fillet, or more if liked
Salt
Freshly ground white pepper
1 medium onion, finely chopped
1 stalk celery, finely chopped
1 leek, using white part only, finely
  chopped
1 medium carrot, scraped and
  chopped
50 g/2 oz juniper berries, crushed
475 ml/16 fl oz tawny port
250 ml/8 fl oz demi-glace (see Basic
  Recipes, page 12)

25 g/1 oz pickled walnuts, finely
  chopped
Vegetable oil
125 ml/4 fl oz double cream
  (optional)

For the Garnish:
2 tablespoons butter
250 g/8 oz black grapes, halved
125 g/4 oz quartered mushrooms
25 g/1 oz walnut meats
2 tablespoons finely chopped parsley

Cut the beef into 4 slices. Season with salt and pepper and put into a fairly deep dish. Cover with the onion, celery, leek and carrot mixture. Add the juniper berries. Pour in the port wine and leave to marinate in the refrigerator for 24 hours, turning occasionally.

When ready to cook, lift out the beef and pat dry with paper towels. Set aside and make the sauce. Pour all the marinade into a saucepan with the demi-glace and pickled walnuts. Simmer, uncovered, until the liquid is reduced to 250 ml/8 fl oz. Strain, pressing down on the vegetables to extract all the flavour. Rinse out and dry the saucepan and return the liquid to it. Set aside.

In a frying pan, heat a little vegetable oil and sauté the beef to the required degree of doneness, about 4 minutes a side for medium rare.

Make the garnish. In another frying pan, heat the butter and sauté the grapes, mushrooms and walnut meats quickly over moderately high heat.

Add the 125 ml/4 fl oz cream to the sauce if using and simmer until it reaches coating consistency. Taste for seasoning, and add salt and pepper if necessary. Otherwise just warm the sauce through and season to taste.

Place a fillet on each of four heated plates. Cover with the sauce and spoon the garnish over each one. Finish with a sprinkling of chopped parsley. Serve with new potatoes and a green vegetable.

WINE SUGGESTION: A Médoc.

BRAISED OXTAIL

Philip Burgess is a Devonian, and now at the Arundell Arms is back in his native county. Though young, he has had a wide experience of cooking, but still relishes the good things of his childhood. He has developed his own version of this old favourite which he describes as a warming winter dish. It is also very satisfying.

SERVES 4

50 g/2 oz plain flour
Salt
Freshly ground pepper
900 g/2 lb meaty oxtails, cut into
    5 cm/2 in pieces
6 tablespoons of beef dripping or
    vegetable oil
1 large onion, coarsely chopped
1 large carrot, coarsely chopped
1 stalk celery, chopped
1 medium-sized leek, trimmed,
    thoroughly washed, and coarsely

chopped using a little of the green
    part
1 bay leaf
Sprig fresh thyme or ⅛ teaspoon dried
1 clove garlic, crushed
1.4 L/2½ pt beef stock, about (see
    Basic Recipes, page 11)
1 tablespoon tomato purée
2 tablespoons dry sherry
Chopped parsley

Season the flour with salt and pepper and dredge the oxtails with the mixture, shaking to remove the excess. In a large frying pan, heat 3 tablespoons of the beef dripping or vegetable oil and brown the pieces of oxtail, in batches if necessary. Lift them out into a large oven-proof casserole. Add the rest of the fat and sauté the vegetables and herbs until the onion is softened. Sprinkle with a tablespoon of the flour and stir to mix. Continue cooking until the flour is lightly browned. Transfer the contents of the frying pan to the casserole. Pour in enough stock to cover, adding a little more if necessary, stir in the tomato purée and bring to a simmer on top of the stove. Cover, and put into a preheated, moderate oven (180°C/350°F/gas 4). Cook until the meat is tender, about 3 hours.

Remove from the oven and put the oxtail pieces into a serving dish. Keep them warm in the turned-off oven. Skim the excess fat from the casserole and strain the liquid through a sieve into a clean saucepan. If the liquid seems very abundant or a little thin, reduce it over moderately high heat until it is lightly thickened. Season to taste with salt and pepper and stir in the sherry. Pour the sauce over the oxtails and sprinkle with chopped parsley. Serve with plain boiled potatoes.

WINE SUGGESTION: A Beaujolais.

MUSTARD AND TARRAGON SAUCE FOR MEATS

This easy to make, sturdily-flavoured sauce is the creation of Nicholas Knight. It is wonderfully useful for lifting an ordinary meat or poultry dish into a special category. I've also used it with a strong flavoured fish like halibut with great success. The chef feels it is best with white meats like veal, pork, chicken or turkey, and certainly it is good with these. I found, also, that it is surprisingly good with beef. Try it as a sauce topping on a hamburger.

SERVES 4

1 tablespoon butter
2 teaspoons fresh tarragon leaves, finely chopped, or dried tarragon soaked in warm water, squeezed out and chopped
1 tablespoon coarse-grain mustard, such as *moutarde de Meaux*
3 tablespoons chicken stock (see Basic Recipes, page 10)

2 tablespoons dry white wine
Salt
Freshly ground pepper
350 ml/12 fl oz double cream, or fresh white cheese (see Basic Recipes, page 24)

Heat the butter in a saucepan, stir in the tarragon, cover and let it sweat over very low heat for about half a minute.

Add the mustard, stock, wine, salt and pepper and the cream and simmer, uncovered, until the sauce is slightly thickened. If using fresh white cheese, simply stir in and heat through.

MEDALLION OF VEAL WITH LEMON

This is another of the simple yet imaginative recipes of Christopher Grist. It takes very little time to cook and makes an ideal dish for two for an elegant dinner. It is also very good made with boned chicken breast instead of veal.

SERVES 2

1 large lemon
½ teaspoon sugar
5 tablespoons butter
2 slices veal fillet, each weighing about
   150 g/5 oz
Salt

Freshly ground pepper
125 ml/4 fl oz dry white wine
1 tablespoon chopped parsley
2 large leaves, or 2 small sprigs
   watercress

Cut the peel from half the lemon in julienne strips. Put into a small saucepan with cold water to cover and bring to a boil over moderate heat. Drain and refresh in cold water and drain again. Return the peel to the saucepan with the sugar and 1 tablespoon water and cook, over very low heat, until the water has evaporated. This intensifies the colour of the peel. Set aside and keep warm.

Heat 2 tablespoons of the butter in a frying pan. Season the veal with salt and pepper and sauté the veal in the butter, over moderate heat, for about 5 minutes on each side. Remove the veal slices to a plate, cover and keep warm. Pour the wine into the frying pan, scraping up any brown bits. Reduce the wine to 1 tablespoon then beat in the rest of the butter, piece by piece to make a creamy sauce. Add the chopped parsley and season with salt and pepper. Pour any juices that have accumulated on the plate with veal into the sauce. Put a slice of veal on each of two heated plates, and pour the sauce over them. Cut the unpeeled half of the lemon into 2 wedges and put on the side of the plates. Sprinkle the veal with the julienne of lemon peel and place a sprig or leaf of watercress on top. This is nice with rice and a mixture of young spring vegetables tossed in butter.

WINE SUGGESTION: A Beaujolais.

VEAL ESCALOPES WITH STRAWBERRY SAUCE

Denis Woodtli uses the tart sweetness of strawberries to enhance the sauce for this simple, uncomplicated dish.

SERVES 2

2 veal escalopes, each weighing about
   175-200 g/6-7 oz
Salt
Freshly ground pepper
250 g/8 oz ripe strawberries
4 tablespoons clarified butter (see
   Basic Recipes, page 25)

125 ml/4 fl oz double cream

For the Garnish:
Sliced strawberries
Parsley sprigs

Flatten the escalopes to 0.6 cm/¼ in thickness, or have the butcher do it. Season with salt and pepper. Purée the strawberries in a blender or food processor, then strain through a sieve set over a bowl. Set the strawberry juice aside. Spread the pulp on one half of each escalope and fold them over. Secure with a toothpick. Heat the butter in a frying pan and cook the veal over low heat for 5 minutes on each side. Lift out onto a warm plate, cover and keep warm. Add the cream to the frying pan and cook until it thickens to coating consistency. Add the strawberry juice and season to taste with salt and pepper. Put an escalope on each of two heated plates and pour the sauce over them. Garnish with sliced strawberries and parsley sprigs.

WINE SUGGESTION: A Beaujolais.

VEAL AND LOBSTER WITH SHELLFISH AND SHERRY SAUCES

This is one of the wholly delectable recipes Michael Quinn created when he was head chef at The Ritz. When I find good veal hard to get, I make this with skinned and boned chicken breasts. They work excellently well.

SERVES 4

500 g/1 lb fillet of veal in one piece
1 cooked lobster tail, weighing
   175–250 g/6–8 oz
Salt
Freshly ground pepper
250 g/8 oz butter

For the Shellfish Sauce:
250 ml/8 fl oz shellfish stock (see
  Basic Recipes, page 14)
1 teaspoon tomato purée
1 tablespoon dry vermouth,
  preferably Noilly Prat
50 ml/2 fl oz double cream
1 tablespoon brandy

Salt
Freshly ground pepper

For the Sherry Sauce:
2 tablespoons finely chopped shallots
125 ml/4 fl oz dry sherry
125 ml/4 fl oz veal stock (see Basic
  Recipes, page 11)
50 ml/2 fl oz double cream
Salt
Freshly ground pepper

For the Garnish (optional):
Fresh chervil sprigs

Cut a slit in the veal fillet being careful not to cut right through the veal. Insert the cooked lobster tail then tie the fillet into shape with kitchen string. Season with salt and pepper. In a frying pan large enough to hold the veal comfortably, heat 2 tablespoons of the butter and quickly seal on all sides over moderately high heat. Lower the heat to moderate and cook the fillet for 15 minutes, turning often. The meat should remain pink in the centre. Transfer the meat to a warmed platter and let it rest. Keep the meat warm, and when ready to serve cut it into thin slices.

While the meat is cooking and resting, make the sauces. Pour the shellfish stock into a small saucepan with the tomato purée, dry vermouth and double cream and reduce to 125 ml/4 fl oz. Stir in the brandy and taste for seasoning. Add salt and pepper, if necessary. Set aside and keep warm.

In another saucepan, combine the shallots, sherry and veal stock and reduce over moderately high heat to 1 tablespoon. Add the cream, stir to mix and strain through a fine sieve into the rinsed out and dried saucepan. Over low heat, beat in the rest of the butter, cut into pieces, to make a creamy sauce. Taste for seasoning and add salt and pepper if necessary. Add a little more dry sherry. Keep warm.

To serve, spoon the shellfish stock onto four heated plates. Arrange the sliced veal on top of the sauce. Spoon the sherry sauce over the veal. Garnish, if liked, with sprigs of fresh chervil.

WINE SUGGESTION: A dry Sherry.

FILLET OF VEAL STUFFED WITH HERB AND GARLIC CHEESE

This is a very delicate dish with a lively butter sauce sharpened with vinegar. Murdo MacSween of Oakley Court created it. The dish bears the stamp of his originality.

SERVES 2

2 slices veal fillet, each weighing
125-150 g/4-5 oz
50 g/2 oz herb and garlic cheese
Salt
Freshly ground pepper

For the Butter Sauce:
6 tablespoons butter

1 tablespoon white wine vinegar
5 tablespoons dry white wine
1 teaspoon chopped shallots
1 tablespoon double cream
1 tablespoon chopped chives

Slit the veal slices to form a pocket and stuff with the cheese. Season to taste with salt and pepper.

Cut 5 tablespoons of the butter into pieces. Put the wine vinegar, dry white wine and shallots in a saucepan and reduce by half. Add the cream and bring to a simmer. Remove from the heat and whisk in the butter piece by piece to form a creamy sauce. Stir in the chives and keep warm.

Heat the remaining tablespoon of butter in a small frying pan and sauté the veal over moderate heat, turning once when lightly browned on the first side. They take only minutes to cook.

Arrange the sautéed veal on two heated plates and pour the sauce over them. Fresh noodles are a good accompaniment with a green vegetable such as green peas.

WINE SUGGESTION: A Côte de Nuits or a Margaux.

VEAL KIDNEY WITH CABBAGE AND MUSTARD VINAIGRETTE

Lovers of veal kidneys will welcome this unusual, simple, and most delicious dish, the creation of Simon Hopkinson, of Hilaire restaurant. It makes a perfect supper dish for friends.

SERVES 4

2 veal kidneys, cleaned and thickly sliced
Salt
Freshly ground pepper
Flour
125 g/4 oz butter
1 tablespoon olive oil
1 large Savoy cabbage, thinly sliced
1 clove garlic, finely chopped

For the Vinaigrette:
2 tablespoons Dijon mustard
2 tablespoons sherry vinegar
125-175 ml/4-6 fl oz olive oil, according to taste
Salt
Freshly ground pepper

Season the sliced kidneys with salt and pepper and dredge lightly with flour, shaking to remove the excess. In a heavy frying pan, heat 2 tablespoons of the butter with the tablespoon of olive oil and sauté the kidney slices for 1 minute on each side. Transfer to a warm plate, cover and keep warm.

Add the remaining butter to the frying pan. Season the cabbage with salt and pepper and sauté in the butter with the chopped garlic, quickly over moderate heat, stirring, for 4-5 minutes. The cabbage should remain green and fresh tasting.

In a bowl, beat the mustard and sherry vinegar together. Beat in the oil gradually, using 125-175 ml/4-6 fl oz to taste. Season with salt and pepper.

Divide the cabbage among four heated plates in neat mounds. Arrange the slices of kidney on top. If any juices have collected on the plate with the kidneys, add them to the vinaigrette. Pour the vinaigrette over the cabbage and kidney. Serve with mashed potatoes.

WINE SUGGESTION: A Chianti.

CALVES LIVER WITH AVOCADO

Melvin Jordan has an original way with calves liver, this dish with avocado, and a variation with blackberries, both delicious.

SERVES 2

8 slices calves liver
Salt
Freshly ground pepper
125 g/4 oz butter
16 fresh sage leaves*
250 ml/8 fl oz dry white wine

2 tablespoons lemon juice
1 large, ripe avocado, peeled, pitted
 and cut into 8 slices lengthways

* Instead of the sage leaves, add
 250 g/8 oz ripe fresh blackberries.

Season the liver slices with salt and pepper. In a large heavy frying pan, heat 2 tablespoons of the butter and sauté the slices of liver over moderate heat for no longer than 1 minute a side. Lift out onto a heated plate, cover and keep warm. Add the sage leaves and wine to the frying pan, stir to scrape up any brown bits and simmer until the liquid is reduced by half. Stir in the lemon juice then whisk in the rest of the butter, cut into pieces. The sauce will have a light coating consistency. Arrange the liver slices on two warm plates and pour the sauce over them. Top with avocado slices.

WINE SUGGESTION: A Chardonnay.

FILLET OF LAMB WITH FRESH HERBS

This is one of the simple and attractive dishes that John Hornsby worked out while he was head chef at the Castle Hotel in Taunton, Somerset.

SERVES 2

250 ml/8 fl oz veal stock, or chicken
 stock (see Basic Recipes, pages 10,
 11)
125 ml/4 fl oz dry white wine
2 tablespoons very finely chopped
 fresh herbs such as tarragon,
 rosemary, thyme, basil, mint and
 parsley

4 tablespoons butter
Salt
Freshly ground pepper
2 × 125-175 g/4-6 oz slices boneless
 loin of lamb, trimmed of fat

In a small saucepan, combine the stock and wine and simmer, uncovered, over moderate heat until reduced by half. Stir in the herbs. Cut 2 tablespoons of the butter into pieces and beat into the sauce, a piece at a time until they are all absorbed. Season the sauce with salt and pepper to taste and keep warm.

In a frying pan just large enough to hold the lamb comfortably, heat the remaining 2 tablespoons of butter. Season the lamb slices with salt and pepper and sauté in the butter for 3-4 minutes over moderately high heat, turning once. The lamb should be pink. Pour the sauce onto two heated plates and arrange the slices of lamb on top. Serve with new potatoes and an assortment of green vegetables such as green beans, peas, and cauliflower on a separate plate.

WINE SUGGESTION: A Côte de Beaune or a Côte de Nuits.

BEST END OF NECK WITH SAFFRON AND GARLIC SAUCE

Martin Rowbotham has created a pleasantly different dish, with the saffron-flavoured sauce in gentle contrast to the spinach.

SERVES 3

1 best end of neck, about 6 chops
Salt
Freshly ground pepper
500 g/1 lb spinach, washed and
   trimmed
2 tablespoons butter

1 small clove garlic, crushed
125 ml/4 fl oz dry white wine
250 ml/8 fl oz lamb stock (see Basic
   Recipes, page 11)
⅛ teaspoon saffron threads, crumbled

Ask the butcher to cut the lamb so that the chops can easily be carved. Pare away all excess fat. Season to taste with salt and pepper and roast on a rack in a preheated, moderate oven (190°C/375°F/gas 5) for 25 minutes for rare, 30 for medium rare. Remove the lamb from the oven and keep it warm.

While the lamb is cooking, blanch the spinach in a large saucepan of briskly boiling, salted water for 4 minutes. Refresh under cold water and drain thoroughly. When ready to serve, reheat the spinach by tossing lightly in the butter.

Pour off the excess fat from the roasting pan. Add the garlic and cook for about 30 seconds, then add the white wine and let it reduce, over moderate heat, to about one-third. Add the lamb stock and the saffron and simmer until the sauce is reduced to 175 ml/6 fl oz.

Divide the spinach between three heated plates. Carve the lamb and put 2 chops on top of the spinach on each plate and pour the sauce over it.

WINE SUGGESTION: A Médoc or Margaux.

NOISETTES OF LAMB WITH PLUMB SAUCE

David Harding, of Bodysgallen Hall Hotel in North Wales, specifies Welsh lamb for this dish. Welsh lamb is exceptionally sweet and tender but lamb from other parts of the world will also do very well.

SERVES 4 or 6

1 × 1.4 kg/3 lb loin of lamb, fat removed, boned and rolled
Salt
Freshly ground pepper
500 g/1 lb plums
2 tablespoons sugar, or to taste

125 ml/4 fl oz dry red wine
4 tablespoons clarified butter (see Basic Recipes, page 25)

For the Garnish:
Watercress

Cut the lamb into 12 slices. Season with salt and pepper and set aside while making the sauce. Put the plums into a saucepan with the sugar and wine and simmer until they are soft, 10–15 minutes. Put the plums through a fine sieve and return the purée to the saucepan. Taste and add more sugar if necessary. The sauce should be quite tart. If the plum purée is very thin, reduce it over moderate heat, to the consistency of double cream. Cool.

In a large, heavy pan, heat the butter and sauté the noisettes of lamb for about 2 minutes on each side. They should remain pink. Coat four heated plates with the plum sauce and arrange 3 noisettes on top of the sauce. Garnish with watercress. For a lighter meal, serve 2 slices of lamb per person and serve 6.

WINE SUGGESTION: A St-Emilion.

CHARLOTTE OF AUBERGINE WITH NOISETTES OF LAMB

Shaun Hill has a simple and delicious way with lamb and aubergines that enhances the flavour of both meat and vegetables. A charlotte mould is deep in proportion to its size. Use any 350 g/12 oz fairly deep oven-proof mould.

SERVES 4

2 best ends of lamb	Salt
2 tablespoons butter	Freshly ground pepper
250 g/8 oz scraped and diced carrots	Olive or vegetable oil for frying
50 g/2 oz finely chopped well-washed leeks or onions	750 g/1½ lb aubergines, sliced thinly
50 g/2 oz diced celery	500 g/1 lb shallots (about 32 medium-sized)

Have the butcher remove the fillets from the lamb, or do it yourself. Chop the bones and meat trimmings. Heat the butter in a large saucepan and add the carrots, onion or leek and diced celery. Sauté over moderate heat until the vegetables are soft. Add the meat trimmings and bones and sauté for 2 or 3 minutes longer. Pour in enough cold water to cover, bring to a boil, lower the heat and simmer, covered, for 2–3 hours. Strain through a sieve into a bowl, pressing down on the solids to extract all the flavour. Discard the solids. Rinse out and dry the saucepan and return the liquid to it. Simmer, uncovered, over very low heat until the liquid is reduced to 250 ml/8 fl oz and is slightly thickened. Season with salt and pepper and set aside.

Heat enough olive or vegetable oil to cover the bottom of a large frying pan and lightly sauté the aubergine slices, turning them once and adding a little more oil if necessary. Do this in batches. Set aside.

Sauté the shallots in oil in the frying pan until they are soft. Drain. Make a layer of the aubergine slices in four 375 g/12 oz oven-proof moulds. Follow with a layer of shallots, seasoning each layer lightly with salt and pepper. Continue until all the ingredients are used up, ending with the aubergine. Set the moulds on a baking sheet and bake in a preheated, moderate oven (180°C/350°F/gas 4) for 30 minutes, or until they are heated through. When ready to serve, turn them out of the moulds onto kitchen paper to absorb any fat.

Cut the lamb fillets into slices of about 2.5 cm/1 in thickness. Heat a little oil in a frying pan and quickly sauté the lamb over moderately high heat, turning once, about 2 minutes a side for rare lamb.

Put an aubergine mould in the centre of each of four heated plates, surround with lamb slices and the lamb sauce.

WINE SUGGESTION: I would suggest a Médoc or St-Emilion.

BONED BEST END OF NECK WITH FLAGEOLETS AND PORT SAUCE

This makes a change of pace from the usual lamb dish, and is uncomplicated to cook. Robert Gardiner developed the recipe which has his own special touches in the way the beans are cooked, and in the port wine sauce.

SERVES 3

For the Beans:
275 g/9 oz flageolets, soaked in cold water overnight
1 onion, stuck with 2 or 3 cloves
2 tablespoons butter
1 tablespoon vegetable oil
1 medium onion, finely chopped
125 ml/4 fl oz dry red wine
250 g/8 oz tomatoes, peeled, seeded and chopped
2 tablespoons tomato purée
2 cloves garlic, very finely chopped
Salt
Freshly ground pepper

2 tablespoons finely chopped parsley
1 best end of neck, boned but with fillet still attached to the 'flap' of meat, trimmed of fat

For the Sauce:
6 tablespoons butter
2 tablespoons chopped shallots
125 ml/4 fl oz tawny port
300 ml/½ pt veal or lamb stock (see Basic Recipes, page 11)
50 ml/2 fl oz single cream (optional)
Salt
Freshly ground pepper

Drain and rinse the soaked beans and put them into a large saucepan with cold water to cover by about 5 cm/2 in. Add the onion stuck with cloves, bring to a boil, lower the heat and simmer, covered, until the beans are just tender, about 1 hour. The time will vary according to the freshness of the beans. Discard the onion. Strain the beans and put into a bowl. Reserve 250 ml/8 fl oz of the cooking liquid.

Rinse out and dry the saucepan. Heat the butter and oil and sauté the onion until it is soft. Add the wine and reduce over moderately high heat by half. Add the tomatoes, tomato purée, garlic and the cooking liquid from the beans. Simmer over low heat for about 20 minutes, or until the sauce is thick. Add the beans, mix thoroughly and season to taste with salt and pepper. Just before serving reheat the beans and stir in the parsley.

Roll up the boned rack of lamb loosely and put into a baking tin with the folded end down. Cook in a preheated, hot oven (220°C/425°F/gas 7) for about 25 minutes for rare, 30 for medium rare. The exact time will depend on the thickness of the flap. Be careful not to overcook as the lamb should be pink. Lift out of the baking tin and set on a warmed platter to rest for 10 minutes.

While the lamb is resting, make the sauce. Pour off the fat from the baking tin and add 2 tablespoons of the butter. Add the shallots and sauté over moderate heat until they are soft. Pour in the port and simmer until reduced almost to a glaze. Add the veal or lamb stock and simmer to reduce until it is thickened. Add the cream, if using, heat through, remove from the heat and beat in the remaining 4 tablespoons of butter, cut into pieces. Taste for seasoning and add salt and pepper, if necessary.

Cut the lamb into 9 slices. Put a pile of beans in the centre of each of three heated plates. Arrange the lamb slices round the beans and spoon the sauce over the lamb, or serve the sauce separately.

WINE SUGGESTION: A white Port, or a Bordeaux-Médoc or St-Emilion.

COLLOPS OF LAMB WITH MORELS AND YOUNG TURNIPS

Martin Lam has a very discriminating palate and a great love for traditional English food. He uses the old term 'collop' for slice but puts together his ingredients in a refreshingly new and modern way. The rich morels are perfectly balanced by the clean taste of the young turnips.

SERVES 6

Fillets from 3 boned best ends of neck
125 ml/4 fl oz olive oil
1 tablespoon chopped fresh thyme
Salt
Freshly ground pepper
8 tablespoons butter
3 tablespoons chopped shallots

250 g/8 oz fresh, or 125 g/4 oz
    dried, morel mushrooms, soaked
250 ml/8 fl oz dry Madeira
125 ml/4 fl oz veal stock (see Basic
    Recipes, page 11)
24 young turnips, peeled and cooked

Marinate the lamb overnight in the olive oil, thyme, salt to taste and a generous amount of freshly ground black pepper.

In a frying pan, heat 2 tablespoons of the butter and sauté the shallots until they are soft. Add the morels and sauté for 2 minutes longer. Add the Madeira and reduce by half. Add the veal stock and simmer for a few minutes longer to blend the flavours. Set aside and keep warm.

Lift the lamb fillets out of the marinade and wipe off the thyme with paper towels. Heat a little olive oil in a large, heavy frying pan that will hold the lamb comfortably, and sauté it for 5 minutes, turning once or twice. It will be nicely pink. Cut the fillets into slices (collops). Have ready six heated plates. Spoon the sauce onto the plates, making sure there are some morels on each plate. Divide the lamb among the plates. Put the turnips alternately with the lamb slices or in any decorative way. Serve immediately.

WINE SUGGESTION: A Médoc or St-Emilion.

LAMB ESCALOPES IN FRESH HERBS WITH POACHED PEARS

I like the straightforward character of the dishes developed by Willie MacPherson. The mixture of flavours here is delicious.

SERVES 4
4 firm pears, peeled
4 tablespoons lemon juice
125 g/4 oz sugar
500 g/1 lb boneless loin of lamb
Salt
Freshly ground pepper
50 g/2 oz mixed chopped fresh herbs
    such as thyme, parsley, mint,
    tarragon, rosemary, chervil or basil

2 tablespoons butter
125 ml/4 fl oz demi-glace (see Basic
    Recipes, page 12)
4 tablespoons dry red wine

Put the pears into a large, shallow saucepan in a single layer. Add the lemon juice and sugar, and cold water barely to cover. Bring to a simmer, cover and cook until the pears are tender, about 15 minutes. Cool in the liquid, lift out, halve and core, then cut the pears into lengthways slices. Set aside.

Season the lamb with salt and pepper then roll in the chopped herbs, pressing lightly so that they stick to the meat. In a frying pan, heat the butter and sauté the lamb over moderate heat, turning frequently so as not to burn the herbs. Cook for about 5 minutes or longer if better done lamb is preferred. Lift the lamb out of the frying pan onto a board and cut it into 4 crosswise slices. Slice each lengthways on a slant and arrange in an overlapping pattern on one side of each of four heated plates. Arrange the slices of pear on the other side of the plate.

Heat the demi-glace in a small saucepan with the wine and bring to a simmer. Pour the sauce onto the middle of the plates and serve immediately.

WINE SUGGESTION: A Médoc or St-Emilion.

BEST END OF NECK WITH MUSTARD AND FRESH HERBS

David Moir, whose cooking I enjoyed when he was head chef at Gleddoch House in Scotland, uses the same cut of lamb and much the same mixture of fresh herbs as Willie MacPherson, but the finished dish is very different. It is wonderfully well flavoured and delightful for a dinner party as it is not difficult or time consuming.

SERVES 6

2 best ends of neck, cleaned of fat, rib bones trimmed
Salt
Freshly ground pepper
3 tablespoons butter
2 tablespoons shallots, finely chopped
1 clove garlic, crushed
2 medium tomatoes, peeled, seeded and chopped

50 g/2 oz mixed chopped fresh herbs such as mint, chives, rosemary, chervil and sage
3 tablespoons freshly-made breadcrumbs
4 tablespoons Dijon mustard
350 ml/12 fl oz reduced lamb stock for gravy (see Basic Recipes, page 11)

Ask the butcher to cut the lamb so that it is easy to carve through the chops. Season the lamb with salt and pepper and put it into a baking tin. Bake in a preheated, moderate oven (180°C/350°F/gas 4) for about 20 minutes. The lamb will be pink.

While the lamb is cooking, heat 1 tablespoon of the butter in a small frying pan and cook 1 tablespoon of the shallots, the garlic and tomatoes for 3–4 minutes. Season to taste with salt and pepper and put into a bowl. Heat 2 tablespoons of the butter in the frying pan, add the rest of the shallots and sauté until they are soft. Stir in the herbs and the breadcrumbs, season with salt and pepper and stir to mix. Put into a bowl.

When the lamb is cooked, remove it from the oven and spread it liberally with the mustard then coat with a layer of the tomato mixture topped with a layer of the herb and breadcrumb mixture. Return to the oven for a few minutes to reheat. Serve on a large, heated platter and carve into 2 chops per person. Serve with the lamb gravy and straw potatoes.

WINE SUGGESTION: A Médoc or St-Emilion.

MELI-MELO OF LAMB WITH GARLIC AND ROSEMARY

This is a most attractive way to serve a medley of lamb, using the innards as well as the loin. It is the inspiration of Paul Gayler, head chef at Inigo Jones Restaurant in London.

SERVES 4

For the Sauce:
6 tablespoons butter
2 tablespoons finely chopped shallots
4 cloves crushed garlic
Bunch rosemary
125 ml/4 fl oz dry white wine
250 ml/8 fl oz lamb stock (see Basic
  Recipes, page 11)
Salt
Freshly ground pepper

For the Lamb:
4 lambs' tongues
Salt
625 g/1¼ lb loin of lamb
250 g/8 oz lambs' sweetbreads,
  blanched
4 lambs' kidneys
1 tablespoon vegetable oil
8 large cloves garlic, unpeeled

Heat 2 tablespoons of the butter in a small saucepan and add the shallots, garlic and 1 sprig of the rosemary. Cover and cook over very low heat until the shallots are tender. Add the white wine and simmer for 3–4 minutes. Add the lamb stock and simmer over moderately high heat until the sauce is thickened. Strain and stir in 1 tablespoon of the butter. Season to taste with salt and pepper. Set aside.

Put the lambs' tongues into a saucepan just large enough to hold them comfortably and add water to cover. Simmer until the tongues are tender, about 1–1½ hours. Add salt halfway through the cooking. Lift out and cool a little. Then skin the tongues and cut into lengthways 0.6 cm/¼ in thick slices. Return to the cooking liquid and keep warm.

Heat 1 tablespoon of the butter in a baking tin and sear the loin of lamb, turning to seal all over. Roast in a preheated, moderate oven (190°C/375°F/gas 5), topped with a large sprig of rosemary, for 20 minutes. The lamb should be pink. Remove from the oven, cover and keep warm.

Put the sweetbreads into a saucepan with salted water to cover and simmer, covered, for 15 minutes. Drain, cover with cold water. When cool remove any membranes and sauté the sweetbreads in the remaining 2 tablespoons of butter. Slice thinly, cover and keep warm.

Cut the kidneys into slices about 1 cm/½ in thick and sauté in the vegetable oil over moderately high heat for about 1 minute.

The garlic cloves can be cooked in the oven at the same time as the lamb. Wrap them in a piece of aluminium foil and put into the oven with the lamb. When the lamb is done, turn the oven up to moderately hot (200°C/400°F/gas 6) and cook the garlic cloves for about 30 minutes longer or until they are soft. Peel off the skins when cool enough to handle.

To serve, have ready four heated plates. Cut the lamb into 4 slices then cut the slices lengthways and fan them out onto the plates. Arrange the tongues, sweetbreads and kidneys round the lamb, then pour the warmed sauce round the meats. Garnish with the garlic cloves and sprigs of rosemary. Serve immediately accompanied by celeriac or spinach on a small plate.

WINE SUGGESTION: A St-Emilion.

VARIATION

POT POURRI OF LAMB WITH TARRAGON SAUCE

Alan Vikops has an interesting variation on the previous recipe, Meli-Melo, which he serves with a tarragon sauce. Instead of loin, he uses the fillet of a boned best end of neck, sliced into 4 and sautéed quickly in butter, about 4 minutes in all. Instead of sweetbreads he uses 2 pairs of lambs' brains which are peeled, blanched and cooked in lamb stock for about 8 minutes, then sliced and kept warm. He does not have the garlic cloves or rosemary as a garnish, instead uses two 5 cm/2 in square puff pastry cases which he stuffs with 8 sautéed and sliced lambs' kidneys.

The sauce is quite different. In a saucepan, combine 250 ml/8 fl oz dry white wine, 2 tablespoons tarragon vinegar, 1 tablespoon chopped shallots, and a few tarragon stalks and bring to a simmer. Simmer, uncovered, until the liquid is reduced by half. Add 1.1 L/2 pt hot lamb stock and continue to simmer uncovered until the liquid is reduced to 250 ml/8 fl oz. Strain, return the liquid to the saucepan and, when ready to serve, warm and beat in 3 tablespoons butter, cut into pieces. Keep the sauce warm. The tongues, simmered for 1–1½ hours in lamb stock, are sliced.

To serve, pour the sauce onto four heated plates. Put the stuffed pastry squares in the centre of the plates and surround with the lamb, tongues, and brains. Garnish with a sprig of tarragon. Serves 4.

PORK, KIDNEY AND CUCUMBER HOTPOT

Graham Flanagan greatly values traditional regional cooking which he feels is of real importance in a nation's cooking. It often needs updating, which he does while still keeping the true spirit of the dish.

SERVES 4

2 tablespoons butter
1 tablespoon vegetable oil
500 g/1 lb boneless pork, preferably loin, cut into 2.5 cm/1 in cubes
2 pork kidneys, cut into 1 cm/½ in slices
Flour for dredging
Salt
Freshly ground pepper
2 medium onions, finely chopped

250 g/8 oz tart green cooking apples, peeled, cored and cut into chunks
375 g/12 oz cucumber, unpeeled, cut into 2.5-3.5 cm/1-1½ in
Pinch dried sage, or 1 fresh sage leaf, chopped
1 bay leaf
1 tablespoon tomato purée
475 ml/16 fl oz brown stock

Dredge the pork cubes and kidney slices in flour seasoned with salt and pepper, shaking the meat to remove the excess.

Heat the butter and oil in a large, heavy frying pan and brown the meats lightly. Lift out the meats with a slotted spoon into a casserole. Add the onions to the frying pan and sauté over moderate heat until the onion is soft. Add the apples and cucumber and sauté for 1 minute longer. Transfer the vegetables to the casserole, season with salt and pepper and add the sage, bay leaf, tomato purée and stock, adding a little more stock if necessary, barely to cover. Cover and simmer over low heat for about 1 hour, or until the pork is tender.

WINE SUGGESTION: A red Rioja.

LOIN OF PORK WITH APPLE AND ONION PURÉE

Brian Prideaux-Brune of Plumber Manor is an unpretentious but highly original chef not interested in cooking whims and fashions. Cooks have long recognized the affinity between pork and apples. Here they become something very special though the recipe is essentially a simple one, easy to cook and taking little time. The chops absorb the flavour of the tart apples and sweet onions. The sauce, rich and unctuous, though served in healthily scanty portions, gives the completed dish a touch of luxury.

SERVES 4

4 tart green apples, such as Granny
   Smiths, peeled, cored and coarsely
   chopped
2 medium onions, chopped
Salt
Freshly ground pepper
4 tablespoons butter

12 thinly cut, boned pork loin chops
75 ml/3 fl oz dry vermouth,
   preferably Noilly Prat
300 ml/½ pt veal stock, or use
   chicken stock (see Basic Recipes,
   pages 10, 11)
150 ml/¼ pt double cream

Combine the apples and onions and 50 ml/2 fl oz water in a saucepan. Simmer, covered, until the apples and onions are both soft. Drain and discard the excess liquid. Mash the mixture to a purée with a fork or purée quickly in a food processor or blender. Season with salt and pepper.

Heat the butter in a large frying pan and sear the chops very quickly on both sides. Transfer the chops to a baking tin large enough to hold them in a single layer, and spread them with the apple and onion purée. Cook in a preheated, hot oven (230°C/450°F/gas 8) until done, about 7 minutes. Transfer the chops to a platter and keep them warm. Pour the vermouth into the baking tin on top of the stove and simmer over moderate heat, scraping up the brown bits. Add the stock and simmer until the liquid is reduced to about 125 ml/4 fl oz. Add the cream and simmer until it is lightly thickened. Taste for seasoning and add salt and pepper if necessary. Spoon the sauce onto four heated plates and arrange the pork chops on top.

WINE SUGGESTION: A Beaujolais.

GARNISHED PORK ESCALOPES

This recipe is another from Michael Collom. His cooking is consistently excellent and his aim is to put together the ingredients that will create the right harmony in a dish. He is open to new ideas but refuses to follow the whims of fashion, as this dish shows.

SERVES 6

4 eggs
125 g/4 oz grated Gruyère cheese
50 g/2 oz grated Parmesan cheese
Salt
Freshly ground pepper
⅛ teaspoon cayenne pepper
2 tablespoons butter
250 g/8 oz finely sliced mushrooms
125 g/4 oz lean ham, cut into
   julienne strips
50 ml/2 fl oz veal or chicken stock
   (see Basic Recipes, pages 10, 11)

6 pork escalopes, each weighing about
   175 g/6 oz
Flour
Oil for deep frying
Savoury rice (see Vegetables and
   Salads, page 192)

For the Garnish (optional):
Watercress sprigs

Break the eggs into a bowl, stir to mix and add the Gruyère and Parmesan cheeses, season with salt, pepper and cayenne. Set aside.

Heat the butter in a frying pan and sauté the mushrooms over moderately high heat until they have given up all their liquid, about 6 minutes. Add the ham and cook for 1 minute longer. Transfer the mixture to a small saucepan, pour in the stock and set aside.

Dredge the escalopes with flour seasoned with salt and pepper, shaking to remove the excess. In a large frying pan, heat about 5 cm/2 in oil. Dip the pork in the egg and cheese mixture and deep-fry in the oil until crisp and golden, turning once or twice, about 15 minutes over moderate heat. Drain on paper towels. Warm the ham and mushroom mixture.

Have ready the Savoury Rice. Serve the pork escalopes on top of a serving of rice with the ham and mushroom mixture at the side. Garnish, if liked, with sprigs of watercress.

WINE SUGGESTION: A Côtes-du-Rhône.

VENISON AND ORANGE STEW

Martin Bredda created this marvellous stew. It could hardly be easier to cook, or more delicious to eat. The recipe can be halved.

SERVES 14 to 16

4 tablespoons vegetable oil
375 g/12 oz sliced bacon, coarsely chopped
6 tablespoons finely chopped shallots
6 tablespoons tomato purée
1 L/1¾ pt dry white wine
1.7 L/3 pt brown stock
4 cloves garlic, very finely chopped
900 g/2 lb mushrooms, sliced
3 tablespoons juniper berries, crushed
Bouquet garni: 1 bay leaf, sprig thyme, 2 parsley sprigs tied with a piece of cotton

Grated rind of 1 lemon
3 oranges, well washed and halved, pips removed
2.7 kg/6 lb boneless shoulder venison, cut into 3.5 cm/1½ in cubes
Salt
Freshly ground pepper
Flour for dredging the venison

In a large heavy casserole or saucepan, heat 1 tablespoon of the oil and add the bacon and shallots. Sauté over moderate heat, for about 8 minutes. Add the tomato purée and stir well to mix. Add the wine, stock, garlic, mushrooms, juniper berries, bouquet garni, lemon rind and halved oranges. Bring the mixture to a boil, and simmer, stirring from time to time, for 20 minutes.

Season the venison with salt and pepper and dredge with the flour, shaking off the excess. Heat the remaining 3 tablespoons of the oil in a large frying pan and sear the venison cubes in it, in batches. Transfer to the casserole or saucepan, cover and cook in a preheated, hot oven (230°C/450°F/gas 8) for 1¾ hours, or until the meat is very tender. Serve with potatoes, or noodles and a green vegetable or salad.

WINE SUGGESTION: A Rioja.

VENISON WITH PEPPERY APRICOTS

This was one of Alan Casey's dishes that I most enjoyed when he was head chef at Culloden House.

SERVES 4

8 medallions (slices) venison, each weighing about 75 g/3 oz
8 tablespoons butter
4 tablespoons brandy
250 ml/8 fl oz game stock (see Basic Recipes, page 12), or brown stock
4 whole cloves
1 bay leaf
1 tablespoon redcurrant jelly
125 ml/4 fl oz double cream
Salt
Freshly ground pepper
16 dried apricots, soaked

Flatten the venison medallions to 0.6 cm/¼ in thickness. In a frying pan, heat 4 tablespoons of the butter and sauté the venison over fairly high heat, turning once, for about 3 minutes a side for rare, 4 minutes for medium rare. Pour 3 tablespoons of the brandy over the meat, and flame it. Remove the venison from the frying pan, cover and keep warm while making the sauce.

Into the frying pan pour the game stock, add the cloves, bay leaf and redcurrant jelly. Reduce to half, then stir in the cream and simmer until slightly thickened. Strain the sauce. Season to taste with salt and pepper and warm through.

Put the apricots, and the water in which they have been soaking, into a small saucepan and simmer them gently if they are at all hard. If they are soft, simply warm them through. Drain and coat them liberally with freshly ground black pepper. Sprinkle with the remaining tablespoon of brandy.

To serve, put 2 medallions of venison on each of four heated plates and pour the warm sauce over them. Garnish with the apricots.

WINE SUGGESTION: A Côtes-du-Rhône.

ROE DEER WITH SOUR CREAM AND CAPERS

Stephen Ross likes his dishes to be well flavoured with plenty of character and he particularly likes to cook with fine, local produce. This dish, like many others that he and chef Antony Pitt created in the Homewood Park kitchen, are the result of fine, or unusual ingredients stimulating creative talent. If the haunch of a young roe deer is not available use tenderloin or round of venison.

SERVES 6
1 small haunch roe deer
125 g/4 oz butter
1 small onion, finely chopped
1 rasher bacon, finely chopped
125 ml/4 fl oz dry white wine
125 ml/4 fl oz chicken stock (see
  Basic Recipes, page 10)

125 ml/4 fl oz lemon juice
Grated rind of 2 lemons
300 ml/½ pt sour cream
2 tablespoons capers
Salt
Freshly ground pepper

Have the venison cut into twelve 1 cm/½ in slices. In a frying pan, heat the butter and sauté the venison slices over fairly high heat, turning once, for about 1 minute a side. Remove to a serving dish, cover and keep warm.

Add the onion and bacon to the frying pan with the white wine and chicken stock and simmer, uncovered, to reduce by half. Add the lemon juice, grated lemon rind, sour cream and capers. Season to taste with salt and pepper. Put 2 slices of venison on each of six heated plates. Spoon the sauce over them and serve with rice or new potatoes.

WINE SUGGESTION: A red Rioja.

MEDALLIONS OF VENISON WITH GREEN PEPPERCORNS

Philip Burgess has a great respect for all types of food and he enjoys cooking with sophisticated as well as simple ingredients. His aim is to produce dishes that are not disguised with heavy garnishes or sauces, and where natural flavours emerge from the cooking at their peak. Like all truly perceptive chefs he has a real appreciation of what he calls peasant-type cookery, and takes a deep interest in working out modern recipes for something as homely as tripe or braised oxtails. He feels it is wrong to neglect these down-to-earth dishes.

SERVES 4

For the Marinade:
1 clove garlic, crushed
1 medium onion, chopped
1 medium carrot, scraped and
    chopped
475 ml/16 fl oz dry white wine
1½ tablespoons olive oil
1 bay leaf
Salt
Freshly ground pepper

For the Venison:
750 g/1½ lb boneless venison loin,
    cut into 8 slices

Flour for dredging the venison
1 tablespoon vegetable oil
4 tablespoons butter
50 ml/2 fl oz dry white wine
1 tablespoon green peppercorns,
    crushed
250 ml/8 fl oz double cream
125 ml/4 fl oz lightly thickened rich
    brown stock
Salt
Freshly ground pepper

Combine all the ingredients for the marinade in an earthenware, stainless steel or enamel bowl, add the venison and refrigerate for 24 hours.

Lift the venison out of the marinade and pat dry with paper towels. Lightly flatten the slices to about 1 cm/½ in thick. Dredge with flour, shaking to remove the excess. In a large, heavy frying pan, heat the oil and butter and sauté the venison for 5–7 minutes, turning occasionally. The meat should remain pink inside. Lift out of the frying pan onto a plate, cover and keep warm.

Pour the excess fat from the pan, add the wine, peppercorns and cream and reduce over moderate heat by half. Add the brown stock and any juices that may have collected on the plate with the venison, and simmer until the sauce is slightly thickened. Taste for seasoning and add salt and pepper if necessary. Arrange 2 medallions of venison on each of four heated plates and pour the sauce over them. Serve with rice or potatoes and a green vegetable.

WINE SUGGESTION: A Côtes-du-Rhône.

NOISETTE OF VENISON WITH LAVERBREAD AND ORANGE SAUCE

Laverbread, a Welsh speciality, is made from purple laver (*Porphyra umbilicalis*) which looks very like sea lettuce except that it is purple-red or brown instead of green. It is cooked down and sold canned in speciality and health food shops and is eaten as a garnish, either hot or cold, with seafood, meat or poultry. It makes a delicious, fresh-tasting and delicate sauce for the richly-flavoured venison. Cooked spinach, very thoroughly drained and chopped, can be used instead, as laverbread is not always easy to find. Tim Cumming developed this unusual dish.

SERVES 6

1 kg/2¼ lb boned and tied saddle of venison, preferably roe deer	Grated zest of 1 orange
6 rashers bacon	125 ml/4 fl oz orange juice
	Grated zest of 1 lemon
For the Sauce:	1 tablespoon lemon juice
250 g/8 oz laverbread or 500 g/1 lb spinach	2 tablespoons butter
	Freshly ground pepper
	Salt

Wrap the venison in the bacon and roast in a baking tin in a preheated, hot oven (220°C/425°F/gas 7) for 10-12 minutes. It should remain pink in the middle. Remove and discard the bacon and cut the venison into 6 slices. Cover and keep warm.

If using laverbread, which is already cooked, put it into a saucepan with all the other ingredients and heat it through, stirring to mix. Season it generously with black pepper. Taste and, if necessary, add a little salt.

If using spinach, wash and trim away any coarse stems. Drop the spinach into a large saucepan filled with briskly boiling, salted water, bring back to a boil and cook for 4 minutes. Drain and refresh in cold water. Drain again very thoroughly and chop. Put into a saucepan with all the other sauce ingredients exactly as for laverbread.

Make a layer of sauce on each of six heated plates and put a noisette of venison on top. Serve immediately.

WINE SUGGESTION: A red Rioja.

MEDALLIONS OF VENISON IN GREEN PEPPERCORN JELLY

Julian Waterer, who was head chef at Greywalls Hotel in Scotland, great venison country, serves this as a starter, attractive in a meal where the main course is fish. I find it makes a perfect main course for two or three people for a warm weather lunch or dinner. It is well flavoured and original in concept like all Julian's recipes.

SERVES 6 as a starter, 2 or 3 as a main course

For the Jelly:
600 ml/1 pt clarified game stock, or beef stock (see Basic Recipes, pages 11, 12)
50 ml/2 fl oz dry red wine
50 ml/2 fl oz tawny port
1 envelope (1 tablespoon) unflavoured gelatine
1 tablespoon red wine vinegar
2 tablespoons sugar

For the Venison and Sauce:
375 g/12 oz boned and tied saddle of venison
1½ teaspoons green peppercorns
3 bunches watercress
Salt
Freshly ground pepper
6 oatcakes (see Basic Recipes, page 19)

Pour the stock, red wine and port into a medium-sized saucepan and reduce to 475 ml/16 fl oz over moderate heat. Sprinkle the gelatine over 50 ml/2 fl oz cold water and stir into the hot stock, simmer for a minute or two to dissolve.

Combine the vinegar and sugar in a small saucepan and simmer until the mixture is syrupy. Stir into the stock and simmer over low heat, stirring, until dissolved. Cool.

Roast the venison in a baking tin in a preheated, hot oven (220°C/425°F/gas 7) for 8–10 minutes. It should be pink inside. Remove from the oven and cool.

If serving as a starter, pour a thin layer of stock into six small (about 250 g/8 oz) ramekins or soufflé moulds and refrigerate until set. Sprinkle with the green peppercorns. Cut the venison into 6 slices and put a slice into each mould. Pour in the rest of the prepared stock to cover the venison and refrigerate for at least 2 hours.

While the jelly is setting, make the watercress sauce. Wash the watercress and remove and discard the tough stems. Put the watercress into a blender or food processor and process to a purée. Transfer to a bowl and season to taste with salt and pepper.

To serve, place an oatcake on each of six plates. Make a border of watercress purée round each oatcake. Unmould the jellied venison and place one on each oatcake.

If serving as a main course for 2 or 3, either serve 2 or 3 venison moulds on larger plates per person, or make them in larger moulds, cutting the venison into thicker slices. If liked, pour the watercress sauce onto the plates and serve the oatcakes separately. The crunchy flavour complements the venison.

WINE SUGGESTION: A red Rioja.

RABBIT

Rabbit is an ideal meat from today's dietary point of view. It is lean, high in protein, with less fat and cholesterol than chicken or beef, yet it has been singularly neglected for years. Its popularity is now increasing and butchers all have rabbit, either cut into serving portions, or whole. Fresh domestic rabbits are sometimes available in butcher's shops. These are of very high quality, and sometimes a member of the kitchen staff of a country house hotel will raise a few domestic bunnies as a sideline. They are tender with white flesh, and some of the best dishes I have eaten have been the rabbit dishes of inspired young chefs. I have collected the ones I have enjoyed most.

ROAST SADDLE OF RABBIT WITH MUSTARD SAUCE

Nick Gill is the originator of this well-flavoured, uncomplicated dish, a delight for all lovers of rabbit dishes.

SERVES 2

500 g/1 lb saddle of rabbit, thoroughly thawed if frozen
Salt
Freshly ground pepper
½ teaspoon dried thyme
2 rashers bacon, halved crosswise
1 carrot, chopped
1 onion, chopped
1 stalk celery, chopped
3 cloves garlic, very finely chopped
1 bay leaf, crumbled

4 parsley stalks
250 ml/8 fl oz dry white wine
1 tablespoon vegetable oil
125 ml/4 fl oz double cream or fresh white cheese (see Basic Recipes, page 24)
1 tablespoon *moutarde de Meaux*, or other French coarse, grain mustard

For the Garnish:
Watercress sprigs

Remove as much as possible of the thin, silvery skin covering the top of the saddle of rabbit. Season the rabbit with salt, pepper and half the dried thyme. Cover the top with the bacon slices.

In a shallow, flameproof casserole just large enough to hold the rabbit, make a bed of the carrot, onion, celery, garlic, bay leaf, parsley stalks and the rest of the thyme. Pour 125 ml/4 fl oz of the dry white wine over the vegetables and put the rabbit, bacon-side up, on the vegetables. Brush the rabbit with oil and roast it, uncovered, in the middle of a preheated, very hot oven (240°C/

475°F/gas 9) for 10 minutes. Add the remaining wine and roast the rabbit for 10 minutes longer, or until it is tender. Lift out the rabbit and keep it warm. Transfer the casserole to the top of the stove and bring the contents to a boil over moderate heat. Reduce the liquid by half. Add the cream and continue to cook the sauce until it has thickened slightly. If using fresh white cheese, simply add and heat it through. Strain the sauce through a fine sieve into a saucepan and season with salt and pepper.

Remove and discard the bacon from the rabbit. Remove the two fillets, each in one piece, and cut them at a 45° angle into 1 cm/½ in slices. Reform the slices into two fillets and return them to the saddle bones. Transfer the rabbit to a heated platter. Bring the sauce to a simmer over moderate heat. Off the heat, stir in the mustard. Pour the sauce over the rabbit and serve garnished with watercress sprigs.

WINE SUGGESTION: Burgundy, either a Côte de Beaune or Côte de Nuits.

VARIATION
Pierre Chevillard has his own version of the dish.

SERVES 2

2 large rabbit legs, each weighing about 375 g/12 oz
Salt
Freshly ground pepper
4 tablespoons butter
2 tablespoons shallots, finely chopped
1 tablespoon *moutarde de Meaux*, or other French coarse-grain mustard

50 ml/2 fl oz dry white wine
50 ml/2 fl oz veal or chicken stock (see Basic Recipes, pages 10, 11)
50 ml/2 fl oz double cream, or fresh white cheese (see Basic Recipes, page 24)
Cooked spinach leaves

Season the rabbit with salt and pepper. In a heavy frying pan just large enough to hold the rabbit legs, heat 2 tablespoons of the butter. Add the rabbit, reduce the heat to low and cook the rabbit, basting it constantly for about 12–15 minutes, or until it is tender. Remove the rabbit legs, cover and keep warm.

Rinse out and dry the frying pan. Add the shallots, mustard and wine to the pan and reduce until the wine has evaporated. Add the veal or chicken stock and the cream. Bring to a boil, lower the heat and cook for 1 minute. Add the remaining 2 tablespoons of butter, shaking the pan until the butter has dissolved.

The main bone can be removed from each leg, but leave the bone in if preferred. Put each leg on a heated plate, surround it by the cooked spinach, and pour the sauce over the rabbit.

RABBIT AND PRUNE TERRINE

This unusual terrine makes a pleasant main course for lunch or a summer dinner served with salads. It can also be served as a starter. It is another of the rabbit dishes invented by Pierre Chevillard.

SERVES 10 to 12 as a starter, 6 as a main course

2 × 900 g/2 lb rabbits	Salt
750 g/1½ lb lean, boneless pork, coarsely chopped	Freshly ground pepper
	50 g/2 oz pistachio nuts, shelled
750 g/1½ lb belly of pork	250 g/8 oz pitted prunes

Bone the rabbits, cutting off as much meat as possible. Chop the rabbit meat coarsely and combine it in a food processor with the pork and 500 g/1 lb of the pork belly, chopped. Process just long enough to mince the meats, or put the meats through a meat grinder. Season to taste with salt and pepper and add the pistachio nuts, mixing them in thoroughly.

Line a 2 L/3½ pt terrine or loaf tin with the 250 g/8 oz pork belly cut into strips, allowing the strips to overlap the terrine. Make a layer of half the rabbit and pork mixture. Make a layer of the prunes in two parallel rows and finish with the rest of the meat. Fold the pork belly strips over the terrine, cover with a lid or with aluminium foil, and put into a baking tin with hot water to come about halfway up the sides of the terrine. Bake in a preheated, moderate oven (180°C/350°F/gas 4) for 1-1½ hours, or until the meats have shrunk slightly from the sides of the terrine. Remove the terrine from the oven and let it cool. Refrigerate until the juices have set. Unmould the terrine and slice.

WINE SUGGESTION: A Burgundy, either Côte de Beaune or Côte de Nuits.

RABBIT STEW MALTAISE

Rabbit becomes something special when cooked according to this recipe, the creation of David Nicholls. His culinary philosophy demands simplicity and the freshest and best produce and he cares a great deal about presentation, as the garnishing of this dish proves.

SERVES 4

For the Marinade:
2 large Spanish onions, finely chopped
475 ml/16 fl oz dry red wine
3 cloves garlic, crushed
4 parsley sprigs
1 teaspoon peppercorns
Sprig thyme
2 bay leaves

For the Rabbit:
1 × 1.1–1.4 kg/2½–3 lb rabbit, cut
  into 8 serving pieces
Salt
Freshly ground pepper

3 tablespoons vegetable oil
475 ml/16 fl oz veal or beef stock (see
  Basic Recipes, page 11)

For the Garnish:
4 small heads purple broccoli
  (calabrese) freshly cooked
4 large, whole, unpeeled cloves garlic,
  sautéed in butter
500 g/1 lb tomatoes, peeled, seeded
  and quartered
Grated zest of 1 orange and 1 lemon
2 tablespoons finely chopped parsley

Combine all the ingredients for the marinade in a large bowl and add the rabbit pieces. Cover and refrigerate for 48 hours, turning the pieces 2 or 3 times.

Lift out the rabbit pieces and pat them dry with paper towels. Season with salt and pepper. In a heavy frying pan, heat the oil and sauté the rabbit until lightly browned all over. Transfer the rabbit to a heavy casserole and pour in the marinade and the veal or beef stock, bring to a simmer, cover and cook in a preheated, moderate oven (180°C/350°F/gas 4) for 2 hours, or until the rabbit is tender. Lift out the rabbit pieces to a heated dish, cover and keep warm. Over moderately high heat, reduce the liquid in the casserole until it is slightly thickened. Taste for seasoning and add salt and pepper if necessary. Strain the sauce and discard the solids. Return the sauce to the casserole and heat it through. Arrange the rabbit pieces on four warm plates and spoon the sauce over them. Arrange the warm broccoli and a clove of garlic beside the rabbit and the quartered tomatoes on the other side. Sprinkle with the orange and lemon zest, then with the parsley.

WINE SUGGESTION: Côte de Beaune or Côte de Nuits.

Vegetables and Salads

Today's chefs have a keen appreciation of vegetables. They dislike the old-fashioned concept of a plate with heaped vegetable servings jostling for space with meat, poultry or fish. They want vegetables to be esteemed in their own right and presented gracefully to the diner. A favourite presentation is a selection of vegetables arranged on a small round or crescent-shaped plate served with the main course. These are often selections of primeurs, tiny little carrots still with their tufted green tops, little new potatoes unpeeled but for a strip round the middle, baby white turnips, tender mangetout, skinny little green beans, baby peas, delicate green asparagus tips, broccoli sprigs and cauliflower florets all at their freshest, youngest best, three or four served neatly arranged.

Many chefs wanting to please vegetarian diners have devised attractive dishes that can be served both to vegetarians and non-vegetarians alike as main courses, and there are more elaborate vegetable dishes that enhance the main course they are served with.

Vegetable purées and purées combining root vegetables are great favourites with today's chefs. They like to present a selection of purées such as beetroots, carrots or broccoli in flavourful heaps separately, or sometimes on main course plates. Potatoes with parsnips, or potatoes with Jerusalem artichokes liven up routine tastes.

There is also a whole new attitude to salads. They can be served as first courses or as main courses, contain meat, poultry, fish or shellfish, and are served warm as well as chilled with a variety of greens and a variety of dressings using different oils and vinegars. There is a whole new dimension of food, taking advantage of today's magnificent abundance.

PURÉED BEETROOTS

Simon Hopkinson serves beetroot purée with roast teal, a most unusual and exciting combination. Teal is a small wild duck not usually available, however the beetroot purée is good with any wild duck, and I have found it agreeable with domestic duckling and other poultry. Beetroots also look very attractive in combination with other vegetables. Serve the purée with mashed potatoes and carrot purée in three neat heaps on the plate with plainly cooked poultry. If liked a gravy or sauce can be served separately.

SERVES 6

900 g/2 lb fresh beetroots	**Freshly ground pepper**
Salt	**2 tablespoons butter, cut into pieces**

Scrub, but do not peel, the beetroots. Trim the stalks. Put into a saucepan of boiling, salted water to cover, and simmer, covered, until tender, about 30 minutes. Drain, cool and rub off the skins. Chop coarsely and purée in a blender or food processor. Return to the rinsed out and dried saucepan, season to taste with salt and pepper, add the butter and heat through, stirring to mix.

PARSNIP AND POTATO PURÉE

Enliven winter dishes with this purée while waiting for the delicious tiny primeurs of spring. The mixture gives bland vegetables a lift.

SERVES 6
500 g/1 lb boiling potatoes, peeled
   and halved
500 g/1 lb parsnips, peeled and
   quartered

Salt
4 tablespoons butter
Freshly ground pepper

In a large saucepan, combine the potatoes and parsnips. Pour in enough cold water to cover, add 1 teaspoon salt, bring to a boil and simmer until the vegetables are tender, about 20 minutes. Drain, cover and shake over low heat for about a minute then purée in a blender or food processor with the butter. Season with salt and pepper and serve with any meat or poultry.

VARIATION
Instead of parsnips, scrape and slice 500 g/1 lb Jerusalem artichokes and cook with the potatoes. Purée as above. Serves 6.

CARROT, BROCCOLI, BRUSSELS SPROUTS AND OTHER PURÉES

Carrots can be puréed in the same way as beetroots. They should be scraped and sliced, then cooked until tender in boiling, salted water. Very young carrots will take about 10 minutes, older ones up to 30 minutes.

Both broccoli and Brussels sprouts are delicious as purées. They seem to have a new and different flavour in this form, and they add a special touch to meat and poultry dishes as their flavour is robust. Many other vegetables are also good puréed. They are all cooked in the same way and puréed in a blender or food processor.

Green peas, green beans and cauliflower florets all take between 5 and 8 minutes in boiling, salted water. Broccoli and Brussels sprouts take about 8 minutes. Check the vegetables when cooking so as not to overcook.

If any of the vegetables seem watery, drain them in a sieve for about 10 minutes then reheat with a little butter to bind them. Vegetables with skins or fibres can be rubbed through a large sieve for a smooth purée then reheated with a little butter. Green peas need this extra step.

John Hornsby, whose cooking I enjoyed when he was head chef at the Castle Hotel in Taunton, Somerset, served two purées, spinach and beetroot with pheasant and other feathered game, and with duckling.

Robert Jones, of Ston Easton Park, serves onion purée with spring lamb, a delicious combination. Young turnips, cooked until tender, puréed and drained in a sieve, then mixed with about a quarter of their volume of potato to give them body, are also good with lamb. Finish them with a little butter if liked.

Julian Waterer serves a leek purée and fresh peaches, lightly poached, with lamb. The combination is equally good with veal or chicken breasts.

Robert Gardiner serves poached cucumber and new potatoes with poached salmon, and Denis Woodtli likes mint with his green beans. I find their ideas stimulatingly imaginative.

CARROT PUDDINGS WITH FRESH HERB SAUCE

Pierre Chevillard has devised this recipe for carrot puddings, to be served either as a vegetable or as a first course. The herb sauce complements the flavour of the carrots.

SERVES 6

750 g/1½ lb young carrots, scraped and thinly sliced
1.4 L/2½ pt chicken stock (see Basic Recipes, page 10)
½ teaspoon sugar
Salt
1 tablespoon olive oil
125 g/4 oz mushrooms, chopped
Freshly ground pepper
4 large eggs, lightly beaten
250 g/8 oz grated Gruyère cheese
3 tablespoons chopped fresh chervil, or 1 tablespoon dried, or use chopped parsley

For the Sauce:
250 ml/8 fl oz chicken stock
1 tablespoon finely chopped shallot or spring onion
250 ml/8 fl oz double cream or fresh white cheese (see Basic Recipes, page 24)
1 tablespoon butter, softened at room temperature
1 tablespoon each chopped fresh chervil, chives, tarragon and parsley, or other fresh herbs
Salt
Freshly ground pepper

Combine the carrots, stock, sugar and salt in a large saucepan and simmer, covered, until the carrots are very tender, about 25 minutes. Let the mixture cool to lukewarm then remove the carrots and purée them in a blender or food processor. Return the purée to the liquid and stir to mix. Pour into a large bowl.

Heat the oil in a frying pan and sauté the mushrooms with salt and pepper to taste over moderately high heat for about 5 minutes, or until all the liquid has evaporated. Cool the mushrooms, then stir them into the purée. Add the eggs, cheese and chervil, mixing well. Taste for seasoning and add salt and pepper if necessary. Pour the mixture into six buttered 175 g/6 oz ramekins and bake in a preheated, moderate oven (180°C/350°F/gas 4) for 30 minutes, or until a knife inserted in the centre comes out clean. Let the puddings cool for a few minutes, then run a knife round the inside of each ramekin and unmould onto six warmed plates.

While the puddings are baking, make the sauce. Combine the chicken stock and shallot in a saucepan and reduce over moderately high heat to 50 ml/2 fl oz. Stir in the cream and simmer until the mixture has thickened lightly, or stir in the fresh white cheese and warm through. Pour through a sieve into a bowl, stir in the butter and herbs, season to taste with salt and pepper and pour over the puddings.

BEETROOTS WITH CELERIAC SAUCE

Michael Coaker, head chef at The Britannia Hotel's restaurant in London, says vegetables should never be dull, and takes delight in creating new vegetable dishes. This is good to eat and anything but dull.

SERVES 4

For the Beetroots:
375 g/12 oz coarsely chopped,
   cooked beetroots
3 tablespoons butter
50 ml/2 fl oz double cream, or fresh
   white cheese (see Basic Recipes,
   page 24) (optional)
Salt
Freshly ground pepper

For the Sauce:
175 g/6 oz celeriac, puréed
2 tablespoons double cream, or fresh
   white cheese (see Basic Recipes,
   page 24) (optional)
1 tablespoon butter
250 ml/8 fl oz chicken stock, about
   (see Basic Recipes, page 10)
1 teaspoon lemon juice

In a food processor or blender, combine the beetroots, butter and double cream or fresh white cheese, if using, and process to a purée. Season to taste with salt and pepper and transfer to a small saucepan. Set aside.

In a saucepan, combine all the ingredients for the sauce. (The cream or fresh white cheese may be left out.) Stir to mix and heat gently. The sauce should be as thick as double cream. Thin with chicken stock if necessary. Keep the sauce warm.

Heat the beetroot purée. It should be thick enough to hold its shape in a spoon. Pour the sauce onto four warm plates. Mould the purée with tablespoons into quenelles and put on top of the sauce.

MUSHROOMS WITH FENNEL

This unusual and simple dish comes from John Evans. It can be served as a vegetable accompaniment to any plainly cooked meat or poultry, or as a vegetarian main course. John created the dish after gathering mushrooms the morning after a rainy night. It gave him the special appreciation of using the fresh grown vegetables and herbs in which he delights.

SERVES 2 to 3 as a main course, 4 to 6 as a vegetable course

7 tablespoons butter
3 tablespoons plain flour
250 ml/8 fl oz milk
125 g/4 oz onions, finely chopped
250 g/8 oz fennel bulb, peeled and
    finely chopped
2 tablespoons finely chopped parsley
500 g/1 lb mushrooms, chopped

1 tablespoon chopped fennel fronds
Salt
Freshly ground pepper
⅛ teaspoon freshly grated nutmeg

For the Garnish:
Fennel fronds

Heat 3 tablespoons of the butter in a small, heavy saucepan. Stir in the flour and cook over very low heat without letting the mixture colour for 2 minutes. Off the heat, gradually stir in the milk. When the mixture is smooth return it to the heat and simmer, stirring from time to time, over low heat for 5 minutes. The sauce will be very thick. Set aside.

In a medium-sized, heavy frying pan, heat the rest of the butter. Add the onion, fennel, parsley, mushrooms and fennel fronds. Season to taste with salt and pepper, add the nutmeg, cover and simmer over moderate heat for 8 minutes, or until the vegetables are tender. Stir in the reserved sauce and simmer over low heat for 1 or 2 minutes to heat through. For a vegetarian main course, serve on a bed of rice and garnish with fennel fronds.

MUSHROOM AND QUAIL EGG TARTLETS

Nicholas Knight, the young head chef at Master's Restaurant in Kensington, London, puts his imagination, combined with his cooking expertise, to work to produce dishes that are simple to cook but complex in flavour and texture. He uses his considerable artistry in the preparation of his dishes. This one, for example, is positively pretty to look at with poached quails' eggs nestling together in tartlet shells. Quails' eggs are now readily available but handling the tiny things requires what I call good hands which not all of us are blessed with, especially when we are in a hurry. I've made the tartlets using ordinary hens' eggs and it works perfectly well. It is a good dish for non-meat eaters, and makes a satisfying main course for lunch. The tarts also make a good cocktail, buffet or appetizer dish made with 7 cm/3 in tart shells and 4 quails' eggs or 1 hen's egg per tart.

SERVES 4

4 × 10 cm/4 in tartlet shells made with shortcrust pastry and baked blind (see Basic Recipes, page 17)
2 tablespoons butter
6 tablespoons very finely chopped shallots
900 g/2 lb mushrooms, finely chopped
Salt
Freshly ground pepper
32 quails' eggs, or 8 hens' eggs
Vinegar

For the Sauce:
250 ml/8 fl oz chicken stock (see Basic Recipes, page 10)
250 ml/8 fl oz double cream or fresh white cheese (see Basic Recipes, page 24)
2 tablespoons very finely chopped chives, or more to taste
Salt
Freshly ground pepper

Make the tartlet shells and set them aside.

In a large frying pan, heat the butter and add the shallots. Cook over very low heat until they are softened. Add the mushrooms and cook over moderate heat, stirring from time to time, until they have given up all their liquid, about 5 minutes. Season to taste with salt and pepper. Let the mixture cool, then spread it over the bottom of the tartlet shells.

If using quails' eggs, have ready a shallow dish of vinegar large enough to hold all of them at the same time. Break the eggs into the vinegar then carefully pour the contents into a large frying pan of briskly boiling, salted water, over high heat. As soon as the water returns to a boil, remove from the heat and lift out the eggs with a slotted spoon and slide them into a bowl of cold water. Set aside until ready to use. If using hens' eggs, break then slide them into a saucepan of boiling water mixed with 1 tablespoon vinegar to each 1.1 L/1 quart of water. Simmer for 3–4 minutes, spooning the white over the yolks as the eggs cook. Lift out into cold water and set aside.

To make the sauce, put the stock, cream and chives into a saucepan and simmer until it is reduced to a light coating consistency. If using fresh white cheese, simply whisk in to mix and heat through. Season to taste.

To serve, put 8 quails' eggs or 2 hens' eggs into each of the tartlet shells and heat through in a preheated, moderate oven (180°C/350°F/gas 4) for 3–4 minutes. Coat lightly with the warm sauce. Serve with a green salad or an assortment of vegetables served on a small separate plate.

CARROT AND GREEN PEPPERCORN SAUCE

This unusual sauce is another of Nicholas Knight's versatile recipes. He uses it as a coating sauce for steak or lamb chops. It is also good with plainly cooked rabbit or poultry, and I have enjoyed it with a bland fish like cod, and a vegetable like broccoli. It is not time-consuming, and when I use fresh white cheese instead of cream it is also pleasantly low in fat.

SERVES 4 generously

250 g/8 oz carrots, peeled and thinly sliced
350 ml/12 fl oz milk, about
2 egg yolks
250 ml/8 fl oz double cream or fresh white cheese (see Basic Recipes, page 24)

Salt
1 tablespoon green peppercorns in brine, drained

Put the carrots into a medium-sized saucepan and pour in enough milk to cover. Bring to a simmer and cook, partially covered, over low heat until the carrots are tender, about 20 minutes. Drain and discard any milk. Purée the carrots in a blender or food processor. Rinse out and dry the saucepan and return the carrot purée to it.

In a bowl, combine the egg yolks and cream or fresh white cheese. Whisk into the carrot purée over low heat and cook, whisking for a few minutes until the sauce is light and fluffy. Season to taste with salt and stir in the green peppercorns. Coat the steak with the sauce, or use to coat lamb chops, poultry, fish or green vegetables.

STUFFED POTATOES

These potatoes are an interesting variation on the usual stuffed, baked potato. Chef Vaughan Archer created them when he needed a lighter version of stuffed potatoes to accompany steak or other meat or poultry dishes. Use your favourite vegetables for the stuffing.

SERVES 2 to 4

2 medium-sized potatoes, each
  weighing about 150 g/5 oz
250 g/8 oz cooked mixed vegetables
  (carrot, celery, green beans, white
  turnips, courgettes, etc.)
2 teaspoons finely chopped truffle
  (optional)

2 teaspoons beaten egg
Salt
Freshly ground pepper
2 tablespoons butter

Peel the potatoes and trim if necessary to a neater shape. A roughly cylindrical potato is the best choice. Using an apple corer, make a hole through the centre of the potato, then simmer in boiling , salted water for 5 minutes. Drain. Mix the vegetables with the truffle, if using, the beaten egg and salt and pepper and stuff firmly into the potatoes. Melt the butter in a small baking tin, roll the potatoes in the butter then bake in a preheated, hot oven (220°C/425°F/gas 7) for about 20 minutes, or until tender. Cut each potato into 6 slices.

VEGETABLE-STUFFED ONION CUPS

This is another of the delectable vegetable dishes created by head chef Vaughan Archer.

SERVES 4

4 medium-sized Spanish onions,
  about 7 cm/3 in in diameter
Chicken stock (see Basic Recipes, page
  10)
4 small carrots, trimmed, scraped and
  cut into 2.5 cm/1 in pieces
4 small turnips, peeled and quartered
4 small courgettes, trimmed and cut
  into 2.5 cm/1 in pieces

125 g/4 oz thin green beans trimmed
  and cut into 3.5 cm/1½ in pieces
8 mangetout sliced into 3 diagonally
4 baby sweetcorn tips, each about
  2.5 cm/1 in
Butter

Peel the onions and trim the root end. Slice off the top of each onion and, using a small serrated spoon, scoop out the flesh leaving a solid shell of 2 or 3 layers. Use the scooped out onion in a soup or stew. Put the onions into a shallow saucepan or frying pan that has a lid. They should fit snugly. Pour in enough stock to come about halfway up the onions, cover and poach until the onions are tender, about 45 minutes. Test with a toothpick or skewer for tenderness.

While the onions are cooking, cook the vegetables in boiling, salted water until they are tender but still crisp. It is better to cook them separately, then divide them into four portions. As soon as the onions are done, lift them out of the poaching liquid and keep them warm. Toss each portion of vegetables in a little butter and fill the onion cups. Serve immediately.

SAVOURY RICE

Michael Collom is head chef at The Priory Hotel in Bath, Avon, and likes to serve this rice dish with his Garnished Pork Escalopes (page 172). I enjoy it with the pork dish, and also with any dish served with rice.

SERVES 6

2 tablespoons butter
2 tablespoons very finely chopped shallots, or spring onions
25 g/1 oz chopped sweet red pepper
500 g/1 lb long grain rice
1 L/1¾ pt chicken stock (see Basic Recipes, page 10)

⅛ teaspoon saffron threads, ground
Salt
Freshly ground pepper
Sprig fresh thyme
1 bay leaf
65 g/2½ oz raisins

In a 2 L/3½ pt flameproof casserole, heat the butter and sauté the shallots and red pepper until they are tender but not browned. Add the rice and cook, stirring, over very low heat for 2–3 minutes. Pour in the chicken stock, saffron, salt and pepper to taste, thyme and bay leaf. Bring to a simmer, cover and cook in a preheated, moderate oven (180°C/350°F/gas 4) until the rice is tender and all the liquid absorbed, about 20 minutes. If preferred, cook on top of the stove over very low heat. While the rice is cooking, soak the raisins in warm water. Drain and add to the cooked rice.

CASSEROLE OF GREEN VEGETABLES

Peter Jackson loves vegetables, especially fresh green ones. This is one of his favourite ways of serving a medley of green vegetables to accompany meat or poultry dishes.

SERVES 4

125 g/4 oz broccoli florets
75 g/3 oz baby peas
50 g/2 oz green beans (haricots vert) cut into 1 cm/½ in pieces
175 g/6 oz sliced courgettes

50 g/2 oz mangetout, sliced diagonally
2 tablespoons butter
Salt
Freshly ground pepper

Cook the vegetables separately in boiling, salted water until crisply tender. Drain and rinse quickly in cold water to set the colour. In a saucepan, melt the butter and toss the courgettes, then add the other vegetables. Season with salt and pepper and serve hot on small side plates.

BUTTERED LEEKS

This is a very simple and quick way to cook leeks, keeping all their delicate flavour and texture. Serve as a green vegetable.

SERVES 6

4 tablespoons butter
6 medium-sized leeks, trimmed,
    thoroughly washed and coarsely
    chopped

Salt
Freshly ground pepper

Melt the butter in a large frying pan that has a lid. Add the leeks, season with salt and pepper and stir to mix. Cover and cook over moderate heat for about 5 minutes, or until the leeks are tender and still crisp. Do not let them brown.

STUFFED, GARNISHED ARTICHOKE HEARTS

Michael Collom has found an increasing number of guests who are vegetarian, and has created dishes to please them. These stuffed artichoke hearts are pleasant for non-meat eaters but also make an ideal dinner party first course, as they can be made ahead of time except for the last minute egg white and cheese topping.

SERVES 6

2 tablespoons butter
2 tablespoons very finely chopped
    shallots or spring onions
Sprig fresh thyme, chopped, or ⅛
    teaspoon dried
250 g/8 oz mushrooms, finely
    chopped

Salt
Freshly ground pepper
6 large, cooked artichoke hearts
6 egg whites
175 g/6 oz grated Cheddar cheese

In a frying pan, heat the butter and sauté the shallots, thyme and mushrooms over moderately high heat for about 5 minutes, or until the mushrooms have given up most of their moisture. Season with salt and pepper. Fill the artichoke hearts with the mixture, and arrange them on a baking sheet.

When ready to cook, beat the egg whites with a pinch of salt until they stand in firm peaks. Fold in half the cheese and spoon the mixture on top of the artichoke hearts. Sprinkle with the rest of the cheese then bake in a preheated, moderately hot oven (200°C/400°F/gas 6) for 10–15 minutes or until the tops are golden brown. Serve with a green salad as a vegetarian main course, or as a first course.

ASPARAGUS TIPS IN CHIVE SAUCE

This is another of Michael Collom's attractive vegetarian dishes that can be enjoyed both as a vegetarian main course or a first course to lunch or dinner. For heartier appetites serve double portions as a main course.

SERVES 6

250 g/8 oz puff pastry (see Basic Recipes, page 15)
Egg wash made with 1 egg yolk mixed with 1 teaspoon water
24 cooked green or white asparagus tips

125 ml/4 fl oz yoghurt
125 ml/4 fl oz whipping cream
1 tablespoon very finely chopped chives
Salt
Freshly ground pepper

Roll out the puff pastry and cut it into six 15 × 10 cm/6 × 4 in rectangles. Place on a baking sheet, brush with egg wash, and if there are any scraps of pastry left over cut them into small decorative shapes and decorate the tops of the pastry pieces. Refrigerate for 1 hour then bake in a preheated, hot oven (220°C/425°F/gas 7) for about 15 minutes or until risen and golden brown. Place on a wire rack to cool. Split in half and put the bottom half on each of six warmed plates. Warm the asparagus tips and put four onto each of the pastry pieces. Put the other half of the pastry on top.

While the pastry is baking, make the sauce. In a small saucepan, combine the yoghurt, cream, chives, and salt and pepper to taste, and heat gently. Pour the sauce round the pastry and serve immediately.

SAVOURY AVOCADO CHEESECAKE

Margaret Brown, has become an expert on early English, particularly Elizabethan and Georgian, cooking. This modern recipe, her own creation, is a delicious departure from her principal area of interest. It can be served as a first course, and also makes a fine vegetarian lunch dish.

SERVES 12 as a starter, 6 as a main course

6 tablespoons butter
125 g/4 oz cream cracker crumbs
4 teaspoons grated lemon rind
Salt
Freshly ground pepper
2 envelopes (2 tablespoons) unflavoured gelatine
3 large, ripe avocados
3 tablespoons lemon juice
3 large egg yolks
250 g/8 oz cream cheese
1 tablespoon snipped fresh chives

1 teaspoon chopped mixed parsley, tarragon and chervil, or ½ teaspoon dried *fines herbes*
250 ml/8 fl oz double cream or yoghurt cheese or fresh white cheese (see Basic Recipes, page 24)
3 large egg whites
Pinch cream of tartar

For the Garnish:
Avocado slices
Watercress sprigs

Melt the butter in a heavy frying pan and stir in the cream cracker crumbs and 2 teaspoons of the grated lemon rind. Season with salt and pepper and cook, over low heat, until the butter and seasonings are thoroughly mixed with the cream cracker crumbs. Have ready a lightly-oiled 23 cm/9 in springform pan. Pack the crumb mixture into the bottom of the pan and chill in the refrigerator for 30 minutes.

Pour 50 ml/2 fl oz cold water into a small saucepan and sprinkle the gelatine over it. Set it aside to soften. Peel and pit the avocados and mash them in a bowl. Add the remaining 2 teaspoons of grated lemon rind and the lemon juice. In another bowl, beat the egg yolks until they are light and lemon-coloured. Mash the cream cheese, chives, and mixed herbs into the egg yolks. Add the avocado mixture and stir until it is smooth. Set the saucepan with the softened gelatine over low heat and stir to dissolve. Stir into the avocado mixture, add the cream, or yoghurt cheese or fresh white cheese, mixing well and season to taste with salt and pepper. Beat the egg whites with a pinch of salt and the cream of tartar until they stand in firm peaks. Stir a tablespoon or two of the whites into the avocado mixture, then fold in the remaining egg whites, gently but thoroughly, and turn them into the springform pan. Smooth the top, cover with foil and chill in the refrigerator for 4 hours, or until it is firm. Remove the sides of the pan and slide onto a flat dish. Garnish with the avocado slices and watercress sprigs.

FRESH PEAR VINAIGRETTE

This imaginative, fresh-tasting salad is another of the felicitous creations of Michael Quinn. It demonstrates his special ability for balancing flavours and textures to contrast and blend, sweet and savoury, firm and soft. It could make the main course of a light luncheon, preceded by soup and followed by pudding or cheese.

SERVES 6

6 large pears
125 ml/4 fl oz white wine vinegar
16 large, fresh mint leaves
10 fresh tarragon leaves

For the Dressing (see Note):
4 tablespoons white wine vinegar
25 g/1 oz fresh mint and tarragon, finely chopped

6 tablespoons lemon juice
Salt
Freshly ground pepper
Caster sugar to taste
125 g/4 oz smoked ham, finely chopped

Using a vegetable peeler, peel the pears, leaving the stalk attached. Put into a saucepan large enough to hold the pears in a single layer with the vinegar, 10 of the mint leaves and the tarragon leaves. Pour in enough water barely to cover and poach the pears, covered, over low heat until they are tender, about 10 minutes. Strain, and allow the pears to cool.

To make the dressing, mix the vinegar, chopped mint and tarragon leaves, and lemon juice in a bowl. Season to taste with salt, pepper and sugar. Stir to mix and dissolve the sugar. Add the chopped ham and mix thoroughly.

Slice the tops off the pears and very carefully scoop out the cores. Using a small spoon, fill the pears with the ham dressing. Pull away the stalks from the pears and replace with fresh mint. Serve with any remaining dressing or with a mint and tarragon flavoured mayonnaise.

Note: The dressing may be too sharp for some tastes. When making it, halve the vinegar and lemon juice and add the rest a little at a time until the right balance of flavour is achieved.

AUBERGINE CASSEROLE

Vaughan Archer likes to serve aubergine dishes to accompany main courses. He serves fresh asparagus tips with his Aubergine Casserole, a delightful combination. His recipe is inspired by a traditional dish from Turkey, *Imam Bayildi* (The Imam Fainted), so called because the Imam is said to have swooned with delight. Chef Archer does not aim to produce fainting fits with this version. His aim is simply to please.

SERVES 4

2 long aubergines, each weighing about 250 g/8 oz, peeled
125 g/4 oz butter
1 tablespoon olive oil
Salt
Freshly ground pepper
125 g/4 oz button mushrooms
250 g/8 oz tomatoes, peeled, seeded and chopped

Cut the aubergines into 20 thin lengthways slices. In a large frying pan, heat 4 tablespoons of the butter and the oil and sauté the aubergine slices until lightly browned on both sides. Fit a slice into the bottom of four 7 cm/3 in ramekins or small soufflé dishes then line the moulds with the slices, leaving the long pieces to hang over the sides. Chop the remaining aubergine finely, sauté it in a little of the remaining butter, season with salt and pepper and set aside. Sauté the mushrooms in the frying pan with a little more of the butter, season and set aside.

Fill the ramekins with layers of aubergine, mushrooms and tomato. Fold over the overhanging aubergine and put the ramekins in a baking pan with water to come about halfway up their sides. Bake in a preheated, hot oven (220°C/425°F/gas 7) for 20 minutes. Remove from the oven, let stand for a few minutes, then invert onto four warmed plates and serve with fresh asparagus tips.

QUAIL BREASTS WITH BACON AND GRAPES ON A MIXED SALAD

Anthony Blake believes that dishes should be presented with colour and imagination and not served in excessively large portions. They should also be simple and light in accordance with modern ideas. This versatile salad could be served as a salad course or make a good beginning to a meal, followed by fish or shellfish as the main course, or be served as the main course of a warm weather lunch or dinner.

SERVES 4

8 quail breasts, skinned, boned and halved
Salt
Freshly ground pepper
Butter
4 rashers bacon, cut into crosswise strips
24 seedless green grapes, peeled and halved
Assorted lettuces: Oakleaf, lamb's lettuce, endive, escarole, chicory, radicchio, soft lettuce

For the Walnut Oil Dressing:
1 tablespoon butter
4 tablespoons finely chopped shallots
Salt
Freshly ground pepper
50 ml/2 fl oz dry red wine
2 tablespoons red wine vinegar
50 ml/2 fl oz walnut oil

Season the quail breasts with salt and pepper. Reserve the rest of the carcasses for making stock. Heat 2–3 tablespoons butter in a heavy frying pan and cook the quail breasts over moderate heat, turning once, for about 4 minutes. They should still be pink inside. Lift out of the frying pan and keep warm. Add the bacon strips to the pan and sauté over moderate heat until crisp. Lift out onto paper towels to drain, then add to the quail breasts to keep warm. Add the grapes to the pan and sauté for 1 or 2 minutes. Lift out and add to the quail breasts.

Choose enough lettuces to serve four people, balancing colour and texture. Wash and dry the lettuces and pile into a salad bowl. Make the dressing. In a frying pan, heat the butter and sauté the shallots until they are soft, but not brown. Season with salt and pepper, add the wine and vinegar and simmer, uncovered, over moderate heat until the mixture is reduced by half and thickened. Remove from the heat and pour into a bowl. Whisk in the walnut oil, and cool.

Toss the assorted lettuces with the walnut oil dressing and arrange them on four plates. Arrange 2 quail breasts on each plate on top of the lettuces and garnish with the bacon and grapes. Serve warm.

AVOCADO AND MELON FILLED WITH CRAB MEAT AND PRAWNS

Allan Holland, chef-patron of Mallory Court, a superb beginning-of-the-century home, now a country house hotel, in Warwickshire near Leamington Spa and Stratford-Upon-Avon, came to cooking from a deep interest in food. Elizabeth David's cookbooks started him off, and he has gone on learning ever since. His eclectic attitude increases his creativity. This dish, classic in its simplicity, is ideal for lunch as a main course, but could be served as a starter for a grand meal.

SERVES 4

175 ml/6 fl oz mayonnaise (see Basic Recipes, page 23)
175 g/6 oz cooked crab meat, picked over to remove any cartilage
125 g/4 oz cooked, shelled prawns
Salt
Freshly ground pepper
Lemon juice

1 large ripe avocado, peeled, pitted and quartered lengthways
1 medium Ogen melon, quartered
1-2 teaspoons tomato purée
125 ml/4 fl oz soured cream

For the Garnish:
Parsley sprigs

In a bowl, combine 4 tablespoons of the mayonnaise with the crab meat and prawns. Taste for seasoning and add salt, pepper and a little lemon juice if necessary.

Have ready four chilled plates. Fill each quarter slice of avocado with a quarter of the crab meat and prawn mixture, and place one on each plate, cut-side down. Arrange a slice of melon next to the avocado, fitting the two together to enclose the filling. Continue with the rest of the ingredients.

Stir the tomato purée into the rest of the mayonnaise to colour it pale pink. Coat the avocado with the mayonnaise. Stir the soured cream until it is smooth and coat the melon with it. Garnish with a sprig of parsley.

AVOCADO, CUCUMBER AND PROSCIUTTO SALAD

Julian Waterer, a young chef whose passion is cooking, is immensely creative and original. This salad can be served as a first course, a light main course, or as an accompanying salad.

SERVES 6

175 g/6 oz sliced prosciutto, cut into julienne strips
¼ large cucumber, cut into julienne strips
3 large avocados, peeled, halved and pitted
250 ml/8 fl oz vinaigrette (see Basic Recipes, page 23) made with lemon juice or wine vinegar and olive oil

For the Garnish:
Watercress sprigs

Arrange the prosciutto and cucumber in the centre of six salad plates. Put each avocado half, cut-side down, on a chopping board and, keeping the narrow ends intact, cut the avocados into thin lengthways slices. Put a half avocado on top of the prosciutto and cucumber and press it gently to spread the slices like a fan. Spoon the vinaigrette over and around the avocado and garnish the plates with watercress.

DUCK BREAST SALAD

John King has a fine feeling for green things, and fresh fruits, and combinations of them with other ingredients, as this salad shows.

SERVES 4

1 whole breast fresh duckling, skinned and boned
Salt
Freshly ground pepper
1 tablespoon vegetable oil
2 tablespoons butter
1 bunch watercress
1 small head chicory
1 small head radicchio
4 sprigs lamb's lettuce
2 pink grapefruit, peeled and segmented
2 seedless oranges, peeled and segmented
3 tablespoons walnut oil
1 tablespoon red wine vinegar

Season the two halves of the duck breast with salt and pepper. Heat the oil and butter in a frying pan and sauté the breasts until they are lightly browned on both sides but still pink in the middle, about 8 minutes. Lift out, cool, slice thinly and set aside but do not refrigerate.

Wash the watercress, chicory, radicchio and lamb's lettuce, drain thoroughly, remove the stems from the watercress and discard any wilted leaves from the cress and lettuces. Dry the salad, and tear it into bite-size pieces. Set aside in a bowl.

Peel the skin from the grapefruit and orange segments and remove any pips. Set aside.

In a small bowl, beat the walnut oil, vinegar and salt and pepper together. Toss the salad greens in the dressing and arrange the salad in the centre of four dessert plates. Lay alternate slices of duck breast, grapefruit and orange segments on top of the salad greens. Pour any fruit juice or vinaigrette over the salad and serve.

WARM CHICKEN AND PEPPER SALAD

Having enjoyed chef Melvin Jordan's Watercress Soup (see page 78), I looked forward to trying his other dishes. His cooking has a simplicity and directness I find appealing, and his presentation is attractive. Green and red peppers with cubes of chicken breast contrast with the salad greens in appearance, taste and texture in this recipe of his.

SERVES 4

1 large clove garlic, crushed
4 tablespoons butter
1 whole chicken breast, halved, skinned, boned and cubed
1 small sweet red pepper, seeded and cut into strips
1 small sweet green pepper, seeded and cut into strips
Salt
Freshly ground pepper

1 recipe garlic croutons (see Basic Recipes, page 24)
1 tablespoon lemon juice
Assorted salad greens (soft lettuce, romaine, radicchio, leaf lettuce, lamb's lettuce, etc.) washed, dried and torn into bite-size pieces
Oil and vinegar dressing (see Basic Recipes, page 23)

Combine the garlic and butter in a small, heavy frying pan and sauté the chicken cubes and pepper strips until the vegetables are tender and the chicken cooked, 4–6 minutes. Season to taste with salt and pepper. Sprinkle the croutons with the lemon juice. Add them to the pan and heat through.

Toss the salad greens in the dressing and arrange on four salad plates. Top with the warm chicken, pepper and crouton mixture. Serve immediately.

VARIATION

Omit the peppers and substitute sliced, roast squab (pigeon) breasts for the chicken. Sprinkle the finished salad with finely chopped parsley.

RADICCHIO AND WARM SCALLOP SALAD

This is one of the elegant salads Michael Quinn created while he was Maître Chef des Cuisines at The Ritz in London. The salad is eye-catching when arranged as Michael does, but is attractive when arranged quite haphazardly. Either way it tastes good.

SERVES 2 to 4

1 recipe oil and vinegar dressing (see Basic Recipes, page 23), using lemon juice instead of vinegar
8 large chicory leaves
½ small radicchio lettuce
8 large scallops, with corals, if possible

Salt
Freshly ground pepper
4 tablespoons butter

For the Garnish:
Chervil sprigs

Make the oil and vinegar dressing using lemon juice. Toss the chicory and radicchio separately in a little of the dressing. Arrange the chicory leaves round the edges of two salad plates. Put the radicchio in a pile in the middle.

Season the scallops with salt and pepper. In a small, heavy frying pan, heat the butter and sauté the scallops over moderate heat until they are lightly coloured. Lift out and arrange on top of the radicchio. Garnish with chervil sprigs and serve the rest of the oil and lemon juice dressing separately.

HUNTER'S SALAD

This is a very grand salad for a special occasion. A whole boned partridge breast is used, but only the suprèmes (the whole breast, halved and boned) of the pheasant and chicken. The other half of the two birds can be used for a simpler family meal. The salad is the creation of Pierre Chevillard, of the Chewton Glen Hotel in Hampshire, taking advantage of the readily available game in the area.

SERVES 4

Oil and vinegar dressing (see Basic Recipes, page 23), using olive oil and adding 2 teaspoons *moutarde de Meaux* or other French coarse-grain mustard
1 whole boned partridge breast
½ boned pheasant breast (1 suprème)
½ boned chicken breast (1 suprème)

1 potato, peeled and thinly sliced
4 tablespoons butter
1 small radicchio lettuce
¼ small head chicory
125 g/4 oz lamb's lettuce, about
Small bunch black grapes, pitted and peeled

Make the oil and vinegar dressing using olive oil and *moutarde de Meaux*. Set aside.

Cut each of the breasts into 4 lengthways slices. In a frying pan, heat 3 tablespoons of the butter and sauté the slices lightly, turning once. The partridge and pheasant should remain pink inside.

Arrange the slices of potato in a grill tin and drizzle them with the remaining tablespoon of butter, melted. Grill under moderate heat, to make potato crisps. Shop-bought crisps can, of course, be used instead.

Wash and dry the salad greens and toss them in the dressing. Arrange the salad on four plates and top with the sliced breasts, making sure each plate has a slice of each meat. Arrange a few grapes on each plate and scatter the crisps over the salad.

FROGS' LEGS AND JUNIPER BERRY SALAD

Andrew Stacey, the young chef Garde-Manager at The Bell Inn at Aston Clinton in Buckinghamshire, has developed dishes that he feels keep their natural flavour and delicately-balanced composition. This unusual salad is refreshing and makes a good lunch or summer dinner main course.

SERVES 4 as a salad, 2 as a main course

2 tablespoons juniper berries
1 tablespoon medium dry, or dry
  sherry
2 pairs frogs' legs per person
3 tablespoons single cream
2 teaspoons lime or lemon juice
Salt
Freshly ground pepper
1 small soft lettuce
½ small head endive
4 leaves radicchio
4 leaves lamb's lettuce

For the Salad Dressing:
2 tablespoons medium dry, or dry
  sherry

2 teaspoons Dijon mustard
2 teaspoons celery seed
2 teaspoons red wine vinegar
Salt
Freshly ground pepper
5 tablespoons olive oil

2 medium tomatoes, peeled, seeded
  and halved
Flour for dredging the frogs' legs
4 tablespoons butter
1 tablespoon each chopped chives,
  parsley and chervil

Put the juniper berries into a small bowl with the sherry and set aside.

Bone the frogs' legs, if liked, or leave them whole. Put them into a bowl with the cream, lime or lemon juice, salt and pepper and turn to coat well. Set aside.

Wash and drain the lettuces and dry thoroughly. Discard any discoloured leaves. Make the dressing by mixing together the sherry, mustard, celery seed, vinegar and salt and pepper then gradually beating in the oil. Toss the lettuces in the dressing. Arrange the salad on four plates. Slice the tomato halves and arrange around the salad.

Drain the frogs' legs and pat them dry with paper towels. Dredge them in flour, shaking to remove the excess. Heat the butter in a large frying pan and fry the frogs' legs until they are golden brown, turning frequently, for about 5 minutes. Drain on kitchen towels.

Arrange the frogs' legs on top of the salad and sprinkle with the herbs. Drain the juniper berries and sprinkle them over the salad.

PIGEON SALAD WITH PINE NUTS

This richly-flavoured, quite hearty salad could easily be the main course of a light meal. It is the creation of Nick Gill, an imaginative cook and a perfectionist.

SERVES 4

2 pigeons
1 medium onion, chopped
1 medium carrot, scraped and sliced
1 stalk celery, chopped
4 parsley stems
1 clove garlic, chopped
6 peppercorns
Salt
Enough mixed salad greens to serve 4, such as lamb's lettuce, spinach, endive, radicchio and chicory, washed and dried

50 ml/2 fl oz vinaigrette (see Basic Recipes, page 23) made with Dijon mustard and 1 tablespoon chopped fresh herbs (parsley, chives, chervil, tarragon)
50 g/2 oz pine nuts
Freshly ground pepper
1 teaspoon chopped fresh thyme, or ½ teaspoon dried
2 tablespoons vegetable oil

Carefully cut the breasts from the pigeons and set them aside. Chop the carcasses of the birds and put them into a large saucepan with the onion, carrot, celery, parsley stems, garlic and peppercorns. Add cold water to cover, bring to a boil and simmer, skimming from time to time, for 2–3 hours. Strain the stock through a fine sieve, pushing down hard on the solids with the back of a spoon or ladle to extract all the juices. Pour the strained stock into a small saucepan and season very lightly with salt. Boil down vigorously to reduce to caramel consistency. Set aside.

In a bowl, toss the salad with the vinaigrette dressing and the pine nuts. Arrange the salad on each of four plates and set aside.

Season the pigeon breasts with salt, pepper and thyme. In a frying pan, heat the oil and sauté the breasts over fairly high heat for 2 minutes on each side. The meat should remain pink. Slice the breasts very thinly lengthways. Arrange in a fan on top of the salad and glaze with the caramelized stock. Serve warm.

BROCCOLI AND RED PEPPER SALAD

This healthy and delicious salad was given me by Alan Casey when he was head chef at Culloden House, Scotland. He likes the new trends in cooking because they emphasize the use of fresh ingredients.

SERVES 4

500 g/1 lb cauli-broc (purple-headed broccoli), trimmed
Salt
6 tablespoons walnut oil
1 tablespoon red wine vinegar
1 tablespoon lemon juice
½ teaspoon dry English mustard
⅛ teaspoon garlic, very finely chopped

¼ teaspoon salt
¼ teaspoon sugar
1 teaspoon finely chopped, seeded, fresh hot green chilli pepper
1 sweet red pepper, seeded and cut into thin strips
2 tablespoons flaked almonds (optional)

Slide the cauli-broc gently into a large saucepan of briskly boiling, salted water and cook, uncovered, at a simmer until it is just tender, 10–15 minutes. Drain, and refresh quickly in cold water. Drain, place in a bowl and chill in the refrigerator.

In a bowl, make a vinaigrette dressing with the oil, vinegar, lemon juice, mustard mixed with a little water, garlic, salt, sugar and hot chilli, beating with a whisk to mix. Pour over the cauli-broc.

Drop the red pepper strips into a saucepan of briskly boiling, salted water for 3 minutes. Drain and refresh in cold water. Drain and pat dry. Arrange the pepper strips round the cauli-broc. Sprinkle the vegetable with the flaked almonds, if liked.

AVOCADO SALAD

This very pretty salad belies all the criticism of the *nouvelle cuisine* idea of the picture-on-the-plate. It isn't gimmicky, or skimpy. It demonstrates the sort of originality that makes the cooking of Murdo MacSween so attractive.

SERVES 2

For the Salad Dressing:
3 tablespoons olive oil
1 tablespoon Dijon mustard
1 tablespoon red wine vinegar
2 tablespoons tomato juice
Salt
Freshly ground pepper

For the Salad:
8 radicchio leaves

½ small head of endive, chopped
10 cooked green beans, cut into 2.5 cm/1 in lengths
2 tablespoons shallots, finely chopped
1 avocado, peeled, pitted and sliced lengthways
2 tablespoons lemon juice

In a bowl, combine all the ingredients for the dressing, whisking thoroughly to blend. Set aside until ready to use.

Arrange the radicchio leaves in a flower shape on two salad plates. Toss the chopped endive and green beans in the dressing and pile them in the centre of the radicchio flower. Sprinkle with the shallots. Brush the avocado with the lemon juice and arrange in a fan shape on top of the lettuce and beans. Drizzle with any leftover dressing.

CRAB, GRAPEFRUIT AND CUCUMBER SALAD

This simple, fresh-tasting summer salad is typical of the cooking of John Evans.

SERVES 4

1 cucumber
1 tablespoon white wine vinegar
2–3 grapefruit, preferably pink, peeled, segmented and chilled
Heart of 1 cos or other crisp lettuce, shredded
250 g/8 oz fresh crab meat, picked over to remove any cartilage

2 teaspoons tomato purée
1 tablespoon brandy
4 tablespoons grapefruit juice
Salt
Freshly ground pepper
⅛ teaspoon of cayenne pepper, or less to taste
Paprika

For the Dressing:
5 tablespoons double cream

For the Garnish:
Parsley sprigs

Score the cucumber with a fork and slice it thinly. Put it into a bowl with the vinegar and 2 cups cold water for two hours. Drain and pat dry. Arrange the cucumber slices round the edge of four chilled salad plates. Arrange a circle of grapefruit segments inside the cucumber. Fill the centre of the plate with shredded lettuce. Arrange the crab meat on top of the lettuce.

In a bowl, whisk together the cream, tomato purée, brandy, grapefruit juice, salt, pepper and cayenne. Pour over the crab meat, sprinkle with paprika and garnish with parsley sprigs.

HOT SCALLOP SALAD

I met Raymond Duthie when he was head chef at the Royal Crescent Hotel and I was very impressed by his cooking and by his meticulous approach to his craft. He sticks to traditional methods of preparation, but does not hesitate to create new dishes when inspiration seizes him. This salad could not be simpler or more delicious.

SERVES 4

Mixed salad greens: radicchio, Batavia
   lettuce, lamb's lettuce, watercress
   and endive
50 ml/2 fl oz olive oil
16 large scallops, sliced
2 tablespoons finely chopped shallots
125 g/4 oz button mushrooms

1 stalk celery, finely chopped
1 tablespoon dry sherry
1 tablespoon sherry vinegar
Salt
Freshly ground pepper
25 g/1 oz parsley, finely chopped
25 g/1 oz chervil, finely chopped

Wash and dry the salad greens and tear them into bite-size pieces. Arrange the salad greens around the edge of a large platter.

Heat the olive oil in a large, heavy frying pan. Add the scallops, shallots, mushrooms and celery and sauté over high heat, stirring constantly, for 30 seconds. Add the sherry and stir, then add the vinegar, stir, and season to taste with salt and pepper. Heap the mixture into the middle of the platter and sprinkle with the chopped parsley and chervil. Serve immediately.

Desserts

D esserts based on fresh fruit are increasingly popular with today's young chefs who like a meal to end on a light note. There are always fresh fruit sorbets on the menu since the sorbet as a dessert has become a universal favourite. Many chefs serve a Champagne, or similar, type of sorbet as a palate freshener during the meal in the old tradition, but fruit sorbets are now an established tradition in their own right as desserts. Ice cream is used imaginatively, and there are still some very rich puddings for self-indulgent moments. A few old favourites like Trifle and Hot Butterscotch Pudding are enduringly popular.

FRUIT SORBETS

Nick Gill of Hambleton Hall has a special way with sorbets which he serves freshly made, either singly or together in smaller quantities with the various fruit colours making an attractive pattern on the plate. They make a subtle and refreshing ending to a meal.

ORANGE SORBET

MAKES 700 ml/1¼ pt
**700 ml/1¼ pt fresh orange juice,
  strained
75 g/3 oz icing sugar, or to taste
1–2 tablespoons orange liqueur,
  according to taste**

For the Garnish:
**Tangerine or mandarin orange
  segments**

Combine the orange juice, sugar and liqueur in a bowl and stir to dissolve the sugar. Taste and add more sugar if liked. Freeze the mixture in an ice cream freezer according to the manufacturer's instructions and serve (see Note). If the sorbet is not to be served immediately, put it into the freezer or freezer compartment then transfer to the refrigerator half an hour before serving to restore the soft texture. Scoop into serving dishes and garnish with a tangerine or mandarin section.

Note: The sorbet can be made in ice cube trays with the dividers removed. After 30 minutes, when partly frozen, remove and beat until smooth. Do this 3 times during the freezing process, which will take about 2–3 hours.

NICK GILL'S LIME SORBET

MAKES 700 ml/1¼ pt
**475 ml/16 fl oz fresh lime juice,
  strained
300 g/10 oz icing sugar, or to taste**

For the Garnish:
Thin slices unpeeled lime

Combine the lime juice and sugar in a bowl and stir to dissolve the sugar. Taste and add more sugar if liked. Freeze the mixture in an ice cream freezer according to the manufacturer's instructions (see Note). Serve immediately, or put into the freezer or freezer compartment and transfer to the refrigerator half an hour before serving to restore the soft texture. Scoop into serving dishes and garnish with a slice of lime.

Note: The sorbet can be made in ice cube trays in the same way as the orange sorbet (see page 208).

NICK GILL'S STRAWBERRY SORBET

MAKES 1 L/1¾ pt
900 g/2 lb hulled and sliced   *For the Garnish:*
   strawberries   **Raspberries**
125 g/4 oz icing sugar, or to taste   **Mint leaves**
2 tablespoons lemon juice

Purée the strawberries with 250 ml/8 fl oz water in a blender or food processor, then rub the purée through a fine sieve into a bowl to get rid of the pips. Add the sugar and lemon juice and stir until the sugar is dissolved. Taste and add sugar or lemon juice as liked. Freeze the mixture in an ice cream freezer according to the manufacturer's instructions (see Note). Serve immediately, or put into the freezer or freezing compartment and transfer to the refrigerator half an hour before serving to restore the soft texture. Scoop into serving dishes and garnish with a raspberry and a mint leaf.

Note: The sorbet can be made in ice cube trays in the same way as the orange sorbet (see page 208).

ALMOND BISCUITS

Nick Gill serves his sorbets with Almond Tuiles, the crisp thin almond biscuits that are shaped like tiles. They are easy to make. This is Nick's own recipe.

MAKES about 40
3 tablespoons unsalted butter,   ¼ **teaspoon almond essence**
   softened at room temperature   **125 g/4 oz blanched almonds, lightly**
5 tablespoons caster sugar   **toasted and ground**
2 large egg whites, lightly beaten **20 g/¾ oz plain flour, sifted**
½ **teaspoon vanilla essence**   **50 g/2 oz blanched sliced almonds**

Cream the butter and sugar together in a bowl until the mixture is light and fluffy. Whisk in the egg whites in two batches. Add the vanilla and almond essence and whisk again until the mixture is lightly combined. Fold in the ground almonds and the flour then stir in the sliced almonds.

Using one quarter of the batter, drop it, a teaspoon at a time 7 cm/3 in apart, onto a buttered baking sheet. Flatten each spoonful into a circle about 6 cm/2½ in in diameter. Bake in a preheated, moderate oven (190°C/375°F/gas 5) for 6-8 minutes until the edges are lightly browned.

Remove immediately from the oven and, using a metal spatula, take the biscuits one by one from the baking sheet and curve them round a rolling pin. Slide off and cool on a rack. Any that cool too much to be easy to curve can be returned to the oven very briefly to soften. Continue in the same way with the rest of the batter.

WHITE PEACH SORBET

This is a most delicious sorbet which Simon Hopkinson created to use his favourite white peaches which are in season only for a short time. He discovered, rather to his amusement, that canned white peaches produce a beautifully textured and flavoured sorbet.

SERVES 6

3 large white peaches, peeled and pitted; or same weight canned white peaches, drained	6 tablespoons lemon juice
250 ml/8 fl oz peach juice, or water	50 ml/2 fl oz blue plum *eau-de-vie* (Quetsch), or yellow plum *eau-de-vie* (Mirabelle) (optional)
4 tablespoons icing sugar, or to taste	

Chop the peaches coarsely and put them into a food processor or blender with the peach juice or water, sugar, lemon juice and *eau-de-vie*, if using, and process to a purée. Taste and add more sugar, if necessary. If using canned peaches, the peach juice in the can will be sweetened so more sugar may be necessary if using fresh peaches. Freeze in an ice cream or sorbet freezer according to manufacturer's instructions, usually 15-20 minutes (see Note).

Note: The sorbet can be made in ice cube trays (see page 208).

ICED BOMB

Terry Boswell invented this dessert to use up some leftover meringues. It happened one summer day when there were also lots of fine strawberries and raspberries to be had. It is a really lovely excuse for creating a dish that is anything but plain and leftoverish dull. It is, in fact, outrageously luxurious and certainly not for everyday.

SERVES 8 to 10
For the Meringues:
4 large egg whites
Pinch salt
¼ teaspoon cream of tartar
250 g/8 oz caster sugar

For the Bomb (see Note):
600 ml/1 pt double cream

½ teaspoon vanilla essence
125 g/4 oz plus 2 tablespoons icing
   sugar
500 g/1 lb chopped strawberries or
   raspberries
1 tablespoon *eau-de-vie de Framboise*
   (optional)
Vegetable oil for terrine

To make the meringues, beat the egg whites in a large bowl with the salt until they are frothy. Add the cream of tartar and beat until they begin to hold their shape. Gradually add 50 g/2 oz of the sugar, beating until the whites hold stiff peaks. Continue to beat while gradually adding the rest of the sugar until the whites are stiff and shiny. Line a baking sheet with buttered and lightly-floured parchment paper and spoon the meringue mixture by tablespoon onto it. Bake in a preheated, very slow oven (100°C/200°F/gas ¼), or as low as possible, and bake for 2 hours or until the meringues are crisp and firm. Take the meringues out of the oven and let them cool. Crumble into pieces the size of walnuts. Set aside.

In a large bowl, beat the cream with the vanilla and 2 tablespoons of icing sugar until it stands in peaks. Toss the strawberries or raspberries in the 125 g/4 oz icing sugar and fold into the whipped cream with the *eau-de-vie* if using. Taste and add more sugar if necessary. Fold in the crumbled meringues gently but thoroughly.

Line a 23 × 12 cm/9 × 5 in terrine or loaf pan with aluminium foil brushed with oil and pour in the cream mixture, banging the pan on the table so that the mixture drops into the corners. With a spatula, level the top. Cover with foil and freeze. Two hours before serving, transfer the bomb to the refrigerator to let it soften slightly. Turn it out onto a serving platter and slice. If liked, serve with double cream or puréed raspberries, sieved to get rid of the pips.

Note: Terry Boswell says this bomb invites the cook's imagination to invent other fillings. 250 g/8 oz of melted chocolate with toasted almonds for example, or experiment with other soft fruit. Cranberry sauce might be interesting.

HONEY ICE CREAM WITH WILD STRAWBERRIES

This is a lovely summer dessert created by Shaun Hill, when he was chef-patron of Hill's restaurant in Stratford-Upon-Avon, before joining Gidleigh Park as head chef. It takes little time and since it can be made ahead is useful for entertaining. Any strawberries can be used, but Shaun prefers tiny *frais des bois*, wild strawberries, which look very pretty on a plain white plate with the golden ice cream beside them.

SERVES 6

250 ml/8 fl oz milk	250 ml/8 fl oz double cream
250 g/8 oz caster sugar	2 tablespoons lemon juice
6 large egg yolks	750 g/1½ lb strawberries, preferably
2 tablespoons clear honey	wild strawberries

Heat the milk. In a bowl, cream the sugar and egg yolks until they form a ribbon. Whisk the warm milk onto the egg yolk mixture and set the bowl over hot water. Cook over low heat until it thickens enough to coat a spoon. Remove from the heat, stir in the honey, cream and lemon juice and pour into an ice cream freezer (see Note). Freeze for 20 minutes.

Arrange the strawberries in a mound on a dessert plate with the honey ice cream beside them. Any imperfect berries may be puréed in a blender or food processor and poured onto the plates as a decorative accent.

Note: Very rich ice creams with a high proportion of egg yolks and cream can be frozen in a mould in a domestic freezer or in the freezer compartment of a refrigerator as they will not crystallize when freezing.

Less rich ice creams can be stirred once or twice during the freezing period to make sure no ice crystals form around the bottom and sides of the tray or other container in which they are freezing.

ICED CRANBERRY SOUFFLÉ

Lyn Hall says her soufflé is ideal for holiday entertaining, and at any time of the year, as cranberries, which freeze well, are always available. It is also easy to make and prepare well ahead of time.

SERVES 6

For the Topping:

300 ml/½ pt sweet cider	2 tablespoons water
Stick cinnamon	Stick cinnamon
Pinch freshly grated nutmeg	2 tablespoons crème de cassis
175 ml/6 fl oz dry red wine	400 ml/14 fl oz whipping cream
2 tablespoons lemon juice	3 large egg yolks
Grated rind of 1 orange	125 g/4 oz vanilla sugar, or use
Sugar to taste	125 g/4 oz sugar and ¼ teaspoon
375 g/12 oz cranberries	vanilla essence
	3 large egg whites

For the Soufflé:

250 g/8 oz cranberries	*For the Garnish:*
50 ml/2 fl oz ruby port	175 ml/6 fl oz double cream,
	whipped

To make the topping, combine all the ingredients in a saucepan and cook over low heat until the cranberries burst. Remove immediately from the heat and leave for 3 hours for the cranberries to absorb the flavour of the liquid.

To make the soufflé, put the cranberries into a saucepan with the port, water and cinnamon stick. Cook over low heat until they burst. Drain thoroughly, reserving the liquid, and chop them roughly. Set aside in a bowl. Reduce the cooking liquid over moderate heat to 2 tablespoons. Remove from the heat and stir in the crème de cassis. Pour into a cup and set aside.

In a large bowl, beat the cream until stiff. Refrigerate. In another bowl, beat the egg yolks with 50 g/2 oz of the vanilla sugar until lemon-coloured and fluffy. In a large bowl, beat the egg whites until they stand in peaks. Gradually beat in the remaining 50 g/2 oz sugar, and the vanilla essence if not using vanilla sugar, and beat until they are very stiff and shiny. Fold the egg yolk mixture into the whites, then gently but thoroughly fold into the cream. Add the crème de cassis mixture and the chopped cranberries, then pile into a 700 ml/1¼ pt soufflé mould prepared with a collar and freeze, uncovered. Remove from the freezer and put into the refrigerator to soften about 2 hours before serving. Pipe or spoon a border of whipped cream onto the top of the soufflé. Drain the poached cranberries that have been soaking and spoon on top of the soufflé inside the whipped cream border. Remove the collar and serve.

BROWN BREAD ICE CREAM

Peter Jackson enjoys brown bread ice cream, so he worked out his own version. It is very rich and good and the breadcrumbs add a pleasant crunch to the soft ice cream. It is also delicious with Kenneth Bell's Butterscotch Pudding (page 225), served sliced and chilled but without the sauce.

SERVES 6

2 large eggs
2 large egg yolks
50 g/2 oz caster sugar
1 vanilla pod
300 ml/½ pt milk
300 ml/½ pt double cream, partially whipped

4-5 tablespoons fresh brown breadcrumbs
1 tablespoon caster sugar
1 tablespoon rum

In a large bowl, beat the eggs, egg yolks and sugar until well blended. Split the vanilla pod and add it to the milk in the top of a double boiler, set over hot water on very low heat. Cover and let it infuse for 10 minutes. Do not let the milk boil. If it gets too hot, remove it from the heat. Strain the milk onto the egg mixture, stirring constantly. Return the mixture to the double boiler and cook, stirring, over low heat until it coats the back of a spoon, about 7 minutes.

Pour it into the bowl and whisk occasionally as it cools. When it is cool, fold in the partially whipped cream and put into the ice cream freezer and freeze according to manufacturer's instructions (see Note on page 212).

Mix the breadcrumbs and sugar together and put on a baking sheet. Put under a preheated, not very hot grill to brown slowly. Do not let them burn. Cool the crumb mixture and stir it into the ice cream with the rum, or a little vanilla essence if preferred. Leave it in the freezer to harden.

JOAN SUTHERLAND BAVAROIS

I never did find out why this dessert is named for Joan Sutherland, the singer, because I was too busy enjoying it, as I always enjoy the cooking of Francis Coulson of the Sharrow Bay Hotel in the Lake District.

SERVES 4 to 6

4 large egg yolks
125 g/4 oz caster sugar
300 ml/½ pt milk heated with a
   vanilla pod or add 1 teaspoon
   vanilla essence
1 envelope (1 tablespoon) unflavoured
   gelatine
1 tablespoon Curaçao

300 ml/½ pt double cream, whipped
4 tablespoons apricot jam
2 tablespoons apricot brandy

For the Garnish (optional):
Whipped cream
Halved apricots

In the top of a double boiler, beat the egg yolks and sugar together until they form a ribbon. Remove the vanilla pod from the hot, but not boiling, milk and pour the milk slowly into the egg and sugar mixture, stirring constantly. If using vanilla essence instead of the vanilla pod, stir it in. Set the double boiler over hot water on low heat and cook, stirring with a wooden spoon, until the custard has thickened and coats the back of the spoon, about 7 minutes. Remove from the heat. Sprinkle the gelatine over 50 ml/2 fl oz cold water to soften, then stir into the hot custard and stir until it is dissolved. Let the custard cool, then stir in the Curaçao. Taste and add a little more if necessary. When the custard is cold, fold in the whipped cream.

In a small bowl, mix together the apricot jam and apricot brandy until smooth. Pour into the bottom of a 1.1 L/2 pt soufflé mould or glass dessert bowl. Spoon the custard on top and chill thoroughly in the refrigerator until set, 3–4 hours. When ready to serve, decorate with rosettes of whipped cream and halved apricots, if liked. Glaze, if liked, with a little warmed and strained apricot jam.

RUM AND BRANDY MOUSSE

This is a simple to make, quick and good dessert, the creation of John Evans. It is useful for a dinner party as it is made ahead of time.

SERVES 6 to 8

5 large egg yolks	400 ml/14 fl oz double cream
125 g/4 oz caster sugar	1 envelope (1 tablespoon) unflavoured
1 tablespoon rum	gelatine
1½ tablespoons brandy	5 large egg whites

In a bowl, whisk together the egg yolks and sugar until they are thick and creamy. Whisk in the rum and brandy. In another bowl, beat the cream until it stands in soft peaks. Fold into the egg yolk mixture. Pour 50 ml/2 fl oz cold water into a small saucepan and sprinkle the gelatine over it to soften, then heat gently, stirring until the gelatine has dissolved. Cool slightly and stir into the egg and cream mixture. In a large bowl, beat the egg whites until they stand in firm peaks. Fold the egg whites into the egg and cream mixture, gently but thoroughly. Pour into a large decorative glass dessert bowl and chill in the refrigerator until set. Serve with brandy snaps. If liked, the mousse may be spooned into individual dessert glasses and chilled.

BLACKBERRY MOUSSE

Roy Richards is the chef-patron of the Manor House in Pickworth but his wife, Veronica, who cooks, and more often than not creates the desserts, merits the title chef-patronne as her desserts, even the more traditional ones, always have a touch of originality because of her creative use of ingredients. I am specially fond of this simple blackberry mousse.

SERVES 6

1 envelope (1 tablespoon) unflavoured gelatine	125 ml/4 fl oz double cream, chilled
500 g/1 lb blackberries	4 large egg whites
50 ml/2 fl oz lemon juice	Pinch salt
125 g/4 oz sugar	Pinch cream of tartar

Sprinkle the gelatine over 50 ml/2 fl oz cold water in a small bowl and leave to soften. Combine the blackberries, lemon juice and sugar in a saucepan, bring to a simmer over moderate heat and cook, uncovered, for 5 minutes. Cool slightly then pour into a blender or food processor and reduce to a purée. Strain through a fine sieve set over a bowl, pushing down hard on the solids. Only the pips should remain. Discard them. Return the purée to the saucepan, stir in the gelatine and warm just until the gelatine is dissolved. Set aside.

In a bowl, beat the cream until it stands in stiff peaks. In a large bowl, beat the egg whites with the salt and cream of tartar until they stand in stiff peaks. Fold the cream and egg whites gently but thoroughly into the blackberry purée. Spoon the mousse into a glass serving bowl and chill in the refrigerator for 4 hours, or until it is set. To serve, divide the mousse among six individual glass dishes.

ALMOND MERINGUE WITH GRAPES

This is one of the uncomplicated, pleasing desserts created by Brian Prideaux-Brune.

SERVES 6 to 8

6 large egg whites	125 g/4 oz slivered almonds
Pinch salt	600 ml/1 pt double cream
375 g/12 oz caster sugar	500 g/1 lb halved and pitted grapes

In a large bowl, beat the egg whites with the salt until they stand in firm peaks. Fold in the sugar and the almonds. Line 2 baking sheets with oiled greaseproof paper and spread the egg white mixture evenly over them. Bake in a preheated slow oven (140°C/275°F/gas 1) for 1¼ hours. Cool.

Beat the cream in a large bowl with a little sugar until it stands in peaks. Fold in the grapes. Lift one of the meringues onto a large, flat dish. Spread the cream and grape filling over it and top with the second meringue. Chill in the refrigerator until ready to serve, then slice and serve.

BURNT GLAVYA CREAM

John McGeever loves to create new and attractive dishes. This one is developed from the traditional Crème Brûlée, or Burnt Cream, which originated a very long time ago at Trinity College, Cambridge, where it is a speciality. Glavya is a Scottish liqueur, based on whisky. If it is not available, use any liqueur based on Scotch.

SERVES 4

4 large egg yolks	50 ml/2 fl oz Glavya (liqueur based
2 tablespoons sugar	on Scotch whisky), or use other
1 teaspoon cornflour	Scotch-based liqueur
300 ml/½ pt double cream	2 tablespoons brown sugar, about

In a bowl, whisk together the egg yolks, sugar and cornflour. In a small saucepan, heat the cream to just under boiling and whisk it into the egg mixture. Stir in the liqueur, return the mixture to the saucepan and simmer, stirring, over low heat until it is thick. Pour it into four 125 g/4 oz ramekins, or small soufflé moulds. Cool and refrigerate for 15–30 minutes. Sprinkle with the sugar and glaze under a preheated, very hot grill.

RASPBERRY SOUFFLÉS

Robert Gardiner, head chef of Ardsheal House in Scotland, loves the fine quality of the summer fruits of his country, especially the big, luscious raspberries. He developed this soufflé to take advantage of their goodness in summer. He freezes a supply so that he can make his favourite soufflé long after the season is over.

SERVES 8

Butter and caster sugar for the soufflé	2 large egg yolks
moulds	8 egg whites
500 g/1 lb raspberries	Pinch salt
1 tablespoon lemon juice	3 tablespoons icing sugar
125 g/4 oz icing sugar	Double cream (optional)

Butter eight 125 g/4 oz soufflé moulds generously, making sure the rims of the moulds are well coated. Refrigerate for 15 minutes. Repeat this process then coat the insides of the moulds with sugar. Refrigerate until ready to use.

In a blender or food processor, combine the raspberries, lemon juice and icing sugar and process until smooth. Add the egg yolks and blend for 30 seconds longer. Scrape the purée into a large bowl. Set aside.

In another bowl, beat the egg whites with the salt until they stand in soft peaks. Add the icing sugar a tablespoon at a time, beating constantly. Beat for about 30 seconds longer after the sugar has been added, or until the whites are stiff and shiny. Mix one quarter of the egg whites into the raspberry purée then fold the raspberry mixture gently but thoroughly into the egg whites. Spoon the soufflé mixture into the prepared moulds and arrange on a baking tray.

Bake in a preheated, hot oven (220°C/425°F/gas 7) for 8-9 minutes, or until they are puffed and lightly set. Serve immediately with the double cream, if liked.

WHISKY AND MARMALADE SOUFFLÉ

Another Scot, Campbell Cameron, head chef of Culloden House Hotel, created this dish using the native drink - Scotch - and marmalade, also credited to Scotland. It makes a very luscious hot dessert. I prefer the hot soufflé without the sauce but when chilled the soufflé makes a most pleasant dessert with the cream and whisky sauce, even though it falls and loses its looks.

SERVES 4

For the Soufflé Base:
250 ml/8 fl oz milk
50 g/2 oz sugar
1 small egg yolk
1½ tablespoons flour

For the Filling:
2 tablespoons marmalade
2 large egg yolks
2 tablespoons Scotch whisky
2 large egg whites

Pour the milk into a small saucepan and bring it to just under a boil. In a bowl, cream together the sugar and the egg yolk until it makes a ribbon. Stir in the flour and mix well. Pour on the milk, stirring constantly. Transfer the contents to the saucepan and simmer, stirring, for 2-3 minutes. Remove from the heat.

Stir in the marmalade, egg yolks and whisky. Beat the egg whites until they stand in firm peaks. Fold gently but thoroughly into the egg yolk and milk mixture and spoon into four 250 g/8 oz soufflé moulds. If liked, the moulds may be buttered and sprinkled lightly with sugar before being filled. Bake the soufflés in a preheated, moderately hot oven (200°C/400°F/gas 6) for 13 minutes or until lightly set and risen. Serve with a sauce made from 125 ml/4 fl oz lightly whipped double cream with 2 tablespoons Scotch whisky and icing sugar to taste, if liked. Serve the soufflés hot as soon as they are cooked.

WHISKY AND OATMEAL SYLLABUB

Murdo MacSween, a nephew of the famed novelist Sir Compton MacKenzie, is a Scot who speaks fluent Gaelic. This is a very Scottish recipe reflecting Murdo's feeling for his native Scotland, but it is not just traditional, it has the special MacSween touch and is very much his creation.

SERVES 6

125 g/4 oz oatmeal
475 ml/16 fl oz double cream,
  whipped

4 tablespoons lemon juice
3 tablespoons golden syrup
4 tablespoons Scotch whisky

Sprinkle the oatmeal onto a baking sheet and toast in a preheated, moderate oven (180°C/350°F/gas 4) for 5–10 minutes, or until lightly coloured. In a bowl, combine the oatmeal and all the remaining ingredients, mixing gently but thoroughly. Spoon the mixture into six dessert dishes and refrigerate for 1 hour before serving. The oatmeal will expand and the mixture be very thick.

PEACHES WITH LEMON AND BRANDY

George Perry-Smith has created a deceptively simple dessert which turns out to be quite exquisitely flavoured. It makes the peach season worth waiting for.

SERVES 6
6 large peaches   3 large lemons
550 ml/18 fl oz water   3 tablespoons brandy
175 g/6 oz sugar

Drop the peaches in boiling water for 1 minute, plunge them into cold water and remove the skins. In a saucepan, combine the water and sugar. Trim the ends of the lemons and slice them very thinly. Remove any pips. Add the lemon slices to the saucepan with the sugar and water and simmer, uncovered, for 10 minutes. Add the peaches and simmer until they are tender, about 10 minutes. The time will vary so test with a toothpick after 5 minutes. Lift them out as soon as they are done. Continue to cook the lemon slices until they are transparent, about 30 minutes. Cool and stir in the brandy, then pour over the peaches and chill in the refrigerator.

MIXED FRUIT IN SAUTERNES JELLY

Joyce Molyneux, chef-patronne of The Carved Angel restaurant, often finds herself with an excess of fresh fruit. This simplest of recipes is an excellent way of turning that excess into a light, refreshing dessert.

SERVES 3 or 4
500 g/1 lb of fruit, apples, pears and   *For the Garnish:*
   peaches*   **Mint sprigs**
250 g/8 oz sugar
250 ml/8 fl oz water   *The jelly can be flavoured with other
250 ml/8 fl oz sweet white wine such   wine or liqueurs. If preferred, a single
   as Sauternes*   fruit may be used, pears for example
1 envelope (1 tablespoon) unflavoured   in red wine and port jelly.
   gelatine
1 tablespoon of lemon juice, or to
   taste

Peel and core the apples and pears and cut into 8 lengthways slices. Drop the peaches into briskly boiling water for a few seconds, lift out and slip off the skins. Cut in half, remove the pits and slice each half into 4 lengthways slices.

In a medium saucepan, combine the sugar, water and wine and simmer just until the sugar has dissolved. Add the fruit and poach, uncovered, until the fruit is tender, 10–15 minutes. Lift out the fruit with a slotted spoon into a bowl. Measure the liquid and reduce it, if necessary, to 475 ml/16 fl oz over moderately high heat. Pour 50 ml/2 fl oz water into a small bowl and sprinkle the gelatine over it. When the gelatine has softened, stir it into the syrup and cook, stirring, until the gelatine has dissolved. Taste and add the lemon juice, adding more if necessary. Pour half the jelly mixture into three or four dessert dishes and chill in the refrigerator until it is set. Arrange the fruit on top of the jelly and pour in the rest of the jelly. Refrigerate until set.

The jelly may be unmoulded and served with yoghurt, cream, or ice cream and sweet biscuits, or served plain garnished with a sprig of mint.

STRAWBERRY OMELETTE

Willie MacPherson, while head chef at The Feathers Hotel in Woodstock, delighted me by having Strawberry Omelette on the menu. Dessert omelettes are not often served on menus with food as innovative and modern as Willie's. It is an essential part of his cooking philosophy to unite the good things of the past with the best of the new. I had forgotten how luscious a strawberry omelette can be. The recipe can easily be doubled for two people.

SERVES 1

175 g/6 oz strawberries
50 ml/2 fl oz Grand Marnier, or
   Curaçao, or other orange liqueur
1½ teaspoons caster sugar
1 large egg

1 large egg yolk
1 tablespoon whipped cream
Pinch salt
1 tablespoon butter
Icing sugar

Put half the strawberries, half the orange liqueur and ½ teaspoon of sugar in a small saucepan and cook over low heat for a few minutes, just until the strawberries have softened. Transfer to a blender or food processor and purée. Cut the other half of the strawberries into quarters and put into another small saucepan with the rest of the liqueur and cook over low heat until the strawberries have softened. Set aside.

In a bowl, combine the egg, egg yolk, cream, the remaining teaspoon of sugar and salt and mix well. Heat the butter in an omelette pan and pour in the egg mixture tilting the pan rapidly back and forth, stirring the egg with the back of a fork to spread the mixture evenly. As soon as it begins to set, in about 4 seconds, spoon in the quartered strawberry mixture and fold the omelette in half. Slide it off onto a buttered oven-proof dish, sprinkle with icing sugar and brown it quickly under a preheated grill. While the omelette is cooking, warm the strawberry purée and pour it onto a plate. Lift the omelette onto the plate, using a spatula. Serve immediately.

STRAWBERRIES ON ORANGE SABAYON

When strawberries are at their largest and finest, red-ripe and luscious, Murdo MacSween likes to serve them in an orange sabayon which brings out the tart sweetness of their flavour. It is a pretty dessert, and simple to make.

SERVES 6
6 large egg yolks
250 g/8 oz sugar
50 ml/2 fl oz dry white wine
50 ml/2 fl oz orange juice
750 g/1½ lb strawberries, large if
   possible, washed and hulled

For the Garnish:
6 mint leaves

In the top of a double boiler set over hot water, beat the egg yolks with the sugar, wine and orange juice and cook over low heat until thick enough to coat a spoon. Pour the sauce onto six dessert plates.

Cut the strawberries in half lengthways and arrange, cut-side down, on top of the sabayon round the inner rim of the plate. Glaze under a hot grill and decorate each plate with a fresh mint leaf.

VARIATION
Sam Chalmers has an interestingly different version of the above, a rather more elaborate one. Instead of wine and orange juice, add 2 tablespoons Grand Marnier to the sabayon. Soak an assortment of sliced fresh fruit in Grand Marnier for 3–4 hours then arrange the fruit on the base of a dessert plate. Pour the sabayon over the fruit, sprinkle with slivered almonds and glaze under a hot grill.

CRÈME BRÛLÉE WITH TANGERINES

Allan Holland has transformed an ancient English dessert, burnt cream, into something excitingly special. The unctuous custard contrasts with the deliciously tart fruit.

SERVES 6
6 tangerines, peeled and segmented
600 ml/1 pt double cream
8 large egg yolks
50 g/2 oz caster sugar

2½ tablespoons Mandarin Napoleon
   liqueur, or any tangerine liqueur
Light brown sugar

Peel the tangerine segments and remove seeds, if any. Divide the segments among six small soufflé moulds, about 250 g/8 oz size.

Rinse a heavy saucepan with cold water and leave wet. Pour in the cream and heat to just below simmering point. Beat the egg yolks and sugar together in a bowl until they form a ribbon. Pour the hot cream slowly onto the egg yolk and sugar mixture, stirring constantly with a wooden spoon. Gradually stir in the liqueur. Pour the mixture into the top of a double boiler and set over simmering water on very low heat. Cook the custard, stirring constantly, until it is thick enough to coat a spoon. Pour the custard into the moulds and refrigerate for at least 6 hours, or overnight. An hour before serving, sprinkle a layer of soft brown sugar over the custards, about 0.6 cm / ¼ in thick, and put under a preheated grill just long enough to caramelize the sugar, only minutes. Set in a cool place but do not refrigerate.

RHUBARB BRÛLÉE

This is a deliciously fresh tasting dessert created by Sheena Buchanan-Smith to take advantage of an abundance of fresh rhubarb. I have found that it also works well with frozen rhubarb when fresh is not available.

SERVES 6

500 g/1 lb fresh rhubarb, cut into 1 cm/½ in pieces, or 500 g/1 lb frozen chopped rhubarb, thawed	75 g/3 oz sugar 250 ml/8 fl oz chilled double cream 125 g/4 oz light brown sugar

Put the rhubarb, fresh or frozen, into a saucepan with just enough water to prevent it burning. Add the sugar, cover and simmer over low heat for about 8 minutes, or until it is soft. Cool and spoon into a 1 L/1¾ pt gratin dish. In a chilled bowl, beat the cream until it holds firm peaks. Spread the cream over the rhubarb and chill in the refrigerator for at least 1 hour, preferably longer. Sift the brown sugar over the cream and set under a preheated grill, about 10 cm/4 in from the heat, for about 2 minutes or until the sugar is just melted. Serve the dessert immediately, or chilled.

MOUSSE OF TWO CHOCOLATES

This simple to make dessert lends itself to all manner of attractive presentation. Its creator, Paul Vidic, head chef at Michael's Nook, spoons layers of each mousse alternately into glass dessert dishes. It also looks attractive served in two small moulds, one of white chocolate mousse, the other of dark. It is very good served with halved strawberries set upright round the edge of the dish with a whole strawberry in the middle. The flavours marry well.

SERVES 6

For the Dark Chocolate Mousse:
125 g/4 oz semi-sweet dark baking
   chocolate
2 egg yolks
125 ml/4 fl oz whipping cream,
   whipped
2 egg whites
Pinch salt

For the White Chocolate Mousse:
125 g/4 oz white chocolate
2 egg yolks
125 ml/4 fl oz whipping cream,
   whipped
2 egg whites
Pinch salt

Melt the two chocolates separately. Place each with 2–3 tablespoons water in the top of a double boiler over hot water on low heat, and stir constantly with a wooden spoon until the chocolate has melted and is smooth, about 5 minutes or less. Cool and stir the egg yolks into each chocolate. Fold the cream into the mixture.

It may be more convenient to whip all the egg whites together with a pinch of salt and fold half into each chocolate mixture instead of beating them separately. When the whites stand in firm peaks, fold them into the two mixtures and spoon in alternate layers into six chilled dessert glasses and refrigerate for at least 6 hours. Decorate according to personal taste with strawberries, crystallized violets, chopped crystallized ginger, or rosettes of whipped cream or, if preferred, leave plain.

TRIFLE

Chris Pitman has an interestingly different version of the traditional trifle. The addition of black coffee sounds very odd, but it works well.

SERVES 6 to 8

1-day-old sponge cake, cut into
   2.5 cm/1 in cubes, about 375 g/
   12 oz
900 g/2 lb blackberries, strawberries
   or raspberries, according to taste
   and the season
4 tablespoons apricot or other jam
125 ml/4 fl oz strong black coffee
125 ml/4 fl oz medium sherry

For the Custard:
4 large eggs

75 g/3 oz caster sugar
¼ teaspoon salt
350 ml/12 fl oz milk
250 ml/8 fl oz double cream
½ teaspoon vanilla essence

For the Garnish:
475 ml/16 fl oz whipped cream
Seasonal fruits

Put the cake cubes into a large glass bowl. Cover with the fruit. In a small saucepan, mix the jam with the black coffee and sherry and heat, stirring, just long enough to make a smooth mixture. Cool and pour over the cake and fruit. Refrigerate for 24 hours.

Make the custard. In the top of a double boiler, beat the eggs lightly. Beat in the sugar and salt. In a small saucepan, heat the milk with the cream to just under a boil. Cool slightly and gradually pour into the egg mixture in the double boiler set over hot, not boiling, water on very low heat. Stir in the vanilla. Cook, stirring constantly, until the mixture coats the spoon, about 7 minutes. Remove from the heat and cool. Pour it over the trifle and refrigerate until the custard has set. Garnish with whipped cream and seasonal fruits.

BUTTERSCOTCH MERINGUE PIE

This simple, old-fashioned dessert was developed by Ken Stott from a traditional recipe. Scots chefs never lose their old favourites, but constantly and subtly update them so they fit happily into modern menus. This one is a delight.

SERVES 6

1 recipe shortcrust pastry (see Basic Recipes, page 17)
Raw rice for weighting the pastry shell
250 g/8 oz firmly-packed light brown sugar
50 g/2 oz plain flour

250 ml/8 fl oz milk
4 large eggs, separated
4 tablespoons butter, cut into pieces
1 teaspoon vanilla essence
Salt
Pinch cream of tartar
50 g/2 oz caster sugar

On a lightly-floured surface, roll out the dough to about 0.3 cm/⅛ in thick and fit it into a 23 cm/9 in pie plate. Crimp the edge with the fingers, prick the bottom of the shell with a fork and chill in the refrigerator for 30 minutes. Line the shell with greaseproof paper, fill with the rice and bake in a preheated, hot oven (220°C/425°F/gas 7) for 15 minutes. Remove the paper and rice and bake the shell for 10 minutes longer, or until the pastry is golden. Let it cool on a rack. In a saucepan, mix together the brown sugar and flour. Whisk in 50 ml/2 fl oz water and the milk. Simmer, over low heat, stirring for 5 minutes or until the mixture is smooth and thick. Off the heat, whisk in the egg yolks, one at a time, then the butter and the vanilla. Cool the mixture, stirring from time to time, and pour it into the pie shell.

In a bowl, beat the egg whites with a pinch of salt and cream of tartar until they stand in firm peaks. Pipe or spoon the meringue onto the filling, covering it completely. Dredge with the caster sugar. Bake in a preheated, slow oven (150°C/300°F/gas 2) for 20 minutes or until the meringue is golden brown. Serve with cream or ice cream or by itself.

HOT BUTTERSCOTCH PUDDING

This is a fine, old-fashioned dessert to which Kenneth Bell has given his own inimitable touch. It is a wonderful hot pudding. If fresh dates are available, they add to both texture and flavour.

SERVES 6 to 10
For the Pudding:
175 g/6 oz sugar
4 tablespoons butter
2 large eggs
1 teaspoon vanilla essence
½ teaspoon baking powder
250 g/8 oz plain flour
250 ml/8 fl oz warm milk
1 teaspoon baking soda

150 g/5 oz chopped dates or raisins
   tossed in flour

For the Sauce:
125 g/4 oz butter
125 g/4 oz dark brown sugar
250 ml/8 fl oz double cream
50 ml/2 fl oz dark rum (optional)

In a bowl, beat the sugar and butter together until the mixture is light and fluffy. Beat in the eggs, vanilla, baking powder, and the flour, stirring to mix. Pour in the warm milk and add the baking soda. Fold in the dates or raisins, or fresh dates, pitted and chopped, if available. Butter a 23 × 12 cm/9 × 5 in non-stick cake tin, pour in the pudding mixture and let it stand for 1 hour. Bake in a preheated, moderate oven (180°C/350°F/gas 4) for 1 hour, or until a cake tester inserted into the middle comes out clean.

While the pudding is baking, make the sauce. In a small saucepan, melt the butter and stir in the dark brown sugar. When the sugar has dissolved, add the cream and continue to cook, stirring, until well blended. Stir in the rum, if using, as it greatly improves the sauce. Turn the pudding out onto a serving dish and cut into 8-10 slices. Arrange the slices on dessert plates and pour some of the sauce over them. Serve the rest of the sauce separately. If liked the pudding may be cut into more generous slices to serve 6.

GLAZED PRUNE TART

I have always admired the versatility of prunes in cooking, since they are equally at home with braised pork, in a pâté, or, as here, in a tart. Pierre Chevillard created this delicious tart.

SERVES 6

1 recipe sweet shortcrust pastry (see Basic Recipes, page 17)
500 g/1 lb pitted prunes
475 ml/16 fl oz double cream

3 large eggs, lightly beaten
125 g/4 oz caster sugar
75 g/3 oz apricot jam

Make the pastry and roll it out on a lightly-floured surface into a round about 0.3 cm/⅛ in thick. Fit it into a 25 cm/10 in flan tin with a removable rim and trim the edge. Prick the shell with a fork and chill it for 30 minutes.

Put the prunes into a saucepan with water barely to cover. Cover, and simmer for 10 minutes over low heat. Cool the prunes, drain thoroughly and arrange them in the flan shell. In a bowl, combine the cream, eggs and sugar, whisking to mix well. Put the flan on a baking sheet and pour the custard over the prunes. Bake in a preheated, moderate oven (180°C/350°F/gas 4) for 30–35 minutes, or until the custard is set. Cool the tart at room temperature then carefully remove the rim. Slide the tart from the baking sheet onto a serving plate. Melt the apricot jam in a small saucepan over low heat just until it begins to bubble. Rub the jam through a sieve to get rid of any bits of skin and brush it over the tart.

VARIATION

PRUNE AND ALMOND TART, FLAVOURED WITH ARMAGNAC

John Armstrong has an interesting version of the above. The pastry is made in the same way as for Glazed Prune Tart, using a 20 cm/8 in flan tin. Soak 250 g/8 oz pitted prunes in warm water for 15 minutes, lift out and pat dry with paper towels. Arrange the prunes on the pastry. In a bowl, whisk together 2 eggs, 5 tablespoons whipping cream, 4 tablespoons caster sugar, 3 tablespoons finely ground almonds and 2 tablespoons Armagnac, or other brandy if Armagnac is not available. Melt 2 tablespoons butter in a small saucepan and when it is cool whisk it into the egg and cream mixture. Pour the mixture over the prunes and bake in a preheated, moderate oven (190°C/375°F/gas 5) for 20–25 minutes or until the custard is set. Sprinkle the tart with 2 tablespoons of Armagnac and serve warm. Serves 6.

CHOCOLATE LAYER CAKE WITH COFFEE CUSTARD SAUCE

This is not a difficult dessert to make but it does take time. It is richly flavoured with a delicious sauce. It is worth the effort for a special occasion. Mark Napper created the cake when he was head chef at Cromlix House.

SERVES 6 to 8

For the Cake:
2 large eggs
50 g/2 oz caster sugar
30 g/1 oz plain flour
2 tablepoons cocoa
2 tablespoons clarified butter (see
  Basic Recipes, page 25)

For the Pastry Cream Filling:
600 ml/1 pt milk
6 large egg yolks
125 g/4 oz caster sugar
50 g/2 oz plus 2 tablespoons plain
  flour
125 g/4 oz butter, cut into pieces and
  softened at room temperature
2 teaspoons vanilla essence
2 teaspoons instant espresso powder
  dissolved in 1 tablespoon hot water

For the Chocolate Cream Filling:
125 ml/4 fl oz double cream
4 tablespoons dark rum
375 g/12 oz semi-sweet chocolate,
  chopped fine
2 tablespoons butter, cut into pieces
  and softened at room temperature
2 tablespoons dark rum to brush on
  cake layers

For the Coffee Custard Sauce:
600 ml/1 pt milk
3 tablespoons ground espresso beans
6 large egg yolks
125 g/4 oz caster sugar

Make the cake. Line the bottom of a buttered loaf tin 23 × 12 × 7 cm/9 × 5 × 3 in with buttered greaseproof paper. Dust the tin with flour, shaking out the excess. In a bowl, beat the eggs and sugar together until the mixture is light and fluffy. Set the bowl over a saucepan of hot water and let it warm, stirring from time to time. In a blender or food processor, beat the mixture until it is very light and increased in volume. Scrape the mixture into a bowl and sift the flour and cocoa over it. Fold in the butter, a tablespoon at a time, until the mixture forms a smooth batter. Spoon the batter into the loaf tin and smooth the top with a spatula. Bake in a preheated, moderate oven (180°C/350°F/gas 4) for 25–30 minutes, or until a cake tester comes out clean. Cool the cake in the tin on a rack for 5 minutes then invert the cake onto the rack. Remove the greaseproof paper and let the cake cool, then chill in the refrigerator, covered, for 2 hours or overnight if convenient.

Make the pastry creams. In a saucepan, scald the milk. In a bowl, whisk the egg yolks until they are combined then whisk in the sugar and the flour, then pour in the milk, whisking constantly. Transfer the mixture to a saucepan and cook over moderate heat, stirring constantly, until it has thickened. Simmer, over low heat, for 5 minutes. Strain into a bowl and stir in the butter and vanilla. Divide the custard evenly between two bowls. Stir the espresso mixture into one bowl, mixing thoroughly. Cover both bowls and chill in the refrigerator for about 1 hour.

Make the chocolate cream. In a saucepan, combine the cream and the rum, bring to a boil then remove from the heat. Add the chocolate and stir until the mixture is smooth. Cool slightly and stir in the butter, mixing well. Chill until the mixture has thickened and holds its shape in a spoon.

Using a serrated knife, slice the cake carefully into 4 layers, brushing each layer on both sides with the rum. Clean the loaf tin and butter the bottom and sides of it lightly. Put the bottom layer of the cake, cut-side up, in the tin and spread it with the plain pastry cream. Cover with another layer of cake and spread with the coffee-flavoured pastry cream. Top with a third layer and spread with the chocolate cream. Top with the last layer, cut-side down, cover and chill in the refrigerator for 4 hours or overnight.

Make the coffee custard sauce. Combine the milk and the ground espresso beans in a saucepan and bring to a simmer. Let stand, off the heat, for 5 minutes. In a large bowl, beat the egg yolks with the sugar until the mixture is thick and light-coloured. Transfer to a saucepan and whisk in the milk mixture. Cook over low heat, stirring constantly, until the mixture has thickened to a custard. Do not let it boil. Strain the custard into a bowl and chill it, covered, for at least 1 hour.

Invert the cake onto a serving plate and, using a hot knife, slice it. Pour the coffee sauce on six plates and top with a slice of cake. Decorate with chocolate leaves, if liked.

CHOCOLATE TRUFFLE CAKE

John Martin Grimsey describes this as a rather rich dessert made with the minimum of effort and ideal for a dinner party as you can prepare it at least 24 hours beforehand. I endorse all of that except that I'd change rather rich to very rich and add that the cake should delight all chocolate lovers, that it keeps well and that it goes a long way. Serve it in thin slices as it is most satisfying.

SERVES 8 to 10

250 g/8 oz semi-sweet baking
   chocolate
2 large eggs
50 g/2 oz sugar
125 g/4 oz butter, melted and cooled
250 g/8 oz digestive biscuits, crushed
250 g/8 oz mixed nuts, chopped
   (walnuts, pecans, cashews, almonds,
   filberts)

125 g/4 oz chopped glacé cherries
175 ml/6 fl oz dark rum

For the Garnish:
Whipped cream
Glacé cherries
Nuts

Break the chocolate into pieces and put it, with 4 tablespoons water, into the top of a double boiler set over hot water on low heat. Stir constantly with a wooden spoon until the chocolate has melted and is smooth, about 4 minutes.

In a bowl, cream the eggs and sugar until they are light and fluffy. Stir in the butter, then the melted chocolate, the biscuit crumbs, nuts, cherries and rum. Leave the mixture to set in a cool place, or in the refrigerator, for 12 hours to let the flavour develop. Unmould the cake onto a serving dish. The easiest way to do this is to put the bowl in a shallow dish of warm water for a few minutes. Garnish the cake with rosettes of whipped cream, candied cherries and nuts.

PASSION FRUIT SOUFFLÉ

Passion fruit has an exquisite flavour and Nick Gill has worked out a simple and delicious soufflé recipe using the fruit. The presentation of the dish is charming.

SERVES 6

Butter, flour and sugar for the soufflé moulds
12 ripe passion fruit
175 ml/6 fl oz fresh orange juice
8 large egg yolks
375 g/12 oz vanilla sugar, or add 1 teaspoon vanilla essence

Grated rind of 1 lemon
8 large egg whites
Pinch salt
Icing sugar

Butter, flour and dust with sugar six 250 g/8 oz or slightly larger individual soufflé moulds. Set aside.

Halve 6 of the passion fruit and scoop the contents into a bowl. Add the orange juice, stir to mix and strain the mixture to remove the passion fruit pips. Beat the egg yolks with 175 g/6 oz of the sugar and the passion fruit and orange juice mixture in the top of a double boiler set over hot water on very low heat, until the mixture is light and frothy. Stir in the grated lemon rind. In a large bowl, beat the egg whites with the salt until they stand in firm peaks. Whisk in the remaining sugar. Mix half of the egg whites into the egg yolk mixture, off the heat, then gently but thoroughly fold in the remaining egg whites. Spoon the mixture into the prepared soufflé moulds and smooth the tops with a spatula. Cook in a preheated, hot oven (220°C/425°F/gas 7) for about 8 minutes or until the soufflés are well risen and lightly set. Remove from the oven, dust with icing sugar and serve immediately with the remaining 6 passion fruit, tops sliced off, and put into 6 small egg cups. The passion fruit should be spooned into the soufflé after the first spoonful has been eaten. If liked, serve with almond biscuits (see page 209).

VARIATION

HOT PASSION FRUIT SOUFFLÉ

Michael Croft has a slightly simpler passion fruit soufflé recipe, conveniently scaled down for one, though it can easily be doubled.

SERVES 1
2 egg yolks
125 g/4 oz caster sugar
4 egg whites
250 g/8 oz passion fruit pulp, sieved
   to remove pips*
Icing sugar

*Passion fruit are frequently available fresh. They are also available canned as passion fruit pulp, in speciality food shops. The canned pulp is sweetened so this should be taken into consideration and the amount of sugar reduced.

In a bowl, beat the egg yolks with half the sugar until light and fluffy. In another bowl, beat the whites, adding the rest of the sugar little by little, until they stand in firm, shiny peaks. Add 3 tablespoons of the passion fruit pulp to the yolks, mix well then stir in a quarter of the egg whites. Fold in the rest of the egg whites gently but thoroughly. Have ready a 250 g/8 oz soufflé mould, buttered and sprinkled with sugar. Pour in the soufflé mixture and bake in a preheated, hot oven (220°C/425°F/gas 7) for about 10 minutes or until the soufflé is puffed and lightly browned. Dust with icing sugar and serve immediately with a sauce of the rest of the passion fruit pulp, warmed, and sweetened, if necessary.

PANCAKES STUFFED WITH PEARS

This was a favourite dessert of Raymond Baudon during the time he was head chef at Johnstounburn House. The pancakes can be made ahead of time which makes this a quick dessert to put together for family or friends.

SERVES 4
8 pancakes (crêpes, see Basic Recipes, page 19)
250 ml/8 fl oz double or whipping cream
175 g/6 oz sugar
50 ml/2 fl oz Cognac, or other brandy

4 large, ripe pears, peeled, cored and diced
125 g/4 oz butter

For the Garnish:
Fresh fruit, thinly sliced

Make the pancakes and keep them warm. If they are made ahead of time, warm them through, in a double boiler over hot water, just before assembling the dish.

In a large bowl, whip the cream with 50 g/2 oz of the sugar and the brandy. Sauté the pears in the butter in a heavy frying pan until the fruit is golden but not soft. Sprinkle with the rest of the sugar and cook for a few minutes longer. Divide the pear mixture among the pancakes and top with the whipped cream. Fold or roll the pancakes, transfer to a warm serving dish and serve garnished with the thinly sliced fruits. Serve immediately.

HOT STRAWBERRIES WITH GREEN PEPPERCORNS

Melvin Jordan devised this delicious way of serving strawberries. The medley of flavours is unusual and delicious.

SERVES 4
125 g/4 oz sugar
50 ml/2 fl oz brandy
4 tablespoons lemon juice
250 ml/8 fl oz orange juice
10 green peppercorns

500 g/1 lb hulled and washed strawberries
Vanilla ice cream, preferably home-made

In a small heavy saucepan, caramelize the sugar to a light golden colour. Off the heat, add the brandy, taking care to step back as it will flame. When the flames die down, stir in the lemon and orange juice and the green peppercorns. Stir over low heat to dissolve the caramel, about 5–10 minutes. When ready to serve, add the strawberries and cook for 1 minute. Serve the strawberries and their sauce poured over ice cream in glass dessert dishes.

The Chefs

I am greatly indebted to the chefs who generously gave me, not just their recipes, but their time, each explaining his or her culinary point of view and aims as a cook. They even let me into their kitchens, a rewarding experience.

Obviously, chefs do move around but this information was correct at time of going to press.

Index